Dilemmas
of the
American
Self

JOHN P. HEWITT

Temple University Press
Philadelphia

Temple University Press, Philadelphia 19122
Copyright © 1989 by Temple University. All rights reserved
Published 1989
Printed in the United States of America

The paper used in this publication meets the minimum
requirements of American National Standard for Information
Sciences—Permanence of Paper for Printed Library Materials,
ANSI Z39.48-1984

Library of Congress Cataloging-in-Publication Data

Hewitt, John P., 1941–
Dilemmas of the American self / John P. Hewitt.
p. cm.
Includes bibliographical references.
ISBN 0-87722-656-3 (alk. paper)
1. Social psychology—United States. 2. Symbolic interactionism.
3. Self. 4. Culture. I. Title.
HM251.H493 1989
302—dc 20 89-5179
CIP

Contents

PREFACE

This book is an attempt to revise our understanding of the person in American society. Social scientists and social critics have typically regarded individualism as the most significant problem of American culture, and they have portrayed the self as transformed, disorganized, under attack, or in decline as a result of individualism and of other powerful forces of modernity. I think matters are far more complex. Although individualism is a powerful force in American culture and society, there are countervailing tendencies toward a communitarian view of life and its possibilities. And over the course of American history the experience of self is better characterized by images of ambivalent responses to a divided culture than by images of change or decline.

In this effort to rethink and reconstruct our basic interpretations of self and society I have drawn upon two different streams of thought, hoping to make a contribution to each as well as to reach a wider and less specialized audience. One stream is social psychology, particularly the sociological version known as symbolic interactionism. This approach to social psychology is a contemporary heir to the pragmatism of William James, Charles S. Peirce, John Dewey, and especially George Herbert Mead, philosophers whose work is itself an expression of American culture and in many respects integral to an understanding of it. Symbolic interactionism stresses the centrality of meaning and symbolic communication in the formation of human conduct, and one of its chief achievements has been the elaboration of a theory of the self. The other stream consists of a more heterogeneous body of literature that has examined American society and culture and depicted their impact upon the person. David Riesman, Allen Wheelis, Carl Rogers, and Christopher Lasch are a few of the diverse contributors to this literature. These and other authors have often couched their discussions of self and society in scholarly terms, but their ideas have also influenced a wider audience, through their best-selling books, the media, and the college classroom.

The social critique of individualism, narcissism, and other features of American culture, and symbolic interactionist self theory, are topics not customarily addressed by one scholar within the pages of a single book. Although many practitioners of social psychology have read critiques of American culture and its alleged transformation, corrosion, or destruction of the self, they have not yet fully grasped the implications of this litera-

vii

ture for social psychology. And contemporary social and cultural analysts seem largely to have forgotten pragmatism and to be oblivious to social psychology and symbolic interactionism. By joining these streams I hope to advance them both.

My own intellectual roots lie in symbolic interactionism, but this book departs in scope, style, and substance from much contemporary interactionist work. The continued development of symbolic interactionist self theory depends upon a willingness to theorize in new ways about the relationship between society and the person, upon the revitalization of the concept of culture, and particularly upon a grasp of American culture. George H. Mead, who gave sociologists their understanding of the self in society, wrote from within the framework of American culture. Symbolic interactionists, who have kept the flame of Mead's ideas alive, have found little place for the concept of culture in their analyses of human conduct, let alone for the special themes of American culture. My hope in this book is to reinvigorate and extend the interactionist theory of the self, in part by removing those chains that bind it to an expression of a particular moment of the culture that spawned it. I want to add to the tradition of social psychology Mead created.

At the same time, analyses of American individualism and of the inexorable decline and fall of the self (or, in some versions, of the wonderful opportunities for self-actualization that lie ahead) have been restricted by their own chains binding them to American culture. Critical scholars and intellectuals, through an exaggerated and usually pessimistic attention to individualism, have distorted our understanding of American culture and of the problems and prospects of the person. American culture is best characterized not as relentlessly individualistic or as lacking in the capacity to conceive of or discuss community, but as torn between individualism and communitarianism, thus creating serious, felt difficulties of social adjustment and personal meaning. This body of literature has also suffered because of its theoretical approaches to the self. Christopher Lasch, for example, attempts to force an understanding of American culture and the person into the psychoanalytic concept of narcissism; Robert Bellah and his associates seem to fit their understanding of person and society to no discernible sociological or social psychological theory. Symbolic interactionist social psychology provides a theory of the self useful in understanding the problems and prospects of the person in American society.

This book is addressed not only to symbolic interactionists and to other scholars interested in the self and its vicissitudes but also to a larger audience willing to risk immersion in its scholarly discourse. I have sought to convey the main ideas of a symbolic interactionist reading of the social psychology of the self and of American culture in terms and images that will be of interest beyond the scholarly world. Although this is primarily a theoretical work, I have risked some imprecision and simplification in order to convey my view of self and society more vividly. And I have explained concepts familiar to specialists so that the book as a whole will be accessible to non-specialists. I have done so in the conviction that social scientific analyses, wherever possible, should be understandable to a literate general audience and to students.

I am indebted to many people who have directly or indirectly contributed to this book—to those whose work I have used (and I hope not misused) in these pages and to my present and former teachers, students, and colleagues. Jerry Platt has been a very supportive and encouraging department chair, and Jane Cullen of Temple University Press an enthusiastic and helpful editor. I owe a special debt to Charles H. Page, a teacher and colleague who has been unfailingly supportive of me for over twenty-five years. I began work on this book just as my daughter, Elizabeth A. Hewitt, entered college, and work on it continued as my son, Gary L. Hewitt, started his college career two years later. As they have grown intellectually (and graduated) during these years they have both cheered and challenged me, and my work has gained from their intellectual presence as well as from their love. And Myrna Livingston Hewitt, wife as well as colleague, has through her love and quiet confidence made this book possible.

Dilemmas
of the
American
Self

CHAPTER I

The Ubiquity of the Self

The self is omnipresent in contemporary life. Everyday conversations are larded with references to identity, self-concept, self-esteem, self-image, self-fulfillment, self-actualization. Therapists and best-selling books promise to teach assertiveness, raise consciousness, enhance self-esteem, or improve relationships. Celebrities parade their psychic wounds before television audiences, and the language of self-reference has become a widely accepted part of popular vocabularies of motive. Men and women measure happiness against the standards of "self-actualization" and "self-fulfillment." They speak of "finding themselves" and of their "real" selves, as if the self could lose itself or be mistaken for another self.

It is not only among ordinary folk that self figures so prominently. Social critics worry about the decline of personality, attack the pathological narcissism fostered by a rootless modern society, condemn the emptiness that lies at the core of the contemporary self, and seek relief in social change or in a return to the virtues of family and community. Social and behavioral scientists regard the self as a key element in the explanation of human behavior. Theories of motivation emphasizing a quest for self-esteem, identity, or self-consistency are a basic part of social psychologists' conceptual kit and are offered as explanations of phenomena as diverse as entire social movements and the poor performance of school-children. Sociologists point to the impact of society upon the person and often regard the individual as little more than an aggregate of roles that would disintegrate without its social mortar. Educators, who are major consumers and appliers of ideas drawn from the social and behavioral sciences, view self-concept as central to their strategies for educational reform and individual improvement. Humanistic psychologists chart the wonderful powers of the self and have attracted a loyal following among a public apparently hungry for their ideas.

The self is, in short, an important object of discourse for contemporary people—for cultural critics, social scientists, therapeutic experts, and ordinary folk alike. This discourse about the self—especially that of critics and social scientists—provides the point of departure for this book, a place from which to start a journey whose ultimate destination is a more penetrating analysis of self and its relationship to society in contemporary America. Discourse about self is a text that reveals American culture. My goal is to understand better this discourse and its sources, to show how it in many ways obscures our understanding of American culture and American people even while it expresses fundamental truths about both, and to reformulate it in terms that better capture the relationship between self and society in America.

Optimistic and Pessimistic Discourse

Discourse is talk, whether conducted in the give and take of everyday life and social relationships, the formal setting of a therapist's office, or the more rarified setting of books and academic journals. Americans frequently talk about the self, and when they do they tend to divide into two roughly opposite camps, which I will tentatively and very loosely label "pessimistic" and "optimistic." These two varieties of discourse about the self express responses to transformations in the person that have allegedly occurred over the past century or two or that may occur in the future. The classification is necessarily inexact, for many examples of discourse are a mixture of optimism and pessimism about the self and its prospects, and many people seem prone to shift between one point of view and the other. Indeed, these opposing points of view both depend and feed upon one another.

The "pessimistic" variety of discourse negatively portrays the state of the person in modern society—as having declined relative to some "Golden Age" in the past, as under attack by the forces of capitalism, or as having deteriorated from a previous condition of energy and organization to its current impotence and disarray. This point of view is epitomized in its intellectual form by the commonplace concern about conformity and "other-direction" during the 1950s, by anxieties about the problems of identity in modern life spread by social scientists and psychiatrists during the 1960s and 1970s, and by the frightening picture of the individual's absorption by the state and corporation painted more recently by sociologists, critical theorists, and historians. In its more popular versions, the pessimistic view is expressed in the criticism of "Yuppies" as selfish and self-centered, in similar popular manifestations of alarm over "narcissism" in the pages of news magazines, and in popular discussions of the decline of the "work ethic" in American life.[1]

The pessimistic view places the society over and above the individual, regarding the former as an essential source of support and nurture, as well as of individuality and individual capabilities, and it makes the integrity and well-being of the society its most pressing concern. In general, this approach is pessimistic about the prospects and potential of individuals, except insofar as society can be changed so as to provide individuals with proper support and guidance so that, as members of families and communities, they can feel a sense of security and direct their energies in socially constructive and personally fulfilling ways. Its view of change tends to be negative, for it sees character as having declined, the self reduced to minimal dimensions and powers, and hope residing only in some kind of major social restructuring.

At the heart of much pessimistic discourse about the self, especially that of intellectuals, lies an implicit (and very often an explicit) theory of modernity. Specific versions of this general theory vary with the discipline and ideological bent of its author, but the general themes are surprisingly common. In the past, according to this theory, a more stable social order produced individuals whose lives were bounded by tradition and community, who were not keenly self-conscious, whose identities were secure, and whose perceptions of self were shaped by institutional involvements and commitments. In such times, men and women knew their place in a social order and had little experience of "identity crises." They were self-interested, as human beings may always be, but they were neither self-centered nor pathologically narcissistic. Although their impulses often ran counter to social expectations, they found security and self-definition alike in conforming to established social custom. Usually members of societies with clear-cut social strata, they developed self-images appropriate to their social station. They lived without undue self-consciousness in a network of family, class, and interpersonal relationships in which the psychic security of the individual was purchased at the expense of individuality. But in a world in which individuality had less importance and community more, people experienced the warmth of community ties and not merely the constraints of community bonds.

Somewhere in time—perhaps as early as the Renaissance, perhaps not until the period of full-scale industrialization during the nineteenth century—changes in society began to yield changes in the self. The idea of the individual person, separable from family and community, began to take root during the Renaissance, and this idea would serve as the foundation for much that was to occur during subsequent transformations of European society. Later, industrialization set in motion social changes that disrupted community, severed people from tradition, made identity problematic, and rendered institutions an uncertain resource for the self.

This theory of the modern self has been elaborated by sociologists, historians, and social critics, who have concentrated much of their attention on American society and its transformation from the agrarian world of the colonial period to modern industrial society. At the outset, it is argued, American society had many of the characteristics of the traditional society, with the person firmly anchored in the fixed social world of the self-sufficient agricultural community. But the coming of the industrial age transformed the person as well as the social order. At first driven by an inner urge to excel in the emerging industrial society, people later became driven more by interpersonal considerations than a quest for mobility or achievement.[2] They became "other-directed" rather than "inner-directed."[3] Their sense of geographical and social place was disrupted in a society constantly in flux, and so they searched for identity.[4] Self was transformed from an object spontaneously experienced in the round of everyday life to one cultivated for its own sake. And as the authority of tradition waned and the spontaneity of self declined, men and women began to look for the anchor points of their lives within themselves rather than in social institutions.[5] A concern for "sincerity" gave way to preoccupation with "authenticity," the era of "character" vanished and that of "personality" arrived, narcissism became a form of psychopathology writ large on American culture, and the "therapeutic culture" triumphed.[6]

"Optimistic" discourse about the self is a genre in which the individual is viewed in a positive light, the self celebrated as having the potential not only to achieve whatever it seeks but also to triumph over society's attempted domination of it. This mode of discourse can be seen in such diverse contexts as the tradition of "positive thinking" spawned by the "mind cure" advocates of the nineteenth century, the psychology of self-actualization of Carl Rogers and other "humanistic psychologists," and the conviction that a new form of human consciousness will lead to the "greening" of America. But it can also be seen, in another version, in the American quest for success and the belief in "rugged individualism."[7]

The optimistic view of the self puts the happiness and integrity of the individual before the welfare of society, viewing the person as the creator of society rather than as its product. This discourse is optimistic about the prospects and potentials of individuals, provided that the repressive power of society can be controlled or checked so that people can act in ways that promote success, self-fulfillment, and self-enhancement. The optimistic view generally sees social change either as already proceeding in desirable directions or as capable of doing so. Individuals have the capacity to "be all that they can be," and by acting in self-actualizing ways, they contribute to the building of a society that will be even more supportive of the individual.

At the heart of optimistic discourse about the self lies a different theory of the person in relation to society and, indeed, an interpretation of social change almost the opposite of that discussed above. Where critics of modernity have seen it as undermining the self, optimists have been more apt to see modernity as the liberation of the person from the past and its repressive mores. In this view, the modern transformation of the world has been beneficial to individuals, who have been gradually relieved of the oppressive weight of society, although there is yet a considerable distance to go before men and women are free to construct a good society in which good selves will be possible.

The optimistic view of the self and its possibilities is rooted in *individualism*, and thus takes different forms depending on the variety of this doctrine from which it draws inspiration and support. One form, which in their critique of contemporary American culture Robert Bellah and company label "utilitarian individualism," stresses the pursuit of individual economic ends.[8] The self, in this view, is defined by its accomplishments, and what is most important is the individual's opportunity to make his or her way in life and to use individual energy and initiative in order to succeed. What Bellah and others have termed "expressive individualism" also emphasizes the pursuit of individual ends, but instead of defining the possibilities of individual accomplishment solely in material or status terms, it stresses the pursuit of happiness, the expression of individual talents, and the need for individuals to act in ways that express their own natures rather than the artificial constraints of society.

Utilitarian and expressive individualism seem poles apart in contemporary social life and discourse—the success-driven professional or entrepreneur who wants to "make it" is in many ways very unlike the "New Age" advocate who seeks individual peace and social harmony. Yet both outlooks put enormous faith in the self—in its capacities to flower, to over-come obstacles, to achieve its purposes. Indeed, as the United States Army recruiting slogan—"Be all that you can be!"—suggests, the line between these forms of individualism is often blurred, for they encourage aspirations for mobility as well as for self-expression. The underlying optimism of both forms of individualism endows the individual with the capacity to overcome social constraints, whether they are conceived as economic obstacles to the quest for success or as repressive social forms that hinder the search for happiness.

In contrast to the pessimistic view, which finds its most vivid intellectual expression in the work of scholars in the humanities and social sciences who have been critical of the excessive individualism of modern, industrial, capitalist society, the optimistic view is expressed most clearly in the work of contemporary "humanistic" psychologists. This should come as no surprise, for if "society" has been the intellectual property as well as the chief concern of the former, "the individual" has been the main abstraction and the principal reality considered by the latter. Thus, for example, in the work of humanistic psychologists like Carl Rogers we can find a more or less systematic intellectual expression of the optimistic view. In his and similar work, instead of criticism of the modern social order for its attacks on the self, we find criticism of an old, confining, socially repressive order that can and will be overcome by self-actualizing individuals. Like flowers growing toward the light, people in the world to come will be more "in touch with" their own needs and feelings and be less bound by the artificial constraints imposed by society and its norms.

What are we to make of these contending views of the self and its fate in contemporary American society? Social scientists have variously sought to test the empirical validity of those views of self that have been explicitly formulated from a scientific perspective, to join the chorus of social critics who condemn the excesses of American individualism, and to debunk the psychology of self-actualization.[9] But they have generally neglected the sociologically most interesting aspect of this discourse about the self, namely, that such opposite versions of reality command such attention and that they have seemingly persisted in opposition for so long. The point and counterpoint of optimistic and pessimistic discourse about the self is a major and largely neglected social and cultural fact of American life.

Optimistic and pessimistic discourse is everywhere. Authors, from David Riesman in the 1950s to Christopher Lasch in the 1970s and Robert Bellah in the 1980s, write best-selling and widely discussed books about the transformation or decline of the self, while others, ranging from Norman Vincent Peale to Carl Rogers, write similarly popular books about positive thinking and self-actualization. People refer to these ideas (if not to their authors) in their everyday talk about themselves and their relationships with others. Ideas about "conformity," "identity," "individualism," "positive thinking," and "self-actualization" thus become the intellectual tools of people who have little idea about the origins of these terms, but who find them useful to apply (and often to misapply) to their own circumstances, often shifting between one perspective and another without seeming to recognize their opposition. We find these ideas in news magazines, television talk shows, popular advice manuals, sermons, and many other places where discourse occurs.

Nor is this opposing discourse anything new on the American scene. It is no doubt tempting for those who think they perceive the relentless decline of the self—or those who extol its great powers—to imagine that they have discovered something new, but the pessimistic and optimistic versions of the self in relation to society have been with us for a long time. One may see a nineteenth-century expression of the opposing views by comparing the fiction of Nathaniel Hawthorne with the philosophical speculations of Ralph Waldo Emerson, the former keenly conscious of the decline of the Puritan community and ideology and its consequent isolation of the person, the latter engaging in that characteristic American "refusal of history" (the phrase is Irving Howe's) and attempting to show the way to "self-reliance." [10] One may see it in the sense of alarm about the fate of the person that arose in the second half of the nineteenth century and found expression in the concern with "neurasthenia," depression, and loss of individual interest or energy for life's affairs, but also in the "mind-cure" movement that enjoyed great popularity at that time as well as in the tradition of "positive thinking" this movement spawned.[11] The optimistic and pessimistic versions of the truth are thus not products of the twentieth century, but have their roots in the nineteenth century and earlier.

Where opposing ideas of such force and magnitude persist for so long, one is entitled to the suspicion that matters of great importance to the culture are at stake and that the discourse in which these ideas are expressed is of crucial import to an understanding of the social order as well as the nature of the person. Discourse arises out of the experiences, perceptions, and difficulties of those who share a culture. People talk about life as they experience it, they describe what they see, and they are especially apt to formulate discourses about the things that most excite them, whether because of sensed opportunities or perceived problems. Scholarly and scientific discourses are no less anchored in culture than are more popular varieties. Ordinary people react to life in the heart and gut; intellectuals and scientists may react in a more intellectually rigorous way, but they also respond with the impulses of ordinary people and not simply with those arising from autonomous traditions of thought or the imperatives of science. They respond as possessors of their culture and its view of the world, and their responses work their way into their concepts and theories. This being so, one has license to suspend judgment about the truth of their ideas and to use the discourses that express them as cultural texts to be examined and interpreted.

Discourse and Culture

What can discourse about the self tell us about American culture? A culture is experienced by and known to those who share it, among other ways, in and through their efforts to cope with problems and difficulties. This view, which will be developed more fully in Chapters II and III, reflects the social thought of both Emile Durkheim and George Herbert Mead. The former took the view that the *conscience collective* is aroused particularly by crimes against the moral order, which focus collective attention on those values and ideals that people hold in common and stimulate them to interact and to share explicitly their common sentiments. Crime arouses collective sentiments, and the punishment of crime provides an occasion for the enhancement of social solidarity.[12]

This view is not unrelated to Mead's pragmatist approach to epistemology, which views the problematic occurrence—that which interferes with routine or habitual conduct and prevents it from achieving its goals —as the occasion for human beings to seek knowledge and to assess the circumstances in which they find themselves. Habit is an important force in human affairs, but it is insufficient as a guide to conduct because problematic circumstances continually arise that call for novel solutions rather than the enactment of routines. When this occurs, human beings become conscious of themselves and of their circumstances, of what they have previously taken for granted, and of the need to seek alternative ways of acting. The result is an increased self-consciousness and an enhanced consciousness of ways of behaving shared by members of the group.[13]

From either Durkheim's or Mead's point of view, it is the problematic occurrence that provides the means whereby shared ways of thinking, feel-ing, and acting—which we may for the moment summarize as "culture"—are made visible to those who share them and their significance reaffirmed. From both perspectives, problematic occurrences stimulate talk, whether on street corners, at dining tables, in the pages of magazines, the books of intellectuals, or the laboratories of social scientists. People talk about crimes, expressing their outrage at an offense or their sympathy with the victim. They talk about their inability to feel happy, expressing their feel-ings to spouses or therapists or in the pages of their books on philosophy or sociology. And when people talk about problematic occurrences, they not only reawaken their collective sentiments and shared assumptions but also recreate and shape them. Culture thus thrives on adversity, which provides a main occasion for the talk that reaffirms and reconstitutes culture.

If this is so, then the surest path to the understanding of a given culture is an examination of the discourse in which it lives. The things about which people talk reflect the matters about which they worry, and their discourse both embodies and reflects their culture. Although no single mode of dis-course or single text can tell us all there is to know about a culture, those things people talk about most—and especially those persisting opposi-tions, arguments, and tensions in their discourse—may speak eloquently about their most important ways of thinking, feeling, and acting.

The inference to be made is inescapable: America has produced inces-sant discourse about the self and its fate, its relationship to society, and its problems and prospects, and this is a sure indication that important fea-tures of the culture as a whole are implicated in this discourse. Precisely what these features are and how they may be conceived is a matter I will investigate in some detail in the next two chapters. For the moment, it will suffice to provide a brief overview of where this analysis will lead.

The principal thesis I will develop in the early chapters of this book is that some of the most central features of American culture—and, in a more fundamental way, the modern culture of which it is a prime ex-ample—are revealed by this discourse of optimistic and pessimistic views of the self and its fate. Optimism is often alleged to be an important cultural trait of Americans, who are said to be fundamentally optimistic about the future, about the perfectibility of human beings and their soci-ety, about their own individual prospects. Perhaps because of the im-portance of themes of geographical migration, upward social mobility, and the conquest of the frontier, observers of all kinds have perceived a fundamental (and sometimes a very naive) optimism. Americans seem disposed to move when the fancy strikes them and to imagine they will gain by doing so, to believe that opportunity will respond to the person who grasps it, and to feel that the future holds great hope. It is less commonly understood that there is a nearly equal strain toward pessimism, toward a view of the future as bleak and of the good and rewarding life as lying in a lost past. Thus, nineteenth-century American migrants were not uniformly optimistic about the future, and they left behind kinfolk and fellow citizens who held a dark view of providence and who refused to budge from their secure Eastern communities.[14] If upward social mobility and the promise of the frontier have been important cultural themes, so too have been recurrent worries about declining opportunities for mobility and the much-lamented closing of the frontier in the late nineteenth century.[15] And the pronouncements of humanistic psychologists about the wonders of self-actualization are often met with skepticism and even derision. Americans can be dark, brooding, fearful, and cynical as much as light, cheerful, confident, and naive.

As with the versions of optimism and pessimism focused on the self and its prospects, the point about these more general cultural themes of optimism and pessimism is not to see which is correct, but to understand them as basic constituents of American culture. Their importance as cultural themes lies in their mutual presence as alternative ways of thinking, feeling, and acting. It is not simply that Americans are optimistic or pessimistic, but that these opposing attitudes toward themselves and the world structure their perceptions of the world as well as their responses to it. Optimism/pessimism constitutes what Kai Erikson has called an "axis of variation" in culture—that is, a deep-rooted and persistent polarity in shared modes of thought, feeling, and action.[16] If Americans are prone to be cheerfully optimistic about their prospects, they also fear that their hopes might not be fulfilled and they are apt to turn quickly toward a more pessimistic view. Not simply or uniformly optimistic or pessimistic, they seem to migrate in word and deed between the extremes of hope and despair, confidence and fear, and (in William James's image) "healthy-mindedness" and "sick-mindedness."

Axes of cultural variation will play a central role in my analysis. By examining critical and scholarly discourse about the self, I hope to reveal the main axes along which Americans structure their perceptions of self and society. The most important of these axes is not that of optimism and pessimism, however, but a closely linked yet more fundamental bifurcation we can roughly label with the words *individualism* and *communitarianism.*

Individualism has loomed large, both critically and sympathetically, in Americans' understanding of themselves, as well as in portrayals of American life and culture by outsiders. Indeed, the constant point of reference for both optimistic and pessimistic views of self and society is individualism. Those who are optimistic about the self and its prospects are so fundamentally because they support one version or another of the culture of individualism. Those who are pessimistic are so because their critique of individualism sees it as undermining social stability and community solidarity, and hence preventing the very happiness and self-fulfillment it seeks.

Just as the American proclivity toward optimism is counterpointed by pessimism, however, individualism also has its counterpoint. Although it is clearly true that Americans conceive of the social world from the perspective of one or another variety of individualism, they are by no means locked simply into individualistic modes and forms of discourse, important as these are. Instead, they have access to and regularly employ modes of discourse that recognize the priority of society and the importance of community. "Community" is a much-used part of Americans' vocabulary, and the quest to find or reconstitute community is a familiar cultural practice—to be seen in utopian literature and efforts to put utopian ideas into practice, in the tenacity with which local and ethnic identities persist, and in the striking endurance of images of community as a place of warmth and support in spite of the alleged disappearance of community from the modern scene.

In short, individualism must be viewed as one pole of an axis of cultural variation, the other pole of which is more difficult to label, although I will call it "communitarian" in order to have a simple term with which to express a rather complex idea. It is not simply that Americans are individualistic *or* communitarian in their outlook on themselves and the world, but that a key part of the American cultural dynamic—and, I will argue, of modernity more generally—inheres in the contrast and tension between individualistic and communitarian impulses. If there is a pervasive American belief in the centrality of the individual, so also is there a tendency to regard community and society as important. Indeed, this axis of variation is perhaps best revealed in the American tendency to see individual and society (or individual and community) as both paired and opposite, as separate and yet somehow linked and opposed realities. Our discourse, scholarly and otherwise, tends to see the individual as threatened by society—and the social order as undermined by individual disorder. The contrast and tension between these two is an integral part of our very ways of thinking about ourselves and our relation to society.[17]

Culture and the Self

Why is a better grasp of American culture important to a theory of self? The sociologist who would understand the relationship between self and society in the American context is profoundly handicapped by the fact that students of this topic have worked largely within the framework of understanding provided by American culture. That is to say, the bulk of sociological, social psychological, and other theorizing about and criticism of self and society in America has simply expressed one or another pole of American culture rather than grasping the interplay of these poles and their relevance for the self.

The variety of self theory anchored in social criticism, for example, has tended to articulate the communitarian pole of American culture. Social critics such as Christopher Lasch and Richard Sennett lament the decline of community and the fall of "public man," arguing that the socialization of the individual by the state and corporation and the quest for privacy have led to one version or another of narcissism and a depleted or weakened self. Robert Bellah and associates condemn the excesses of American individualism, decrying the decline of Biblical and Republican traditions. Such critics seem convinced that the communitarian impulse survives only in their own discourse and that of other critical intellectuals. But their illustrations are so consistently drawn either from the discourse of alienated intellectuals or from the more extreme adherents of expressive individualism that they wholly ignore those territories of American life in which various forms of community hold sway and in which discourse emphasizes the value of community. There is a life of self and community, as well as discourse about these things, of which these social critics seem unaware. Because they express one pole of the culture and deny the existence of its opposite, these critics make poor guides for the study of the self in America.

Matters are different, but not better, in academic sociology and social psychology, where theories of the self are similarly constructed without much awareness either of American culture or of the way in which even scientific theories of the self contribute to and express one or another pole of that culture. One of the most visible sociologists in recent decades, for example, was Erving Goffman, whose analyses of self-presentation and the relationship between self and others sparked widespread interest even beyond the sociological fold. For Goffman and others who work in his tradition or the closely related intellectual tradition of symbolic interactionism, the self is nothing without the social framework of roles on which it is hung. Take away the actor's role, in which he or she is always anxious to achieve a favorable self-presentation, and there is nothing left— no core of being, no essence, no thing at all. In Goffman's view of the matter, nothing is safe from sociology, which is to say that none of the illusions Americans (and others) may have about individuality and self are anything other than illusions.

From a scientific perspective, such assertions constitute testable hypotheses about the relation between the individual and the social world. Like many of the theories and hypotheses I will examine in this book, they contain a measure of truth. But it is not the empirical validity of such assertions that makes them seem important, logical, and valuable to social scientists, and especially not to the consumers of social science; it is the fact that they formulate one pole of an axis of cultural variation, one set of cultural themes that is carried and perpetuated, among other places in American life, by social science. The sociological view of the self—expressed in sociology textbooks and taught in sociology courses —is one means by which the communitarian pole of American culture is expressed and perpetuated. When sociologists express it, they are participating in a cultural debate about person and society. It is an important debate, and one that helps define and express American culture, but however unavoidable may be the participation of sociologists in this debate, mere participation is poor social science.

Much the same thing may be said of psychological theories of the self. From the sociologist's vantage point, what psychologists say about the self often seems to neglect the social dimension, to make the individual the only important reality. Although this criticism is surely valid, a more telling point is that psychology is fully caught within the individualistic pole of American culture. Carl Rogers' theory of self-actualization expresses a part of American culture, and like its counterpart theories in sociology, it participates in the American debate about the self and its place in society. Although it may be as difficult for psychologists to escape from participation in the cultural debate as it is for sociologists, participation is no substitute for analysis.

The major problem with existing theories of the self, then, whether of the variety expressed by social critics or by academic sociologists and psychologists, is that these theories express and reflect the culture but are poor analyses of it, and hence poor theories of the self. These theories express one or another pole of American culture, but fail to move sufficiently far outside of the culture to capture its real implications for the person. They are, in other words, insufficiently reflexive, and thus act as carriers of the culture rather than as analyses of it.

I propose in this book to reconstruct the theory of person and society in America in a way that makes it less directly a reflection of American culture as well as more theoretically satisfying and empirically correct. This is no easy task, for if existing critical, sociological, and psychological theories of the person in American society are little more than reflections of American culture, is there reason to hope that any theory can become more than a reflection of culture?

All social theory is, in part, discourse that both reflects and reproduces the culture from which it springs. Social theorists respond to the social world they experience, as well as to traditions of social thought, and their own theories become one means through which the culture of their society is realized and reproduced. Indeed, in a secular age where increasing numbers of people are exposed to their ideas, whether in college or through the mass media, social thought may become an even more important carrier of the culture and of its axes of variation. Sociologists, who take great pains to show their students and the public just how thoroughly social and how dependent on others the self is, do so in part because they are responding to a culture they themselves share, a culture in which people at times readily believe they may think and act independently of others and that the self may make and transform itself. Confronted with one pole of the culture, the sociologist responds by formulating the other pole. Psychologists celebrate the powers of the person to achieve fulfillment and remake society not only as a way of expressing their commitment to individualism but also in response to the communitarian pole of American culture. They too respond to one pole of the culture by formulating its opposite.

That social theory arises in response to and comes to express culture does not mean that it must do so naively or that we must therefore abandon the effort to construct theory or to put it to empirical test. It does mean, however, that we must be aware of the cultural matrix from which our ideas spring and, indeed, make the depiction of culture the very first step in our research and theory. If the work of social theorists of self and society—including social critics as well as those who labor in the more empirically grounded traditions of sociology and social psychology —embodies and expresses American culture, then the first step in reconstructing and improving that theory is by showing its connections with the culture. The result will not be a theory of the self that is in any sense free of the influence of culture. But it will be a theory of the self that is less committed to a particular moment of the culture.

Next . . .

The first task of this book is to examine a range of theories of the person in American society, not in order to criticize their shortcomings, but in order to see how they reflect American culture. Chapter II will examine the discourse of social critics, psychologists, and social scientists and attempt to glean from their interpretations of self and society in America some fundamental clues about the nature of American culture itself.

Chapter III will present a more formal approach to culture—one that incorporates Erikson's concept of axes of variation but that also draws theoretical inspiration from the work of George H. Mead—and apply this approach to American culture. My thesis is that American culture is divided along an individual/community axis of variation. Americans are pulled toward both autonomy and community, and so are confronted with the need to choose between several characteristically opposite ways of seeing themselves in relation to the social world: conformity versus rebellion, staying versus leaving, and dependence versus independence.

Chapter IV continues the analysis of American culture by treating the American experience as the epitome of modernity. The essence of modernity, I will argue, lies in an inherent and continuing contrast between community and society, and not in a simple and unilinear change from one to the other. Society is a large, complex, and open stage that invites individuals to perform as autonomous, individualized beings. Community is a more enclosing, simple, and supporting place that invites identification and promises security. Society has not replaced community; instead these two contrasting modes of social life continue to stand in mutual tension. Chapter IV will explore the implications of this view of modernity for the nature of modern community and examine the forms assumed by community in contemporary American society.

Chapter V returns the focus of the book to self theory by developing a theory of identity grounded in symbolic interactionism as well as in the preceding analyses of modernity and community. From a sociological vantage point, identity is the key concept on which a more general theory of self in society must be built. Identity is rooted in several "natural" processes—a quest for continuity of experience, a drive toward the integration of self-objectifications, a sense of likeness with others, and a sense of differentiation from them. Identity has three key forms—situated, social, and personal—each of which provides in its own way for continuity, integration, identification, and differentiation. Of these, social and personal identity are in a natural state of tension in modern society, the former rooted in community, the latter in society.

Chapter VI extends the theory of identity begun in Chapter V by examining the various strategies of self-construction spawned by American culture. In a culture defined by the tension between individual and community, the person is caught between the attractions of autonomous social participation and exclusive identification with community. This chapter will construct a typology whose purpose is to convey the range of solutions contemporary Americans find to these opposing forms of the person.

Finally, Chapter VII will summarize my reconstruction of self theory, paying particular attention to its implications for a critique of American culture and for social research on self-construction.

CHAPTER II

Social Theory as Cultural Text

The task of showing how theories of the person constitute discourses that realize American culture calls for conceptual tools. At the outset, two concepts—*culture* and *discourse*—will suffice. The conception of culture with which I will begin is that of Clifford Geertz, who summarizes it as

> essentially a semiotic one. Believing, with Max Weber, that man is an animal suspended in webs of significance he himself has spun, I take culture to be those webs, and the analysis of it to be therefore not an experimental science in search of law but an interpretive one in search of meaning.[1]

Although ultimately I will replace Geertz's interpretive approach to culture with a pragmatist one, a conception of culture as "webs of significance" will suffice for the present. Human beings, in this view, are not creatures blindly enacting a code, whether genetic or cultural, but creatures acting in their world as they conceive it and on the basis of the meanings that they have learned and that they bring to it.

To speak of American culture within this framework is to speak of the webs of significance Americans spin, within which they are suspended, and in terms of which they conduct themselves. Clearly it is beyond the scope of this book to capture and describe "American culture" in a comprehensive way. Even a culture more distant from one's own and of greater homogeneity requires painstaking care to grasp and describe, and never yields itself fully or finally to interpretation. Accordingly, my goal here is quite modest: to interpret a portion of American culture, specifically those meanings centered on the relationship between individual and society and on conceptions of what the person should, might, could, or must be. The goal is chosen because, I think, those meanings are key to other meanings.

How does one go about understanding even this limited cultural domain? I begin with the assumption that social theory, broadly construed to include sociological and social psychological theories of the self as well as social and cultural criticism, constitutes a form of discourse that reveals and also sustains a part of the web of meanings centering on the person to be found in American culture. Culture lives in such discourse, as well as elsewhere, and thus one way to understand a culture is to examine that discourse.

Discourse and Culture

In their everyday lives, people continually interpret the meaning of others' actions, attempting to learn the significance of what others are doing in order to formulate their own conduct. They do so in a variety of ways: by inferring the intentions of others so as to anticipate what they will do next; by attaching explicit labels to the conduct of others, considering it to be "stupid" or "dishonest" or a demonstration of "integrity"; by constructing explanations of the unexpected or undesired things that others do or of the unpleasant but inescapable situations in which people find themselves.

The efforts of those who share a culture to make sense of themselves and of the situations in which they find themselves may be termed discourse. Discourse is talk—about the joys and problems, opportunities and constraints of life, about other people and their actions, about motives, about types of people, about character, about sex, about ambition, about anything that matters to human beings. The object of discourse is to make sense—or, more formally, to construct interpretations that create sensible, understandable, meaningful accounts of whatever natural, supernatural, or human circumstance or event has stimulated talk.

In very broad terms, it is the unexpected that precipitates and focuses discourse.[2] People talk about things that are important to them, sometimes because they must do so in order to understand one another or to continue with their lines of conduct, sometimes because they are gathered at occasions like cocktail parties or summer evening street corner encounters with neighbors in which there is little to do except talk. Some topics are important because people are engaged in the business of solving problems, coping with events that threaten their capacity to act, their conceptions of themselves, or their happiness. Thus, parents and children hurl accusations at one another that have to do with "independence" and "freedom" and what "the other kids" are doing because, in American culture, both parents and their children are ambivalent about the prospects of relinquishing parental control or losing parental guidance. Office colleagues talk behind one another's backs and plot strategies of revenge or advancement. By the same token, discourse also focuses on the pleasantly unexpected. A man pursuing a woman finds that she accepts his invitation or returns his gaze, and reflects on what it might mean, and shares his questions and interpretations with his fellows. The salesperson makes a big sale, or a novelist makes the best-seller list, and both talk excitedly with their colleagues about their success and what it means and what they will do with the money they have made and how good the feeling of accomplishment is.

Human talk is both preparatory to action and a form of action in its own right. Whether it occurs in problematic or unexpectedly pleasant or exciting circumstances, discourse brings meaning to a situation and enables subsequent action. It constructs or creates meanings in such a way that people can imagine what they might do next and then decide what they will do. And it is itself a way of doing, a way of taking a stance toward the world and toward one's own place in it. When neighbors shake their heads in dismay at the latest offense of the delinquent who lives just around the corner, they give shape to their world and assign identities to those who inhabit it. When the successful talk about the meaning of their accomplishments, they separate themselves from the unsuccessful and bolster one another's self-esteem.

A great deal of everyday discourse consists of first-order interpretations.[3] When, for example, a *Newsweek* columnist shakes his head in disapproval of Yuppies and their misguided belief that they can achieve and have whatever they may want, he makes a first-order interpretation. When a contemporary Yuppie announces that she has discovered that the meaning of life lies in the appreciating value of real estate, she is, likewise, making a first-order interpretation. For that matter, when a parent accuses a child of dishonesty in secretly frequenting places he has been forbidden to go, another first-order interpretation has been made. Such interpretations use the terms and categories of a culture as they are understood by members to assign meaning to people, situations, and events. First-order interpretations impute motives, cite causes, and assign purpose to people and situations and thus render them intelligible within the more general web of cultural meanings.

Second-order interpretations may be conveniently (although perhaps too simply) defined as interpretations of interpretations. The real estate entrepreneur who attributes her interest in real estate to the feeling of control it gives her over her life and the parent who explains a child's dishonesty by citing a busy life that has made it difficult to give the child proper moral guidance are constructing second-order interpretations. Second-order interpretations often take for granted the validity of first-order interpretations. To the parent, for example, the child *is* dishonest, and the problem is to understand why, a problem solved by making a second-order interpretation that explains the dishonesty.

Viewed in these terms, theories of self and society may be thought of as second- or even higher-order interpretations—that is, as interpretations of interpretations, and sometimes as interpretations of interpretations of interpretations. The theories to be examined in this chapter—which posit changes in social character, the loss of identity, the decline of the self, the hollow core behind the facade of self-presentation, and the powers of self-actualization—are responses to social life that seek to capture the essence of something perceived as problematic and to explain why things are as they are. The theorist's sense of the problematic arises, in part, from a paradigm of observation and analysis maintained within a particular academic discipline or tradition of social criticism. But this sense of the problematic also reflects the theorist's own life and observations, his or her social position, the way the particular theorist or the discipline is engaged with the society as a whole, and, in the last analysis, the culture itself.

American theories of self and society constitute higher-order interpretations that both reflect and shape Americans' first-order interpretations of themselves in relation to the society and to their culture. American culture makes the nature of the person and his or her relationship to others problematic in ways that influence what theorists write about. In several of the examples to be examined in this chapter, theorists assert that the person has been drastically transformed by social changes of the last century. These assertions have their origins at least partly in matters of concern to the culture at large and not merely in the more restricted sense of problems maintained in the disciplines within which these theorists work. At the same time, however, such theoretical ideas, once formulated, enter the stream of cultural discourse and begin to shape both that discourse and the underlying experience it seeks to interpret. A theory that social change produces change in the person thus responds to a widely felt sense of the problematics of experience, but the theory subsequently becomes a way of interpreting that experience as well as an influence upon the experience itself.

The theoretical discourse to be examined enters the culture at several points. Sociologists, for example, theorize about the social foundations of the self or argue that modern society has transformed the self. Their interpretations are presented to their students through lectures and textbooks and sometimes also to the general public when their books reach a popular audience or when their ideas are disseminated by journalists. Psychologists theorize about self-actualization, and their ideas come into the cultural stream not only through their pedagogy and the popularization of their ideas but also through the therapy they give clients or through the efforts of educators and other practitioners to put their theories into practice.

Theoretical discourse has some obvious points of similarity with and difference from everyday talk. In everyday life, there is a more consistent focus on conduct: people often make first-order interpretations because they need a basis on which to act. The parent must assign meaning to the child's action—by calling it "dishonest," for instance—in order to have a basis for doing something about it. Implicit in this formulation is the idea that many first-order (and second-order) interpretations are possible, and that culture does not in any simple way determine conduct, but only provides the framework within which it occurs. Moreover, both first- and second-order interpretations in everyday life are matters of negotiation and conflict: the parent alleges dishonesty, but the child protests that he didn't mean to be dishonest, that circumstances account for his conduct. The parent explains the child's misdeed as a result of parental failure to make the value of honesty sufficiently clear and laments failing to do so; the child thinks to himself that he knows well enough he has disappointed himself and his parent and wonders if, given the opportunity, he would do the same thing again.

Theoretical discourse is public rather than private, and it is protracted, for the rapid give and take of face-to-face conversation is replaced by the almost slow motion of argument and counter-argument, theme and elaboration found in books and academic journals over a period of months or years. And there is likewise much less felt urgency to act, to do something about the situation that has precipitated discourse. Theoretical discourse generates a more diffuse imperative for action, for often those who engage in it urge no specific response to the circumstances they describe and, often, decry. Moreover, theoretical discourse has a life of its own, for although it enters and influences the culture at several points, it also exists within the partially autonomous sphere of the academic disciplines and the world of socially critical intellectuals. Often this discourse feeds upon itself, caught up within its own rhythms and purposes, oblivious to what is going on in the world outside the academy or the intellectual circle.

Even when they lack an explicit or implicit message about what should be done, however, and even when they become self-enclosed, all forms of discourse about human situations have the effect of realizing (in the sense of enacting or making concrete) the culture on whose webs of significance they depend. To speak of the dishonesty of children or write of the decline of the self is to make real the cultural categories of "dishonesty" and "character." To speak of one's failure to make standards of conduct plain to one's children or to write of the growing legions of suburbanites who take their behavioral cues from others rather than from within is to make real those cultural categories of "responsibility" and "conformity" in terms of which we understand our world and act in and on it.

To a great extent, this realization of culture occurs in the responses of individuals and groups to the discourse in question. Whether formal or informal, public or private, discourse elicits some kind of response—agreement or disagreement, praise or condemnation, approval or disapproval—that focuses on and evaluates important cultural objects. Talk about the decline of "character" and the growth of "conformity," we will see, constitutes "character" and "conformity" as meaningful objects of attention and conveys a moral or normative stance toward them.

Discourse about the person and about the character of specific persons or of categories of persons, therefore, is one of the ways in which American culture is realized—that is, made manifest, experienced, and brought into play as a basis for understanding and action. My thesis is that this form of discourse is a crucial way in which Americans interpret themselves and their experiences. To put the matter perhaps too simply, culture lives in discourse, and American culture lives in discourse about the person and about the person's relationship to society. And an important share of that discourse has come to be conducted in the language of the social sciences, psychology, and social criticism.

Accordingly, my purpose here is to build an interpretation of American culture by examining this discourse and its first- and higher-order interpretations. Any such interpretation of a culture must try to understand its central meanings but also to stand somewhat apart from them. My effort will be to comprehend what theorists mean when they talk about such matters as selfishness, individualism, character, personality, identity, and other terms that pertain to the person. The goal is to understand these categories as they are understood by those who employ them. And I must attempt to see things that the natives do not see, to grasp not only how they see the world and how they think they see the world but also themes and patterns in their understandings of which they typically remain unaware. To examine the variety of ways in which Americans talk about the person is to search for an interpretation that will make connections among disparate experiences and categories that do not, in the activities of everyday life, ordinarily seem connected.

This is clearly a task at which one cannot hope fully to succeed, for I am not in the position of a foreign observer who brings a fresh eye to American culture, but am, instead, myself a native sociologist. As a result, I can rise above the second-order interpretations of other natives only with some difficulty—only, in fact, by suspending belief in the validity of native categories that are often implicit in my own world view and by abstaining from taking an interest in the validity of native models, that is, those second- and higher-order interpretations that are the stuff of discourse. I do not know if there really are narcissists, other-directed persons, persons governed by impulse, or any of the other social types created by the discourse to be examined in this chapter. More to the point, these categories do not interest me as empirical categories, nor do assertions made about the categories interest me as empirical propositions that one might subject to test. Propositions about change or decline in character, the self, identity, personality, and the like are interesting not because they can be tested but because they are forms of discourse that reveal something about American culture.

With this minimal theoretical structure in mind, we can turn to specific illustrations of theoretical discourse about the self. Academics, social critics, independent intellectuals, writers, psychologists, literary critics, and others whose job it is to produce social theory are the manufacturers, distributors, and wholesalers of ideas about the person. My task in this chapter is to examine a reasonable sample of their discourse in order to see what it may reveal about American culture.[4]

Institutional and Impulsive Selves

The sample with which I will begin is a relatively obscure but well-focused expression of a more common and broader theme in the sociological analysis of American character. The text in question is a theoretical essay by a social psychologist, Ralph Turner, and its focus is on a transformation from "institution" to "impulse" as anchor points for the experience of "the real self" by Americans.[5] Its broader theme is the soon-to-be-familiar idea that self, character, identity, and other aspects of the person have been drastically transformed by modern society.

Turner is interested in how people experience themselves, and especially in the distinctions they routinely make between those feelings and actions they take as expressions of their "real" selves and those that seem foreign or peripheral. Experience is filled with impulses, sentiments, emotions, actions, and ideas, some of which we take as indicators of who or what we really are, whereas others seem accidental, irrelevant, or, some cases, foreign and threatening to our established self-conceptions. A lawyer who wins a crucial case may treat it as a validation of her conception of self as a good lawyer; a father who loses his temper with his son may apologize, saying that he hasn't been "himself" lately.

There are, according to Turner, two fundamentally different modes of experiencing the self, one labeled *institutional,* the other *impulsive.* The institutional mode of self-experience looks to society and its institutions for the anchor points of the self. In the institutional mode,

> an angry outburst or the excitement of extramarital desire comes as an alien impetus that superficially beclouds or even dangerously threatens the true self. . . . The true self is recognized in acts of volition, in the pursuit of institutionalized goals, and not in the satisfaction of impulses outside institutional frameworks.[6]

In contrast, the impulsive mode of self-experience looks to society, but in a negative way as the source of artificial and distorting restraints on the expression of the real self. In the impulsive mode,

> the outburst or desire is recognized—fearfully or enthusiastically—as an indication that the real self is breaking through a deceptive crust of institutional behavior. Institutional motivations are external, artificial constraints and superimpositions that bridle manifestations of the real self. . . . The real self consists of deep, unsocialized, inner impulses. Mad desire and errant fancy are exquisite expressions of the self.[7]

For "institutionals," the social world and its values are bedrock reality and the self is dependent upon and defined by them. For "impulsives," the self is bedrock, and society and its constraining norms threaten to distort and overwhelm it.

Institutionals and impulsives differ in several fundamental respects: in the motives they deem acceptable for conduct, their views on the origins of the self, the significance of self-control, the nature of hypocrisy, the role performances they value, their perspectives on time, and the form of individualism they espouse. Institutionals accept high standards of conduct for themselves and believe that the person "shows his true mettle under fire." They believe that the self is created through effort, and that "waiting around for self-discovery to occur is ridiculous. The self is something attained, created, achieved, not something discovered."[8] Institutionals place considerable emphasis on self-control, locating the real self in acts of volition and feeling it to be revealed when the person is in control of self and situation. For institutionals, one is a hypocrite when one fails to live up to the standards to which one is committed. One strives for a "polished, error-free performance, in which the audience forgets the actor and sees only the role being played" and one tries to keep one's eye on the future by making commitments to others and to institutionally valued social roles. Individualism consists of the rejection of pressures for mediocrity and the compromise of principle.

Impulsives reverse these attitudes and beliefs. One should do things because one truly wants to, "not because it is good or bad or noble or courageous or self-sacrificing, but because [one] spontaneously wishes to do so." Furthermore, the self is something to be discovered rather than made, for what one truly is can only be known through reflection, by trying out various alternatives. For impulsives, "the true self is revealed only when inhibitions are lowered or abandoned." One is a hypocrite if one asserts and lives by standards that call upon one to do things one does not truly wish to do. One strives to reveal one's human frailties, to show the whole self, warts and all, to others. Life exists in and for the present, not some distant future, and one shows oneself an individual by repudiating institutional claims that would restrict the expression of impulse.

According to Turner, there have been substantial shifts away from institutional selves and toward impulsive selves. That is, people are changing, becoming less accepting of society and its constraints and more inclined to anchor their conceptions of reality within themselves. They are coming to perceive society not as the repository of a set of "values" to be sought or realized, but as a set of "norms" that constrain and restrict the individual. While he argues that this change has occurred "over the past several decades," it is also a longer-term historical development. It is paralleled in literature by a growing disenchantment with culture, and

Turner approvingly cites Lionel Trilling's distinction between "sincerity" and "authenticity," which the distinction between institutional and impulsive self-anchorage resembles.[9]

Relating Turner's views to the culture of which they are higher-order interpretations is a matter of some complexity. He reports on a variety of first-order interpretations Americans use to attach meaning to their own experiences and to the actions of others. A large number of the terms and phrases he uses to capture the contrasting ways in which the self is viewed have the ring of cultural authenticity, and one senses Turner has done a good job as a "native informant" who can convey the distinctions that are relevant in a culture and the ways members use them. Whether there are, in fact, two distinguishable character types is a difficult empirical question, and, in any event, it is quite beside the point here. Turner seems to have captured a language in terms of which the self has been conceived, talked about, viewed, examined, and debated by Americans, particularly during the 1970s, when the article appeared. He has, in other words, captured and described some of the major terms in which discourse about the self is conducted.

It is not entirely clear from Turner's discussion whether the characterological typology of institutionals and impulsives is of interest to ordinary people or only to the social scientist. On the one hand, the distinction between "institutionals" and "impulsives" looks to be of relevance to the social scientist interested in social change, but not to those whose self-orientations it distinguishes. The "natives," one might infer from some of the presentation, go happily about their way oblivious to the fact that some of them are institutionals and some are impulsives.

On the other hand, there are hints in the discussion that perhaps the distinction between institutionals and impulsives—or at least between some of the particular constituent elements of these types—is of relevance to ordinary people and does, in fact, describe a way they think about one another. When, for example, Turner tells us that institutionals find "waiting around for self-discovery" to be "ridiculous," he hints that institutionals and impulsives have one another in their sights and that at least part of the experience of self in this society is of a contrast between one's own sense of where the real self lies and how others differ from one in this respect. In other words, it is not simply that people have either an institutional or an impulsive experience of the real self, but that the adoption of one mode requires both knowledge and explicit rejection of the other. If we adopt this reading of Turner, institutionals are those who do not merely experience the attractive warmth of social institutions but who also reject what to them are the absurd antics of impulsives. For their part, impulsives do not simply find the reality of the self in impulse, but give meaning to this experience by comparing it with the rigidity and repression of the institutionals.

On this framework of interpretations Turner builds an interpretation that is of interest here as cultural discourse. His "native model" emphasizes social change, viewing the zenith of the institutional mode of self-anchorage as falling in the past and that of the impulsive as in the present or perhaps the future. This is not a conclusive, or even a forcibly stated interpretation, however, for toward the end of his essay, Turner wavers, telling us that there are still some institutionals around and that perhaps most individuals will seek both kinds of anchorages at one point or another in their lives.

The propensity to see change in the person, as in the family, religion, education, politics, and other social institutions—and, by and large, to attribute it to urbanization, industrialization, modernization, or capitalism—is a pronounced cultural pattern among sociologists. I do not mean to allege that sociologists are imagining things when they see such changes. The point is more simply that sociologists are disposed not only to look for change but to cast their interpretations of contemporary society in terms of contrasts between what was and what is, between some state of affairs that once existed and that which now exists or is coming to be. The reasons for this cultural pattern perhaps lie in the origins of sociology in the political and industrial revolutions of the eighteenth and nineteenth centuries, when the intellectual response to change, whether conservative, liberal, or radical, formed what we now know as the social sciences.

It is questionable, however, whether the apparent cultural ease with which Turner formulates an hypothesis of a changing self is simply and only a reflection of this cultural proclivity of the social scientist to see change. For there is a more plausible alternative explanation, which sees this social science paradigm as a mirror of its culture. If the social psychologist sees a self transformed by history, it is in part because change is an important interpretive framework in the very culture itself—not just the culture of social science, but American culture more generally, and perhaps even, in very broad terms, the culture of the modern world. The self as an object of contemporary concern and interest seems suspended in a web of cultural significance in which *change* is a necessary component.

Turner struggles with a variety of explanations of why the self has changed its locus from institutional to impulsive, and these are as instructive about the cultural origins of his theorizing as is his assumption of change itself. Turner reviews the possibility that broader cultural changes have led to the transformation of the self. Secularization, for example, may have made psychological explanations of behavior more believable, and thereby opened the way to the increasing credibility of impulse. Or, perhaps, it was the growing recognition of cultural diversity that undermined the unquestioned authority of any particular culture and thereby also its social institutions. Another line of reasoning involves the change in dominant cultural orientations from production to consumption. During the nineteenth century, with its pronounced industrial growth, such qualities as discipline, ambition, dedication to work and family were essential and this encouraged institutional allegiances. As the emphasis shifted from production to consumption, a different set of qualities became important, including "the cultivation of personal tastes, expressive styles, and distinctive psychological 'needs'" that can be interpreted as more closely linked to an impulsive mode of self-anchorage. Finally, Turner theorizes that perhaps the locus of the self has been transformed as institutions have become undependable sources of reward either because institutions themselves have become disorderly or because the spatial and temporal distance between what the individual does and the rewards earned for that action has become too great. If people do not feel rewarded for their institutional commitments, they are likely to find reality within narrower and more private spheres of existence.

Turner realizes the complexity of the explanatory problem that confronts him, and his is no naive attempt at theorizing. The alternative explanations he considers do, however, represent something of a precis of various theories of social change with which sociologists and other social scientists have been preoccupied and that constitute a major part of the "webs of significance" through which they interpret the world: the decline of religious and the rise of secular theories as ultimate explanations and justifications of human behavior; the declining authority of fixed social institutions and the rise of cultural relativism; the degradation of work and the ascendancy of consumerism; the decline of warm communities and the growth of impersonal bureaucracy. The suggestion I wish to advance is that we look at this body of ideas—here enlisted in the task of explaining the transformation of the self—not only as social theory but also as a part of the culture that Americans, and members of Western societies generally, share.

To put the matter somewhat more forcibly, Turner's analysis of the real self and its transformations is an expression, couched in the language of social science, of a cultural complex of ideas, beliefs, and assumptions that is widely shared in American society. There is an assumption of the importance of the self as an object, a propensity to view the present as either a drastic improvement over or a lamentable decline from the past, a view of social life that emphasizes contrasting, and in some degree, even conflicting orientations, and, perhaps surprisingly, an emphasis on character.

In common usage, "character" denotes the person's inner nature, moral fiber, "backbone," and self-control, those elements of inner constitution that make one a moral person who, by the effort and example of conduct, will earn the respect and admiration of society. "Personality," in contrast, denotes more superficial and transitory attributes of the person, those surface appearances that should be cultivated so that one will be liked by others. In one of the standard social science paradigms for viewing and explaining the transformations in society and person from the nineteenth to the twentieth century, character has declined in significance and personality has gained. Twentieth-century Americans are supposedly less concerned with moral fiber and more concerned with appearances, less interested in respect and admiration and more interested in popularity, less driven by conceptions of higher morality and more by expediency.[10]

Although the empirical validity of this paradigm is inherently difficult to assess, it is in some ways a self-undermining form of discourse. That is, the very existence of discourse about types of character contradicts the premise that matters of "character" are no longer of interest. Talk about the "real self" necessarily employs conceptions of character as well as of personality, of desirable elements in the makeup of the person and not simply of how persons appear. And when conceptions of character are formulated, even by the social scientist who believes that interest in character has declined, we have a bit of evidence of a continuing interest in character. The social scientist's sermon is oblique, but it is no less a warning that something significant has occurred or is occurring.

The distinction between institutional and impulsive selves—in whatever particular terms it may be formulated—is a cultural interpretation of importance and use to cultural members. It is not simply an analytical device of the social psychologist, but seems to be one of the ways in which an underlying cultural polarity of views of the person is expressed. The social scientist writes about types of character in order to follow the theoretical and research mandates of the discipline. But, in effect, such discourse renders palpable something that is more ambiguously and viscerally felt—namely, a tension between a conception of the person as a derivative of society whose character is tested by loyalty and devotion to it, and a conception of the person as the creator of society who is entitled to the expression of individuality and "personality." Social scientists give one of several voices to a less articulated but widely shared tendency to see society and the person as in opposition or tension. "Character" and "personality" and "institution" and "impulse" formulate this felt tension in specific ways and thus make available a more focused way for people to understand themselves in relation to society.

What use do people make of such constructions of types of character? In the case of Turner's work the relevant question is really, how do undergraduate students respond to the chore of reading his essay on the "real self"?

Student audiences do not simply absorb and believe the implicit assumptions, categories, and supposed facts that are presented to them. Some students see themselves in these types, some seem offended by one type or the other, some dispute either the morality or the technical possibility of constructing such typologies, and some find Turner's interest in the topic a relic of a bygone era. Here, as in all aspects of social life, the meaning of a gesture, of an act, of any effort to communicate or influence conduct lies in the response it arouses in those to whom it is directed.

One important and common element in such responses to the moral neutrality of the social psychologist, who tries not to express a preference for one character type over another, is the introduction of normative considerations. The person becomes an object of normative interest and emerges either clean-smelling or foul; the important point is that the moral nostrils are stimulated, even though the social scientist had in mind something much different—namely, the objective portrayal of the human condition. Undergraduates learn about "institutionals" and marvel that other people could be as repressed as their parents, while breathing a sign of relief that their generation, at least, has managed to escape this predicament; or they learn about "impulsives" and now have a label to attach to those of their friends whose lack of commitments and plans have mystified them.

To put this in a slightly different way, the social types created by social scientists, which are typically intended solely as description, engender responses of normative judgment and of identification that give continuing voice to the opposing conceptions of the person that characterize American culture. The range of responses to the types constructed by social scientists is broad: one may think of Turner's institutionals as impossibly rigid and old-fashioned or as holding high the banner of personal responsibility in an age of selfishness; one may see the impulsives as breaking the chains of the past or as a sign of social decay. But, whatever the particular response, it seems to involve a normative dimension, a concern with what is right and proper and desirable in the person as against what is not. Identification—whether in a positive or a negative way—is a sign of this concern, for when people seek either to be like or to be different from the models that are presented to them, we have evidence that normative judgments are being made. And, at bottom, it is in the making of such judgments that contradictory conceptions of the person are expressed and reproduced.

Conformity

Ralph Turner's 1976 analysis of "the real self" followed a path broken in 1950 by *The Lonely Crowd*, a classic work in the annals of social science and in the interpretation of American culture.[11] This book, co-authored by David Riesman, Ruel Denney, and Nathan Glazer, is a classic as much because it became a surprise best-seller as for its substantive contributions to social science. Indeed, it is the fact that it did become a popular book that makes it especially noteworthy. Riesman and his associates contributed a new classification of character types to social science, but they also struck a responsive chord in the public, resulting in the comparatively rare phenomenon of an academic book not only contributing to the vocabulary of the self but also becoming a commercial success. That the chord to which the book-buying public and the scientific and literary critics responded was not precisely the chord the authors had struck adds another note of cultural significance to their work.

The main lines of the argument are familiar. Building on, but also endeavoring to go beyond, the analysis of national character that had commanded the attention of psychoanalytically inclined anthropologists during World War II, Riesman focused on what he called "social character." The concept takes both a broader and a narrower meaning, the former drawing upon a psychological conception of character as "the more or less permanent socially and historically conditioned organization of an individual's drives and satisfactions" and the latter incorporating the more sociological idea of conformity to social and cultural dictates. Thus, social character is defined as "that part of 'character' which is shared among significant social groups and which . . . is the product of the experience of these groups."[12] In actual usage, however, Riesman narrows his focus to a definition of social character that reflects a question of considerable interest to sociologists—namely, how a society manages to induce its members to do what the society wants them to do. That is, the focus of Riesman's concept of social character is narrowed to conformity and how it is socially ensured, and his famed typology of character types turns on differences in the way societies have, at different times, ensured conformity to their demands.

For the bulk of human history, economic, technological, and demographic circumstances have favored a "tradition-directed" social character in which "the conformity of the individual tends to reflect his membership in a particular age-grade, clan, or caste; he learns to understand and appreciate patterns which have endured for centuries, and are modified but slightly as the generations succeed each other."[13] The tradition-directed social character is adapted to a society in which there is little in the way either of real change or of efforts to promote change. The society lives in a kind of equilibrium with its material environment, and its way of life is sustained by a "tight web of values" in which legitimation rests upon established, familiar, and "traditional" ways of doing things.

The "inner-directed" and "other-directed" character types have made a more recent appearance on the historical scene. "Inner-direction," which developed in "the kind of society that emerged with the Renaissance and Reformation and that is only now vanishing," entails a very different mode of social conformity: "The source of direction for the individual is 'inner' in the sense that it is implanted early in life by the elders and directed toward generalized but nonetheless inescapably destined goals."[14] The society in which the inner-directed social character is found is one of social change and growth. It is a developing, modernizing society, in which the premium for behavior shifts from the careful enactment of patterns of behavior that have served well in the past to the capacity to adapt to changing circumstances and to make one's mark in a world in which tradition has been splintered. The inner-directed person, typified by the nineteenth-century entrepreneurs and pioneers who settled the United States and developed its industry, has a "psychological gyroscope," a guidance system developed in childhood that enables the individual to maintain "a delicate balance between the demands upon him of his life goal and the buffetings of his external environment."[15]

The society in which inner-direction develops is a changing, growing society in which a strong emphasis is placed upon production. Savings, personal discipline, commitment to long-range goals, and the deferral of gratification are encouraged. But as the society achieves its goals, the emphasis begins to shift from production to consumption, from discipline to enjoyment. And production itself shifts from small-scale to large-scale organizations—the division of labor grows both larger and more complex. The result is the emergence of the third of Riesman's character types, the "other-directed" social character.

The other-directed person is equipped with a "psychological radar" rather than a moral gyroscope, for the essence of life for this character type is sensitivity to the needs and expectations of others:

> What is common to all the other-directed people is that their con-temporaries are the source of direction for the individual—either those known to him or those with whom he is indirectly acquainted, through friends and through the mass media. . . . The goals toward which the other-directed person strives shift with that guidance; it is only the process of striving itself and the process of paying close attention to the signals from others that remain unaltered throughout life.[16]

The other-directed person is sensitive to others, to what they are doing and to what their actions imply for his or her own conduct. There is an "insatiable psychological need for approval" that goes well beyond what is a normal human wish for the liking of others because, for the other-directed person, this need is the "chief source of direction and the chief area of sensitivity."

Different modes of social conformity imply different instrumentalities of motivation and social control. The tradition-directed person is in part motivated to conform by the sentiment of shame, for although this person is under no compulsion to be a certain kind of person, there is strong pressure to act in approved ways, and one fears the shame that will surely result if one does not. The inner-directed individual is held on the straight and narrow path by an inner gyroscope, and should this person veer from the proper course, the result is guilt. For the other-directed person, sensitive to a far wider range of social signals and operating in a far more heterogeneous and cosmopolitan milieu, the important mechanism of social control is more likely to involve a diffuse anxiety.

There is one final complication to be considered. For Riesman, social character is not a perfect replica of the society. In other words, although there is a dominant mode of social conformity, a society is never fully successful in integrating everyone into its orientations. If most people are adjusted, orienting themselves to a prevailing mode of conformity and accepting its constraints, others are either *anomic* or *autonomous*. The anomic are those who are unable to live within the dominant mode— unable, that is, to reproduce expected patterns of behavior in a tradition-directed society, to establish and follow a life course in an inner-directed society, or to act on the basis of an appropriate sensitivity to others in an other-directed social world. The autonomous are able to conform, but somehow have the capacity to rise above social demands, to see further than their peers, to think of new ways of doing things, to choose to act in non-conforming ways.

In an inner-directed society, the autonomous are those who are not so blindly driven by their gyroscopes, who have the capacity to choose their goals and set their own pace in pursuing them. It is more difficult to understand who the autonomous are in an other-directed society, for the quest for autonomy is itself more difficult. The autonomous person in an inner-directed world has something concrete against which to rebel —a set of internalized goals with which to struggle and above which to rise. But the other-directed person has a more nebulous enemy, for in a world where people are sensitive to one another and wish only to take one another's wishes and feelings into account—to exaggerate the conception of other-direction slightly—social demands "appear so reasonable, even trivial." [17]

Although we are informed that there is little we know about autonomy, it is clear that here is where Riesman's sympathies lie. Each mode of social conformity offers at least some opportunities for individuals to rise above it. Those who live in tradition-directed societies have the fewest such opportunities, for the circumstances of life, especially material conditions, encourage people to think that there are no other ways of being. In inner-directed societies, there is the possibility of choosing one's own goals. And in the other-directed societies coming into being, there is perhaps even less need than ever before in history for people slavishly to conform to social demands. As the importance of work declines in relation to the significance of leisure, Riesman hopes, the opportunities for the other-directed person to become autonomous will increase.

Social scientists of Riesman's day responded to his work critically, in part because it had made too much of the relationship between the demographic transition and change in character. It was also criticized by some who felt that it failed to make an empirical case for the predominantly inner-directed character of Americans in the nineteenth century and their growing other-directed character in the twentieth. Historians and sociologists alike pointed out what seemed to them to be its selectivity in perceiving character traits, and they provided numerous examples of ways in which Americans of the nineteenth century seemed equally as other-directed as those of the twentieth.[18] There was, among social scientists, a tendency to underplay Riesman's references to autonomy and to give most stress to the three modes of conformity.

The Lonely Crowd was an unexpected best-seller. Far from being used only as a reading for courses in social science, as the publisher and authors expected, it sold well in its first publication by Yale University Press and later in an abridged paperback edition. Not surprisingly, it was widely interpreted as an attack on conformity, which was associated with the other-directed character type. It helped stimulate and sustain a spirited discussion of "conformism," a word that came into common use during the 1950s and was a central term for the apprehension of self then, just as "identity" would become in the 1960s and 1970s. The most common public perception seems to have involved a sense of decline from the "good old days" of inner-direction, when people weren't conformists, to the "bad new days" of other-direction, when they were rapidly becoming "organization men" in grey flannel suits, faces in the crowd of mass society, keeping up with the Joneses without any independent sense of morality or direction.

What can we make of Riesman's analysis as discourse that reflects American culture? As with Turner's analysis, the point in looking at Riesman's work in this way is not to discredit it as social science, but rather to draw from it themes that may tell us more about the webs of cultural significance in which Americans live. Even if one were to accept the conceptual structure as a valid basis for conducting historical research on changing character, there would be ample warrant for considering it as a cultural document. For no work of social science is thoroughly immune from influence by the categories and meanings of the culture in which it is created. *The Lonely Crowd* is certainly not immune, for in conception and execution it is not merely a neutral work of social science but an ethically and critically involved study of the American character that is deeply concerned with what might become of it as well as with the task of describing it.

As a document of the culture, *The Lonely Crowd* elicited a normative response in spite of the fact that it reduced the treatment of character to a neutral sociological conception of conformity. Even though conformity is sociologically inevitable and varies only in the way it is ensured, as the authors pointed out, the book was widely interpreted as a warning against the growth, in post-war American life, of a tendency to conform to the dictates of others. Descriptions of the inner-directed character of the nineteenth century evoked nostalgia for a time when, as the common misinterpretation went, people were not conformists because they listened to their inner voices rather than to the crowd around them. Conformity was thus equated with other-direction and autonomy with inner-direction.

Why such a response? Although Riesman and his associates were careful to point out that their analysis was tentative and suggestive and that the other-directed character was just beginning to appear, their analysis was granted the status of fact, at least by those sympathetic to its message. Given that the message was apparently so badly misinterpreted by a great many readers, it is an intriguing and important question as to why it found such an eager audience. The paradox lies in the fact that Americans of the 1950s, who were supposedly becoming other-directed, were alarmed by the prospect and took up the cry against the dangers of conformity by purchasing and talking about a book that could easily have been read as a sympathetic depiction of the other-directed character.

The interest generated by *The Lonely Crowd* is easily explained by positing an interest in the nature and character of the person as a significant cultural theme. American culture seems to put people in a position of ambiguity about themselves. Although relatively few are now actively preoccupied with anxiety about the status of their souls as were the Puritans, whose Calvinism encouraged not only a view of the self as depraved but also ongoing worry about whether one was among those predestined for salvation, the heritage of this general self-doubt lingers in a more general form. There seems to be a persistent impulse among Americans to worry about whether they are what they should be, whether they have the sort of personal traits, abilities, skills, social manners, or inner strength they should have. The sense of ambiguity does not stem from individual lack of adjustment to social life, but is an inherent part of the culture and its system of meanings.

We must posit more than a cultural concern with the meaning of the self in order to explain why this book met so ready a reception and generated so characteristic a misinterpretation of its main point. Previously I suggested that American culture holds up conflicting conceptions of what the person should be. *The Lonely Crowd* enables a clearer specification of that idea, for its reception suggests that a cultural opposition between *conformity* and *autonomy* is one of a number of pairs of terms that give concrete and specific content to the more general conflicting conceptions of the person. Each term in this pair formulates a kind of person that is viewed both positively and negatively by Americans. The widespread attack on "conformism" in the 1950s should not obscure the fact that Americans, in other contexts, value precisely those traits of other-direction depicted in the book, as well as the fact that conformity is itself viewed as a virtue under many circumstances. Similarly, the tendency of its audience to emphasize what they saw as a warning against conformity rather than to perceive Riesman's preference for autonomy does not mean that no value is placed on autonomy by Americans. For just as conformity is both a positive value and a term of derision for Americans, so, also, autonomy is both something feared and a term of approbation.

Both conformity with and autonomy from the expectations of others are perceived, in American culture, as desirable qualities of the person. Each is both encouraged and discouraged, sought and avoided, praised and condemned. Riesman's book thus found an audience not only because it formulated ideas about the fate of the person in American society but also because it resonated with one of the key dimensions of ambivalence in terms of which this fate is experienced. The key to the book's appeal lay in its formulation of social character in terms of the concept of conformity, which was read by the public not in its sociological sense, but in relation to a culturally spawned anxiety that one might conform too much—or not enough.

The Lonely Crowd was an interesting book because of its apparent focus on the troubling issues of conformity and autonomy. Its virtue lay in the way it was able to provide a culturally meaningful resolution of these issues. Like the discourse about the real self considered earlier, the resolution was achieved by incorporating the dimension of social change. There once was a time, the book appeared to say, when people were not slavishly conformed to the opinions of others, when they followed the dictates of their own consciences, of their inner sense of direction and purpose. All of that has changed, for conformity rages in the very being of the other-directed person. Such an interpretation simultaneously allows an expression of the fear of conformity and of the value placed on autonomy.

Yet it is a curious interpretation, for autonomy is anchored in a character type, the inner-directed, that lies safely in the past, and, indeed, one in which some of the attributes of conformity to the needs and interests of society can readily be perceived. Moreover, Riesman's description of other-direction, misinterpreted as conformity, could readily be interpreted as a warning against excess, as a danger signal that, once sounded, might alert readers to be careful about what they do and what they are. In this sense, discourse about what is for a time perceived as a problem with the national character not only gives voice to opposing conceptions of character but introduces hope for the future, for what can be described in American culture is also what can be improved, prevented, changed, or ameliorated.

Taken together, the discourses considered thus far seem to have explored several facets of a more fundamental cultural division about the proper nature of the person. Both Turner and Riesman seem either to respond to or describe a cultural imperative that the individual come to some kind of self-understanding—whether by discovering and experiencing the true self or by achieving some resolution of the issue of conformity versus autonomy. But the terms in which this self-understanding may be achieved are not simply presented, for the person seems confronted with contrary advice. One should look within oneself for the resources and the direction with which to live one's life; at the same time, one should be loyal to society and its institutions, for it is only in the company of others and through the dutiful performance of one's social roles that one realizes a proper character. One should be autonomous, but one should also conform to the expectations of society; one should listen to one's own inner voice, but one should also listen to the needs of others.

American culture, at least insofar as it pertains to the self and is revealed by discourse about the person, thus consists not of a dominant set of meanings, but of a set of meanings defined by opposing terms and conceptions. The culture thus to a great extent exists in and through a continuing debate about what the person is and should be. The terms of this debate have been increasingly provided by social science, which interprets the contemporary world largely by contrasting it with the past. But this social science conception itself reflects a more widespread way of defining the relationship between self and society and is not simply a source of terms by means of which the contrast can be grasped. Americans act within a set of meanings that make the nature of the person an important matter, but also one that is difficult to grasp. They do so in a social context in which a variety of images of what is, what was, what could be, and what should be are under continual discussion. They are made self-conscious by the culture itself—by its emphasis on the person, by its conflicting conceptions of what the person should be, and by its provision of an interpretive frame that emphasizes change in the culture itself as well as in the person.

The American cultural debate about the person is conducted in diverse terms, for there are several polarities that make the person problematic and discourse about them is, like other forms of discourse, subject to fads and fashions and to the periodic introduction of new terms of analysis. One of these terms, *identity*, achieved considerable prominence beginning in the late 1950s and is still in common use. Analysis of it will reveal some familiar cultural meanings as well as new dimensions of ambiguity and anxiety.

Identity

In 1958, a psychiatrist, Allen Wheelis, published *The Quest for Identity*, which addressed issues similar to those Riesman and his colleagues had considered almost a decade earlier, but which adopted the language of the professional psychiatrist and promoted adoption of the term "identity," which was by then coming into widespread use. Its focus was

> a change in the character of the American people. . . . The change is within the lifetime of most persons of middle or advanced years, and the process of change is still underway. The social character of ourselves and our children is unmistakably different from what we remember of the character of our grandparents.[19]

Wheelis saw a change in character that he described in terms that mirror the popular conception of *The Lonely Crowd* rather than Riesman's own conception of the social transformation that had occurred. According to Wheelis, the change in character involved the ascendancy of the group over the individual. "Man is still the measure of all things," he wrote, "but it is no longer the inner man that measures; it is the other man. Specifically, it is the plurality of men, the group. And what the group provides is shifting patterns, what it measures is conformity. It does not provide the hard inner core by which the value of patterns and conformity is determined."[20] In this transformation, people have become more aware of their identities, but less satisfied with them.

What is identity? In a formulation that encompasses some of Erik Erikson's vision of mature identity, but which is broader and more diffuse,

Wheelis makes identity dependent upon meaning, upon the extent to which the person's efforts in life "make sense. . . . It depends also upon stable values, and upon the conviction that one's actions and values are harmoniously related. It is a sense of wholeness, of integration, of knowing what is right and what is wrong and of being able to choose."[21] This conception of identity embraces both of two meanings conveyed by this term. On the one hand, identity conveys the idea of "identification with" others and a sense of likeness with them. To have an identity in this sense is to identify with a social group of some kind. On the other hand, identity also conveys the sense of continuity over time. To have an identity in this sense is to have a sense of self as a continuously whole and distinct entity, one that varies from one situation to the next yet remains fundamentally the same.

Identity was once an easily attained sense of personal meaning, for one was accorded an assured place in the social world. If anything, Wheelis explains, the problem our ancestors had to cope with was that they were too clearly placed and had little leeway in the construction of identity. In the modern world, an assured sense of self is harder to achieve, for there is little that the person can exclude from consciousness. Contemporary people have more things to integrate than did their ancestors. They are more aware of themselves, have a greater range of experiences, encounter a broader array of meanings. Although their lives are more narrowly specialized, and in spite of the fact that the nation as a whole is more homogeneous than it was a century ago, contemporary people experience a more diverse culture. As a result, the authority of the superego has declined, and "there has occurred in society as a whole during the past two generations a development analogous to that which occurs in an individual during psychoanalysis, an expansion of awareness at the expense of the unconscious."[22] During the nineteenth century, Wheelis tells us, values were relatively stable and were transmitted to the person by parents and established as "a relatively permanent and autonomous agency." But, in this century, values are not stable, for the world changes too much and too fast. Accordingly, the superego has declined and the role of the ego has expanded.

Thus, the person of the twentieth century faces different problems than the person of the nineteenth. Formerly, when the superego was strong, powerful drives that ran counter to its guidance had to be repressed, and if those drives were strong enough, the result was the classic symptom neurosis of psychiatry. But in the contemporary world, the person is caught in a real dilemma:

> If out of the multitudinous choices of modern life he commits himself to certain values and with them builds a durable identity, he is apt to lose contact with a rapidly changing world; if he does not commit himself, but maintains an alert readiness to move with the current, he suffers a loss of the sense of self. Not knowing what he stands for, he does not know who he is. This occasions the anxiety which is coming to be the name of our age.[23]

Thus, the contemporary psychoanalyst does not deal with the classic symptom neurosis, but with "vague conditions of maladjustment and discontent."

The social character of the present age, then, is one adapted to fit a "culture of change." The person must be more malleable, more able to change his or her mind and to shift from one set of values to another. In the new social character,

> the light touch supplants the firm grip; the launcher of trial balloons replaces the committed man. One avoids final decisions, keeps everything subject to revision, and stands ready to change course when the winds change. The key words for our time are flexibility, adjustment, and warmth—as, for our grandfathers, they were work, thrift, and will.[24]

But this kind of social character implies a diminished drive for achievement, a lessened sense of direction, a weakened sense of purpose. With nowhere to go and few commitments, the modern person has a sense of restlessness and longing that provides a reserve energy for mass movements. Although people are not satisfied with themselves and their lives, they seemingly can't escape this situation.

The Quest for Identity thus anchors its analysis of the changing self in a depiction of a transformed social world that in some respects resembles that of *The Lonely Crowd*. The stable, fixed world of the past, in which people had a clear sense of purpose and commitments to goals established early in life, has given way to a fluid, changing society in which people feel cast adrift and, accordingly, follow the feet of others rather than their inner compasses. It is a world described in terms of a profound sense of loss of what was and of concern about what will be, for Wheelis evoked an even stronger nostalgia than did Riesman, in spite of his vivid portrayals of nineteenth-century cultural rigidity. Although it would be an overstatement to say that Wheelis locates good only in the last century and evil solely in this one, there is no question but that he casts a concerned and sometimes stern eye on the present and the future.

The Quest for Identity helped popularize identity as a new term in the American vocabulary of self, but in many respects its vision of past and present resembles that of Riesman, Turner, and others. Instead of the sociologist's anchor points of conformity and social control, Wheelis used the psychiatrist's language and the concept of identity that had been gaining currency since Erik Erikson's development of the concept of ego identity. Still, there was the same hearkening back to a past in which values were more certain and more stable, the person looked inward for a sense of direction, and life therefore had meaning and purpose. Although Wheelis clearly portrayed the personal costs of such a sharply crystallized sense of identity, he also evoked a nostalgia similar to that evoked by Riesman. One imagines that readers misinterpreted Wheelis's work in much the same way as they did Riesman's, attributing autonomy to those clear-sighted and hard-headed nineteenth-century men and women and conveniently forgetting the darker, sterner, more repressive side of their culture.

The cultural message of *The Quest for Identity* thus closely resembles that of *The Lonely Crowd* in its portrayal of conformity as a major problem of twentieth-century America. But in its adoption of the concept of identity it also helped to stimulate the use of a catchword that was even more easily assimilated into American usage than were Riesman's concepts of inner-direction and other-direction. "Identity" captured a different aspect of the American dilemma of the self, for it described and seemed to explain the felt paradox of life in a society seemingly in constant change.

"Change," it appears, is an interpretive device of general utility in American culture. Americans look for evidence of change, lament change, welcome change, and, in general, interpret both personal experience and social life in terms of the idea that change is ubiquitous. As a result, the person seems suspended in a web of conflicting meanings. On the one hand, if change is good, then one had best be prepared to accept it and to cope with it, and that seems to imply a readiness to change the kind of person one is. The implications of such a stance are reasonably clear: one must avoid entangling commitments, chart a course from which one may easily deviate, and be open, loose, and adaptive. But, if change is bad, then one must try to steer a steady course in the midst of shifting currents; one must strive to remain constant in an inconstant world; one must try to maintain one's commitments to others in a social world in which people are prepared to break their promises.

Discourse about identity formulates an analysis of the problems of the individual in a culture that fosters both commitment and mobility. The portrayal of a former era in which identity was strong and stable because people had an assured sense of place and of a present era of identity diffusion and anxiety is, in one sense, a pessimistic diagnosis, for it seems to imply that the best lies in the past. At the same time, however, this form of discourse is also optimistic, for it meshes with a cultural pattern of optimism in which the diagnosis of a personal or social ill is seen as preface to the search for a solution. If Americans are so receptive to diagnoses of changing and declining character, it is not because of a penchant for self-flagellation, but because of a belief that what is broken can be repaired. The cultural significance of a problem lies in the related belief that a solution can be found.

Talk about identity formulates the problem in both a sociological and a psychological way, although it is the latter formulation that generally gains the upper hand. On the one hand, because the causes of identity problems are social, their solution is seen to lie at least partly in the reform of, if rarely in wholesale changes in, the social order. On the other hand, identity also defines a problem in such a way that it can be dealt with through individual therapy, as well as through independent activity. The person who can attribute all manner of discontents to problems of identity has gained a warrant to explore his or her place in the world and to attempt to gain a new sense of self, through therapy or through changes in occupation, leisure activity, beliefs, or group membership.

Identity as a term of discourse about the person thus helps to sustain the very culture that produces it. "Identity" is an ideal associated with the past as well as a way of formulating individual goals in the present. It evokes nostalgia for a sense of place even as it reminds the individual of the need to make a place in the contemporary world. It provides a way of focusing and directing self-consciousness as people act in a culture in which self-consciousness is imperative. It formulates a dilemma that all members of the society face and few can fully resolve, the simultaneous attraction of a known place in a fixed social world and a potential place in a world to be made in the future. To adopt the language of identity is to be self-conscious, to attempt to make sense of one's personal relationship to social change, to face this common dilemma—and, crucially, to reproduce the very web of meanings that gave rise to discourse about identity in the first place.

Narcissism

During the 1970s a new term, *narcissism,* became the predominant metaphor in attempts to characterize the self and its transformation in the contemporary world. Although used by Richard Sennett in his critique of privatism in modern life, the concept of narcissism is most closely associated with the work of historian and social critic Christopher Lasch.[25] In *The Culture of Narcissism,* which became a best-selling book, and later in *The Minimal Self,* Lasch uses the psychoanalytic theory of secondary narcissism as a way of characterizing the condition and fate of the person in the modern world of powerful state and corporation.

According to Lasch, the sense of historical time and connection that once united the generations and made individuals interested in something outside of themselves has waned. People no longer act either under the guidance of their ancestors' ways of living or with any thought to the impact of what they do on succeeding generations. Instead, a new generational selfishness has arisen: "To live for the moment is the prevailing passion—to live for yourself, not for your predecessors or posterity. We are fast losing the sense of historical continuity, the sense of belonging to a succession of generations originating in the past and stretching into the future."[26] This loss of continuity does not result merely from untrameled individualism or the decline of community, however, for powerful social and historical forces are at work.

At the root of the contemporary problem, it seems, are state and corporate bureaucracies that have stripped cultural competence from ordinary people, undermined whatever independence individuals may once have possessed, and made contemporary people dependent upon them. The state, corporation, schools, helping professions, and other bureaucratic centers of power have captured control of culture—of the fundamental ways of thinking, feeling, and acting once controlled and passed on from one generation to another by people within their own communities and families. This loss of culture puts the modern person in a position of dependence.

> Having surrendered most of his technical skills to the corporation, he can no longer provide for his material needs. As the family loses not only its productive functions but many of its reproductive functions as well, men and women no longer manage even to raise their children without the help of certified experts. The atrophy of older traditions of self-help has eroded everyday competence, in one area after another, and has made the individual dependent on the state, the corporation, and other bureaucracies.[27]

Contemporary individuals are not merely isolated from their fellows, lacking in any sort of commitment to a common life, but lack the very inner resources that might compensate for this isolation. Unlike the "rugged individualists" or "inner-directed" men and women of the nineteenth century, who sought to make the world according to their image of what it should be, late twentieth-century people are fundamentally incompetent, lacking in skills—and in self-confidence.

Narcissism is the psychological result of this dependence on centralized, bureaucratic expertise. The narcissist is preoccupied with self, not because he or she has a clear sense of a self to be imposed on the world, but because of deep-rooted anxiety and insecurity that comes from not having much of a self.

> Notwithstanding his occasional illusions of omnipotence, the narcissist depends on others to validate his self-esteem. He cannot live without an admiring audience. His apparent freedom from family ties and institutional constraints does not free him to stand alone or to glory in his individuality. On the contrary, it contributes to his insecurity, which he can overcome only by seeing his "grandiose self" reflected in the attentions of others, or by attaching himself to those who radiate celebrity, power, and charisma. For the narcissist, the world is a mirror, whereas the rugged individualist saw it as an empty wilderness to be shaped to his own design.[28]

The contemporary narcissist suffers, in short, not from selfishness or excessive individualism, but from the loss of self and from the incessant anxiety this loss causes.

The loss of self is partly due to the decline of institutionalized authority, for neither tradition itself nor the authority figures of present or past generations who represent that tradition command much interest or respect. This decline of traditional authority has not, however, produced any simple liberation from social demands, and, in particular, it has not freed the person from the demands of the superego. Indeed, the decline of authority has promoted a harsh and punitive superego. "As authority figures in modern society lose their 'credibility,' the superego in individuals increasingly derives from the child's primitive fantasies about his parents—fantasies charged with sadistic rage—rather than from internalized ego ideals formed by later experience with loved and respected models of social conduct."[29] This destructive superego lies at the heart of the problem of narcissism.

There is, Lasch argues, an incessant struggle to maintain psychic equilibrium in modern life. The individual is expected to submit to the demands of social intercourse, but there is no accepted code of moral conduct nor any structure of authority to support it. The result is a craving for "peace of mind," and in this quest for the modern equivalent of salvation—mental health—the individual turns to therapists, who "become his principal allies in the struggle for composure." Their focus is exclusively on meeting the emotional needs of the patient, and they find any notion of the sublimation of individual needs into self-sacrifice or subordination to the needs of others "intolerably oppressive." Thus, the emerging modern sensibility rejects tradition, authority, and obligation to the needs of others and puts in its place not simply self-interest and self-gratification but the interest and gratification of an ill-formed and incapable self, one that cannot be satisfied even when it is getting what it thinks it wants.

The narcissistic personality is, says Lasch, the characteristic pathology of our age, and hence also the most useful metaphor for understanding its problems. Narcissists, as psychiatric patients,

> "act out" their conflicts instead of repressing or sublimating them. These patients, though often ingratiating, tend to cultivate a protective shallowness in emotional relations. They lack the capacity to mourn, because the intensity of their rage against lost love objects, in particular against their parents, prevents their reliving happy experiences or treasuring them in memory. Sexually promiscuous rather than repressed, they nevertheless find it difficult to "elaborate the sexual impulse" or to approach sex in the spirit of play. They avoid close involvements, which might release intense feelings of rage. Their

personalities consist largely of defenses against this rage and against feelings of oral deprivation that originate in the pre-Oedipal stage of psychic development.[30]

Narcissism, and not the symptom neuroses of the late nineteenth century, thus provides the characteristic psychiatric illness of the age. There is no battle between the demands of instinct and a severely constraining culture; instead, there is no guidance from the culture and no competence in the individual. Hence, there is only emptiness, rage, and unhappiness within.

Narcissism seems to Lasch to be an inevitable result of life in the modern world. In an age without tradition and authority, with no realistic figures from whom to take direction and to use as models for the ideal self, the individual is the victim of a punitive superego and is able to develop no ego that can counter or moderate its powers. The individual is also the victim of a culture in which all have suffered a loss of everyday competence, so that the person's isolation from tradition, authority, and community is reinforced by a culture in which one is always dependent upon experts. As a result, there is no moral certainty, but only the advice of experts; and there is no personal salvation, but only the limited satisfactions to be gained through therapy. There is, indeed, only the pathology of narcissism, or, as Lasch expressed it in a later book, a "minimal self," one reduced merely to surviving in a difficult, unpredictable, harsh world.

The reception accorded *The Culture of Narcissism* shows strong parallels to the fate of *The Lonely Crowd*, and this fact helps in the task of interpreting it. Like Riesman, Lasch expressed surprise that the book became a best-seller, as well as considerable discomfort at the way it was interpreted. Just as the popular readership took *The Lonely Crowd* as a critique of and warning against conformity, so the popular readership of *The Culture of Narcissism* took it as an attack on selfishness. Where Lasch meant the concept of narcissism in its psychoanalytic complexity, readers, apparently including President Jimmy Carter, took it to be a critique of individual selfishness and a call for a return to traditional American virtues—this in spite of the fact that the book is partly grounded in a radical critique of capitalism.

The reception afforded Lasch's book, like that Riesman's received almost three decades earlier, suggests a characteristic relationship between American culture and works of cultural criticism. The cultural critic relies on images of decline to contrast the present sorry state of affairs with a world that once was. In doing so, the critic does not necessarily intend to

honor the past or to argue that present problems will be solved by returning to it. Rather the device of contrasting past and present has come to be
one of the major ways in which social ideals are portrayed. The past, or at
least some of its features, becomes utopia in order to dramatize the dys-
topian present. Lasch, for example, neither glorifies the past nor proposes
a return to Victorian culture, and he appears to use images of the past
mainly as a means of portraying the possibilities of human life as a basis
for reconstructing it in the future. Nonetheless, his portrayal of the past
has the ring of utopia—a better, more perfect world that we have lost.

The critic's images of change and decline, as well as whatever conceptual apparatus has been created to convey them, thus quickly become
assimilated to common sense. That is, the critic's main terms and ideas—
"inner-direction," "other-direction," "narcissism"—become labels useful
in formulating interpretations consistent with the inner meanings and
contradictions of the culture. Just as Riesman's analysis became a way of
formulating the dilemma of conformity and autonomy, Lasch's analysis of
"narcissism" became a way of formulating the dilemma of individualism
and community. For Lasch, narcissism has a complex and subtle meaning
anchored in Freudian theory, and his advice was that ordinary people in
their communities begin to reclaim the sense of competence and cultural
authority that had been taken from them by state and corporation; for the
public that bought and responded to his work, narcissism was taken as a
synonym for selfishness, and his advice could readily be interpreted as a
call for a restoration of traditional values.

It thus seems that, however much the social critic or commentator
wishes to instruct the public in the causes and complexities of contemporary ills, the diagnosis begins to resonate with important cultural themes,
which, in the end, assert their interpretive simplicity over the critic's intellectual subtlety and complexity. Narcissism is a difficult idea, as Lasch
takes great pains to remind the reader, even in some sense daring the
reader to attempt to grasp it. Whatever judgment one makes of the concept's applicability to American culture, it is significant that even this
complex psychoanalytic concept readily becomes assimilated to cultural
themes. It becomes a synonym for selfishness and excessive individualism. Authority and tradition evoke positive responses in Americans, and
a psychoanalytic theory of how their decline manifests itself in the individual psyche becomes converted into little more than moral exhortations
for their restoration.

In short, Lasch's critique of the modern state and corporation and its impact on culture and psyche thus becomes, by virtue of the reception afforded it, a statement of the communitarian pole of American culture. Lasch favors community, to be sure, and would no doubt see himself and the intellectual and critical tradition in which he writes as a bastion of communitarian sentiment. Yet it is not only the expression of the communitarian view in the pages of his book that makes it a statement of this pole of the culture but its reception by a public that probably does not well understand its main ideas. The book does not seem merely to express communitarian sentiments—as well as sentiments that fear the decline of tradition and authority—but to tap into and reinforce sentiments that are already present in the culture.

A strong case can be made that social criticism—much like the "scientific" perspective of Turner or the more dispassionate but still critical stance of Riesman—provides one of several alternative languages in which the main dilemmas of the culture can be expressed.[31] In both Riesman's and Turner's work we saw that a scientific vocabulary could be a way of depicting social reality and eliciting normative responses to it. The same seems true of the critical discourses of Lasch. "Narcissism" provides a term through which the individual's own state of being as well as his or her relationship to others can be grasped and expressed. This term, which begins life as a scientific concept, acquires a normative character, for the portrayal of the narcissist elicits a normative and not a clinical response. The term is seized—and the book becomes a best-seller—because it addresses important cultural issues and provides one of several possible ways in which they can be discussed and understood.

The result of this process is that "narcissism," much as "other-direction" before it, becomes an objectification of the culture. That is, the social critic creates a typification of a personality that itself stands metaphorically for the culture and its problems. The social type is interesting and gains currency as a way for people to interpret their experience because people recognize themselves in this type and because they do not like all of what they see. The type captures—at least for the duration of the public's attention span—some of what people experience in themselves and others. It becomes a way of visualizing what is wrong, but also a way of imagining how the social and personal condition might be improved.

It thus seems that the pessimism of the social critic—who feels that things can only get worse unless radical steps are taken to change the social conditions under which people are socialized and live—stimulates an essential optimism in those who respond to the criticism. The critic diagnoses a social and personal ill, but the diagnosis contains the implicit message that if certain things are done, the condition will improve.

Sociology and the Self

The theories just considered explicitly focus on alleged changes in the self and, except for Turner, who adopts a more neutral social scientific perspective, the theorists are either critical of or at least concerned with American culture. As a result, it is not difficult to find many points at which this body of work responds to and manifests American culture. But what of the vast body of social science literature, which purports to offer the scientific truth about human beings and their relationship to society? Can we find similar responses to and reflections of the main axes of American culture in one of this society's cultural products—namely, sociology?

From many sociologists' perspectives, of course, it is subversive to suggest that this might be the case, for sociology is either supposed to be about facts and not ideology or its critical stance is itself held outside the range of criticism.[32] But both experience and the sociology of knowledge teach that neutrality is unlikely and difficult. The origins of ideas may well be irrelevant to their empirical validity, but these ideas nevertheless emerge and live in a particular cultural setting and arise in part from its sense of what needs explaining. Thus, if the cultural polarities discussed so far are as important and pervasive as depicted, we should expect to find them expressed in one form or another in the sociology of the self.

American sociologists have generally taken their theory of the self—although not without some important modifications—from George Herbert Mead, whose course in social psychology attracted a great many University of Chicago sociologists and whose basic explanation of the process of socialization was widely appealing in sociology at large. Although rooted in a sophisticated version of pragmatism that made the organism and environment mutually dependent and determinative, Mead's theory was appealing to sociologists largely because it provided a way of assigning priority to the environment, which for most sociologists meant "society."

Mead argued that the human being, through the use of symbols, is able to conceive and act toward the self, not directly, but indirectly, by adopting the perspectives of others in social life. Not present at birth, the self develops during the process of socialization as the individual comes to

grasp the structure of group life and to acquire a variety of perspectives
—roles—from which to experience the self. So conceived, the self—specifically, what Mead termed the "Me," which was the aspect with which
sociologists most concerned themselves—consists of a structured series of
objectifications of the self. Interacting with various others, the person must
imaginatively assume their perspectives in order to interact with them.
This imaginative taking over of the role perspectives of others—"taking
the role of the other"—gives the individual a series of glimpses of himself
or herself, but always from another point of view. Gradually, the person
acquires the capacity to take the perspective of the group or society as a
whole—taking the "role" of the "generalized other"—and thus comes to
have not merely a discrete series of images of self but a more organized
conception of self in relation to others. The self becomes organized in a
way that reflects the organization of society: the parts of the self become
the roles found in the social division of labor, and the organization of
these parts in the person is given in their organization in social life.[33]

Mead's conception of the self is actually much more complex than this
portrayal, for in addition to a concept of the self as an object experienced
from the perspective of others Mead also had a conception of the self as
an internal process. In constructing their behavior, human beings learn
to respond to themselves as they imagine others would respond to them.
But they are not, in Mead's view, fully tractable creatures. The individual
is no thrall of society, for every act begins with an impulse that is the
property of the individual and that need not meet social demands. Human
beings have impulses—drives, interests, needs, wishes—that are not fully
socialized, and the individual in some sense exists in tension with society. This aspect of the self, which Mead called the "I," taking the term
and at least some of the imagery from William James's conception of the
self as knower and known, represents the insurgent properties of the organism: acts begin with impulses that are not consciously produced and
cannot be controlled until they are underway and can be grasped from the
perspective of a role.

For Mead, then, the experience of self resembles an ongoing internal
conversation. Experiencing an impulse to act in a particular way, the person next imaginatively regards the impending act from the vantage point
of others, and sometimes redirects conduct so as to take their possible
objections or preferences into account. In this sense, the self is society internalized. But even anti-social impulses may occasionally be released, not
just by mistake but also because the person is capable of resisting those

real or imaginary others who threaten disapproval or of calculating that self-interest outweighs the good of the community.

As Anselm Strauss has observed, mainstream sociology did not adopt the whole of Mead's theory of the self.[34] Sociologists were often confused by Mead's concept of the "I," which they found to be either unnecessary or so muddled that it had to be thrown out. Indeed, sociologists generally ignored Mead's complex philosophical and social psychological views of the relationship between the organism and the environment. But they found the concept of self as an organization of roles very appealing, for reasons that relate directly to my thesis that the sociological theory of the self responds to and manifests American culture.

Strauss argues that, in an era in which sociologists were struggling for the legitimacy of sociological explanations of behavior as against biological and psychological explanations, Mead's theory of the self as role was particularly appealing because it clearly made the person a social product and therefore made human conduct a matter of sociological explanation. No doubt this view is partially correct, for Mead did provide the materials out of which sociologists could not only construct a conceptually neat model of the relationship between the person and society but also offer it as a counter to biological and psychological explanations. By modifying Mead's view of the self so as to make it even more decidedly sociological, sociologists since the 1920s have been able to claim a distinctive way of accounting for behavior. Moreover, such a view of self and society fits with the functionalist model of society, with its assumption of normative consensus and its neglect of conflict, that came to dominate American sociology after World War II.

But there are other, more fundamental reasons why this view of the self was so appealing. A version of the self as fully social and fully socialized was also consistent with sociologists' sense of mission—of their own contributions to the society, especially as teachers. Joseph Gusfield has argued that sociology in this country has had its major impact not as social technology, but rather "in its contribution to the popular consciousness of Americans about themselves and their America."[35] According to Gusfield, sociology has reinforced consciousness of America as a society, and the sociologist has brought an emphasis on "group identities, loyalties, and typical situations." Moreover, like their European predecessors, American sociologists were anti-individualists:

> In the United States, it was crucial for the sociologist to counteract the force of a heroic individualism, one that saw collective aspects of

life as surmountable and even unimportant. The sociologist brought
to the public arena an accent on the person as a group phenomenon:
a figure of role and status, class and ethnic group, region and religion.
No sociologist could subscribe to the applause that Walt Whitman
gave to the self: "One's self I sing, a simple, separate person."[36]

Thus, according to Gusfield, sociologists posed a rhetoric of group membership and societal influence against the rampant individualism of Americans, and thus contributed to the more general "reconsideration of the
individual in the mid-twentieth century."

There is little question about the fact that sociologists have deployed
a distinctive rhetoric in the service of a more "collective" orientation to
life and in opposition to the "individualism" they perceive in American
society. Whatever other objectives they have, sociologists typically see
themselves as applying a corrective to what they perceive as their students' misguided belief that they can do and achieve whatever they wish,
that "everybody is different," that the individual is everything and society nothing. The sociologists' sense of pedagogical mission includes many
goals, of course, but central among them is a desire to combat what seems
to them to be the naive individualism of their students.

It is the origin and cultural standing of this sense of sociological mission that seem to me to be misconceived not only by Gusfield but by
the sociological community more generally. What Gusfield conceives as
a sociological contribution to consciousness of society and the reconsideration of the individual is really an expression of long-standing themes
within the culture itself. Sociologists did not invent the critique of individualism, nor, indeed, should we accept the view that this critique is an
intellectual contribution alone and that, were it not for intellectuals, it
would not exist. American culture is not a culture of individualism, but a
culture in which "individual" and "society" are posed against one another,
each appealing in its vision of the good life and the nature of the person,
each with its partisans who assert its virtues and condemn the vices of the
opposing vision, each having an impact on the society as a whole.

Sociologists have to a great extent defined themselves as the "party" of
society and community and made the correction of excessive individualism one of their major goals. Their scientific ambitions should not blind us
to the fact that sociologists participate in the very same web of meanings
as those whose lives and behavior they seek to study and hope to improve.
The origins of sociologists' deep concern with the excesses of American
individualism do not lie exclusively in the sociological community and its

subculture. And although sociologists do in fact constitute a community defined in part by its critique of individualism, their community is not alone in portraying the evils of individualism or in defending the social order against them. The anti-individualism of sociologists is a reflection of the culture in which these views originate, for they are cultural members who respond to the same cultural dialectic as do other members. Thus, we cannot take what sociologists say about such matters merely as scientific analyses of the culture but as documents of it—as interpretations that provide insights into how and what the natives think.

The sociological theory of the person thus expresses one extreme of the American polarity of individual and society. From the perspective of one pole of the culture, people derive from society, they owe it loyalty, and the needs of the community come before those of the individual. The sociological perspective that has been taught to several generations of American college students offers a theoretical and "factual" basis for this normative preference. The sociological concept of the individual as derivative of the society and as following its norms, even if unwittingly, and even if under the illusion of individual volition, provides a "scientific" basis for the communitarian thrust of the culture.

By no means does this mean that sociologists intentionally adopted this view of humankind in order to espouse a particular normative perspective. The relationship between culture and social thought is too complex for so simple a connection. I do argue, however, that it is natural for sociologists to adopt a view that gives priority to society over the individual. It is natural not simply because there is an individualistic thrust in American culture that sociologists sought to counter but also because there is a communitarian thrust they sought to espouse and promote. This is a case where values more or less unwittingly influence social theory, and especially the emphasis it gives to one topic or another.

One of the best-known sociological approaches to the self is that of Erving Goffman, whose first book, *The Presentation of Self in Everyday Life*, became a classic of social science, read by every generation of sociology students since it was first published in 1959.[37] This book adopted an explicitly "dramaturgical" approach to the self, arguing that impression management was an inevitable feature of social interaction, at least in Anglo-American culture, and that the self could be seen as a result of collaboration between a performer and an audience. The person seeks to enact a character before an audience, and when the performer is successful in doing so—when, for example, the waitress succeeds at her task of being the kind of character a waitress is supposed to be—then the parties to the interaction impute a self to the performer. But this self is no inner core, no essence, no thing that has caused the performance, for it is an effect rather than a cause. The self, which people imagine to be substantial, is really a collectively produced illusion.

Goffman's book, like many social science books, resembles a debate with an invisible partner. One reads Goffman's responses, but one does not see, and so must infer, the questions and points of the opponent. Thus, for example, one reads the following assertion:

> A correctly staged and performed scene leads the audience to impute a self to a performed character, but this imputation—this self—is a product of a scene that comes off, and is not a cause of it. The self, then, as a performed character, is not an organic thing that has a specific location, whose fundamental fate is to be born, to mature, and to die; it is a dramatic effect arising diffusely from a scene that is presented, and the characteristic issue, the crucial concern, is whether it will be credited or discredited.[38]

We must infer the argument to which this assertion responds. That "argument," of course, is the belief that there is a unique, potent, causal self, a self that acts and that makes a difference, a self that has William James's "will to believe" in its own capacity to exert judgment. It is all an illusion, Goffman seems to say, a necessary illusion, one that human beings must in some sense sustain if they are to be able to act.

Goffman's analysis of character and performer, as well as the sociological view of the self more generally, can also be seen as a way of both formulating and responding to the same cultural concerns that have preoccupied those who posit change or decline in the American self. Earlier I argued that the assertion of change in the self is a way of intellectually formulating, and even to some extent of coming to terms with, culturally polarized views of the self and its relation to society. Those whose preference is the communitarian pole can simultaneously express this preference and reject individualism by adopting the pessimistic view that the self has declined or changed as the forces of community have weakened and those of individualism have strengthened. The social criticism formulates and thus also helps preserve the culture—not simply the cultural emphasis on community, as it thinks, but the individualistic/communitarian axis of variation.

Goffman formulates this axis in a slightly different way, not by creating images of decline and drastic transformation, but in the more cynical voice of the debunking social scientist. Nonetheless, by implicitly formulating the axis he provides a way for people to come to terms with it and thus helps to sustain it. There is circulating, he implicitly tells us, a view that self-conscious, acting, deciding individuals are impressing their shape upon the social world, that each of us has some active center of being that decides what to do and then does it. But when you examine what people do, he tells us, the only thing the active center of our being seems to be concerned with is impressing others—that is, with managing the impressions they form of us so that we appear to be the kind of character we are supposed to be. When we and they collaborate in this work of impression management, we are able to create the collective illusion of acting, individual selves.

Goffman's disturbing, seemingly cynical view of the self in its own way perpetuates the dialectic of individual and community that is so central to American culture. It does so, first of all, because the response it engenders, both in those who believe it and those who do not, is not that of neutral scientific inspection, but that of strong conviction that he is correct or an equally strong belief that he is wrong. Undergraduate students in particular tend either to strenuously reject or to vociferously agree with Goffman. Some of them find it hard to recognize themselves in his portrayal, arguing that they usually behave spontaneously and without the kind of calculation Goffman seems to portray. Others seem drawn to Goffman's view of the person as constituted by society and chorus their approval, even deriding the naiveté of those who disagree.

It seems unlikely that forceful responses to social science of the kind elicited by Goffman's ideas (and those of sociologists more generally) spring from a deep concern with empirical evidence. Instead, one suspects, these ideas either support or undermine existing views of the world, and the sociologist thus earns either approval or condemnation on this basis. Sociologists find in their classrooms students prepared to respond both positively and negatively to their messages about the social world and the origins and nature of the self. The sociological message is thus not the news its proponents think it is, for some have already been converted and others apparently never will be.

Moreover, the very existence of debate strengthens and preserves this cultural polarity. "Individual" and "community" (or "society") are, at bottom, ways of thinking about and comprehending experience, of making sense of one's own conduct and perceptions and those of others. Ways of thinking about things are preserved to the extent they are exercised, and the discourses of sociologists with their students provide contexts for using and thus for exercising these aspects of culture. To be sure, sociologists no doubt convince some of their students that the self is a collaborative project, fully social in its motivation and origins. But, because the classroom is a place where this idea meets with opposition, they may also reinforce the individualistic sentiments of other students.

Self-Actualization

Discourse about the self articulates cultural meanings, and the social and character types it creates give shape and substance to the conflicting ideas about the person toward which these meanings point. In the specimens of discourse examined thus far, discourse has had a decidedly pessimistic tone. The decline of self-direction and the rise of conformity were lamented; the loss of identity was cited as a major problem of the present era; the self was regarded as under voracious attack by the corporation and state; and the person was sociologically construed as helplessly enacting social rituals. Such formulations assert one set of cultural prescriptions —those we might label in a very general way as stressing the importance of institutional allegiances, character, and identity.

There is, however, another mode of discourse that takes a different tack, celebrating rather than criticizing the transformation of the self in contemporary society, and expressing a positive rather than a negative view of personality and of the impulsive side of human life.[39] It has appeared in countless works of popular psychology and books of advice as well as in more academic formulations, and it has gradually acquired academic respectability. This discourse goes under such names as the "human potential movement" and "humanistic psychology," and it was especially prevalent during the late 1960s and throughout the 1970s. One can find an almost limitless supply of examples of this kind of discourse, each with its particular emphasis or twist, but for my purposes, the theories of psychologist Carl Rogers are an excellent specimen.

Beginning with the publication of *Client-Centered Therapy*, Carl Rogers was identified generally with the humanistic wing of psychology and specifically with a view of psychotherapy in which the object of the therapeutic process is to help free the individual from obstacles that prevent growth.[40] Client-centered therapy (and, later, a more broadly and politically styled "person-centered approach") is based on an optimistic view of human nature: "There is in every organism, at whatever level, an underlying flow of movement toward constructive fulfillment of its inherent possibilities. There is a natural tendency toward complete development in man."[41] This tendency, the self-actualizing tendency, is "the foundation on which the person-centered approach is built," for if human beings are like plants growing as best they can toward the light, then the goal of therapy should be to remove those obstacles that stand in their way. And, similarly, given this view of human nature—which seems to see people as inherently good—those who are able to free themselves of the obstacles that thwart their self-actualizing tendencies gain enormous power and capacity to change the world.

The self-actualizing tendency reflects the fact that all life is, says Rogers, "an active process, not a passive one": "The organism is self-controlled. In its normal state it moves toward its own enhancement and toward an independence from external control."[42] The self-actualizing tendency is a constructive tendency, for organisms have a great many potentialities —for pain or self-destruction, for example—that they do not strive to develop. The implication is clear: the natural tendency of living things is to fulfill themselves, to realize whatever potential they have as organisms, to become all that they are capable of becoming. It is a principle as true of people as it is of plants.

Yet, says Rogers, it is clear that a great deal of human experience does not seem to reflect the unfettered operation of the self-actualizing tendency. People are often divided against themselves, the unconscious side of them striving for self-actualization, but the conscious side failing to be aware of or to accept what the unconscious is doing. Rogers gives as an example of this division a woman who thinks of herself as submissive and compliant, but who occasionally erupts in hostile and resentful behavior that "surprises her and that she does not own as a part of herself." This presents a problem to be explained: "Why this division? How is it that a person can be struggling with one goal while her whole organic direction is at cross purposes with this?"[43]

The answer Rogers constructs depends on a long tradition of American pragmatism and functionalist psychology, although it is not presented in these terms. Attention is a function of interest, and it is when the smooth and unimpeded functioning of the organism in its surroundings is disturbed that the organism becomes sharply self-conscious. When functioning without any obstacles from the environment, and thus without sharp self-awareness, "the person is whole, integrated, unitary." When obstacles occur, self-awareness develops as a means of eliminating them, "by modifying the environment or altering the behavior of the individual." Thus, although the capacity for self-awareness is portrayed as having developed as a means of coping with the environment, it is clear that the preferred mode of functioning, in the Rogerian system, is unconscious: "When a person is functioning in an integrated, unified, effective manner, she has confidence in the directions she unconsciously chooses, and trusts her experiencing, of which, even if she is fortunate, she has only partial glimpses in her awareness."[44] In short, "man is wiser than his intellect" and "well-functioning persons come to trust their experiencing as an appropriate guide to their behavior."

Why, then, is a rift between conscious and unconscious so prevalent? Given the terms in which Rogers constructs his analysis, the answer must be found in the environment rather than in the individual. That is, there is a rift not because of something located within the person—such as the inherently anti-social nature of human beings posited by Freud—but because of the individual's fate in the social world. In effect, the social world, for Rogers, tries to convert the person, to exert control, to adapt natural urges, such as sexuality, to its own uses. As a result, people have natural and honest impulses and feelings that they must consciously deny in order to live in society and secure the love and acceptance of others. Ultimately, the source of the problem is culture, and especially "Western culture," which imposes "rigid concepts and constructs" that interrupt the organismic flow, the self-actualizing tendency.

The result is the dissociated person, who is "best described as one *consciously* behaving in terms of introjected, static, rigid constructs, and *unconsciously* behaving in terms of the actualizing tendency."[45] The solution lies not just in client-centered therapy, which posits an approach that can aid in the growth of those who experience this dissociation, but more broadly in the person-centered approach, which, in adapting the methods of therapy to life, constitutes a revolutionary politics of interpersonal relationships. In this transforming politics, people act as themselves, putting up no fronts or facades, allowing themselves to experience the world at a "gut level" and to be honestly aware of this experience and to share it with others. Moreover, people give one another unconditional positive regard, acceptance, caring, and prizing. And they strive for empathic understanding, to sense with accuracy and to respect the feelings and meanings of other people.

The result, says Rogers, is an "emerging person" who will be the "spear-head of the quiet revolution" that will change American institutions from within. The new person has a "deep concern for authenticity," for honest rather than hypocritical communication, for straightforward talk. "One of the deepest antipathies of emerging persons is directed toward institutions. They are opposed to all highly structured, inflexible, bureaucratic institutions. The firm belief is that institutions exist for persons, and not the reverse."[46] The new person will replace bureaucratic institutions with smaller groups and more flexible, less structured social arrangements—free schools, smaller and more personal business enterprises, work teams instead of assembly lines. The new person will not seek power for its own sake but only in order to do good, and he or she will be a caring, generous individual who seeks "new forms of community, of closeness, of intimacy, of shared purpose." The new persons will explore "inner space," be willing "to be aware of self, of inner feelings, of hangups. These individuals are able to communicate with themselves more freely, with less fear."[47] As a result, the new persons will trust their own experience more than external authority. They will eventually build a better society, one that will allow this now-emerging person to flourish and become the predominant type.

Whatever their scientific or intellectual merits, these ideas are interesting as samples of a culture and its meanings. Although couched in the universal language of psychology, they have a more particular resonance with certain themes in American culture. Indeed, whatever the scientific and intellectual origins of Rogers' words, they are filtered through an American cultural view of the world and of human nature, and they reveal one facet, one side, of the web of meaning in which Americans conduct their lives.

I have suggested that there are two contending definitions of the person within American culture. One emphasizes society as the source of those values and standards on which the person depends and to which the person is responsible. The other emphasizes the person as the creator of society, as the creature whose needs must be met and as the measure of its success in doing so. These opposing conceptions of the person supply a web of meanings with which Americans must contend. Thus, American culture does not specify a single ideal kind of person, but, instead, makes the cultural meaning of the person problematic.

Like the other specimens of discourse I have discussed, Rogers' theories of the person formulate this opposition in a concrete way and thus supply members of the society with a way of conceiving of themselves and their relation to it. In doing so, it makes use of a basic set of cultural conceptions, which, although filtered through the language of humanistic psychology, are as present in Rogers' books as they are in discourse about narcissism, institutional and impulsive selves, types of social character, or the problems of identity.

Rogers' theories give voice to a conception of the person as the source and measure of society, and as corrupted by society. It is a rigid, repressive, unbending society that, in seeking to enlist individuals to its purposes, makes it difficult for them to be self-actualizing beings. If people were left to their own devices, free to act on the basis of their unconscious (and inherently good) desires and to construct the social arrangements they see fit, there would be far less unhappiness and the needs of individuals would be better met. And, by following the program of the person-centered approach, a new and better society can be constructed, one in which people are more satisfied with their lives, more caring about one another, and more able to realize their potential.

It would be a mistake to see this version of humanistic psychology as expressing only one side of the conflict about the relationship between the person and society that is so deeply rooted in American culture. For, in fact, just as the other specimens of discourse formulate a character type that embodies both sides of this conflict and posit a specific resolution of it, so does Rogers through his concept of the "new" or "emerging" person.

The emerging person is apparently well on the way toward overcoming the wounds inflicted by a rigid and controlling society. But this twentieth-century version of the "New Adam" will by no means be an asocial being, for imbedded in the character type Rogers has created is a powerful sense of mission to transform American society. Rogers says that American society has become more rigid and intolerant, with the result that the rift between conscious and unconscious selves is greater than it has ever been. But, at the same time, the emergence of a new kind of human being bodes well for the future. The new person is, in fact, a quiet revolutionary who will transform the society from within, creating new forms of social organization, new forms of intimacy and community, and, ultimately, a better society. The new person is caring, wanting to do good for others and not just for self.

It thus seems that society remains an important focus, even though it is society that is the source of those restrictions that impede the self-actualizing tendency. People, even in the Rogerian scheme of things, still have responsibilities to one another—to be open and honest, to provide unconditional acceptance and caring, and to strive for empathic understanding. In this scheme, the interpersonal relationship is the goal to be sought, not a more formal and authority-based form of social organization. Nevertheless, the Rogerian view gives positive voice to that side of American culture that makes the person responsible to others, just as it gives negative voice to a conception of the person as derivative from society by making society the main source of personal troubles.

There is even a sense in which one can find a normative conception of character buried amidst the neutral psychological language of Rogers' theories. It is not simply that human beings can be self-actualizing when given the opportunity, but that they ought to be. It is not simply that honesty, openness, and empathy will facilitate self-actualization in others, but that people ought to be honest, open, and empathic. These are, in their own way, traits of an ideal character, of someone conducting life in the manner in which it should ideally be conducted.

It thus seems that while the character type formulated by Rogers differs in important matters of emphasis from other character types, there are also significant points of similarity. Rogers' self-actualizing new person clearly bears little surface resemblance to the inner-directed, achieving, nineteenth-century person of "character," for this new person tries to overcome introjected demands rather than live in accordance with them, to follow inner impulses rather than seek external goals, and to display "personality" rather than live up to some externally imposed conception of character. But there are more similarities between these types than meet the eye trained to see within the framework of American culture. The self-actualizing person, much as the Puritan or the nineteenth-century industrialist, feels compelled to look within, to find and follow some vision, to know the real self. The self-actualizer evidently feels this urgency to look within, and the desired vision of self is expressed in relation to a perceived tension between the individual and society.

Thus, although in many respects it is far more optimistic about the prospects of the person in the future American society than the other forms of discourse I have examined, Rogers' view of the person and society falls within the same range of conceptions of the person and society. Rogers theorizes about human nature, but conveys a distinctively American conception of the person. He expresses the individualistic side of the culture, and yet pays homage, as typifications of character in American culture evidently must, to community and society. The society is a source of woe for the person, and yet those who are healed by the person-centered approach will one day develop warm and humane communities that will themselves foster self-actualization. Rogers works with the same cultural ideas as Turner, Riesman, Wheelis, and others, and engages in a discourse that, like theirs, reproduces these ideas and their inherent contradictions.

Next . . .

In this chapter I have begun to develop a view of American culture that departs from the conventional wisdom of social science; indeed, I have argued that the social sciences, psychology, and psychiatry are major vehicles for the reproduction of this culture. Theories of change in society and character reflect not only the intellectual and scientific imperatives of various disciplines but also more deeply rooted cultural meanings that shape what sociologists, psychologists, psychiatrists, and critics talk about and how they do so. All have in common a concern with the nature of the person, a preoccupation with social and generational change, and a divided view of the relationship between the person and society.

My task now is to move from discourse about self as a mirror of American culture to a more direct examination of the culture itself. Chapter III will essay a brief theory of culture and then attempt a portrayal of the main themes and counter-themes of American culture.

CHAPTER III

A View of American Culture

Contemporary discourse about the self weaves its account of the nature and fate of the person in American society from the strands of three related cultural themes. First, there is a preoccupation with the nature, essence, constitution, meaning, significance, and substance of the person. Although this interest in the person is now far more apt to be expressed in scientific discourse than in the language of religion, there are strong echoes of a Puritan past in which the individual's state of grace was a matter both of inner preoccupation and of public discussion. In the discourse of psychologists, social critics, historians, and social scientists one sees reflections of a deeper cultural interest in the person.

Second, ideas about generational and social change provide salient interpretive devices through which this preoccupation with the person enters discourse. Social theorists organize their discourse by positing various ways in which a changing social structure or culture has induced change in the nature of the modern person. Psychologists, particularly in the humanistic wing of their discipline, posit the individual as the source of capabilities that will, in helping to transform the society of the future, also transform the sort of person the society will produce.

Third, discourse about the self reveals two contending views of the relationship between the person and society. On the one hand, the person is viewed as a loyal creature of society, as one whose essence is derived from society, as responsible to others and charged with maintaining the integrity of a way of life held in common with them. On the other hand, the person is viewed as the creator of society, as prior both in fact and in rights to others, as the main point of reference in measuring the success of those forms of community life that are voluntarily constructed. These views are in conflict; neither by itself defines the meaning of the person in American culture, for it is their very opposition that does so.

In extracting these features of American culture from discourse about the self, I have relied upon a conception of culture as "meaning" and as "webs of significance." The latter metaphor is useful only up to a point, for while it properly emphasizes that humans act on the basis of meaning and that they are suspended (and sometimes caught) in its many strands, it says little about how people actually use and sustain these meanings. Indeed, it is vague about what people actually do other than making interpretations. Thus, a more precise conception of culture and its relation to conduct is called for.[1]

The Concept of Culture

The clearer conception of culture and its relation to conduct that we need can be constructed by examining George H. Mead's concepts of *symbol* and *object*.[2] A symbol is anything—word, painting, icon, sound—whose function is to point to and to serve in place of something else. "House" is a symbol, a word that stands for a certain kind of structure in which human beings cook, eat, sleep, bathe, and engage in many other everyday acts. "Justice" is a word that stands for something much more abstract, a set of ideas about how people will treat one another in certain contexts, such as the "administration of justice" in the enforcement of laws or "economic justice" in the distribution of goods and services. In the same way, the sound of a car's horn stands in a general way for "danger" or "something to look out for," and in the particular instance for "Watch out, for I'm coming and I won't stop!" or "What a stupid thing you did!"

An object is the "that" to which a symbol points. As a word, "house" is a fragment of a speech act; as an object, a house is that thing designated by the symbol. As may be obvious, the meaning of a symbol is not inherent in its physical form, but derives from its consistent use. A symbol has meaning when it is used in approximately the same way by the members of some group, collectivity, or community of users. A house is a house only as long as those who employ this word to designate a part of their world have the same thing in mind when they utter it. Or, as Mead would have put it, a significant symbol arouses in the one who uses it the same attitude as in those who hear it.

An attitude is a readiness to act toward an object in a certain way. When I think of my "house," all sorts of feelings and dispositions are aroused in me: depending on the circumstances, I may want to seek out the bedroom and get some much-needed rest, visit the kitchen and prepare a snack, or just sit in the back yard and contemplate the garden. I am prepared or ready to act toward this object in a variety of ways, and its meaning for me effectively consists of those actions I am prepared to take toward it. An object such as a house encompasses one or more actions I might take in which this object figures centrally either as the main goal—*object, objective*—of my act or as a key implement I use in attaining some other goal. "Meaning" thus lies not in some imaginary space or in "webs of significance," but in actual and possible responses to objects. And the object, the thing designated by a symbol, takes its reality from the way people act individually and collectively toward it.

Objects both invite and impede action. On the one hand, to speak of my house is to imagine something that invites me to act toward it in a variety of ways. It is not simply that I can or may assume a certain attitude toward it, but that the object positively invites me to take that attitude. My house is a repository of my experience, a thing that stimulates memories and arouses expectations. It reminds me of pleasurable (or painful) experiences and teases me with the possibility of new experiences in the future. A part of me is invested or embodied in this house; when I look at it or walk through it, I see myself—my previous acts, failures, accomplishments, flaws, and fine points—reflected in it. When I walk into my study, my chair invites my sitting down in it or my using it as a stepladder to reach a book on a high shelf, and as it receives my frame I may remember what I was thinking or writing when last I sat in it.

On the other hand, objects also get in the way of action, preventing it or redirecting it. I must walk around a large and ill-placed filing cabinet when I walk into my study; if I am not careful I will bump into it and hurt my foot. My house is an investment—of memories as well as of funds—and I cannot walk away from it lightly. If I leave for the day, I check to see that the doors are locked and that appliances are turned off. If I contemplate selling it, I take care to see that I realize a gain, or at least do not suffer a financial loss, and I worry that life may not seem the same in another house, in spite of its greater luxury or more attractive neighborhood.

Many human objects seem quite tangible—a house, after all, is a solid thing of walls and floors and roof that one can see and touch, a thing that first did not exist, was then built, and may, if I am not careful, burn to the ground and no longer exist. But, while it exists, it is tangible, material, a thing. It resists my touch; when I push against it, it pushes back. "Love," "liberty," "justice," "happiness," and similar objects are, by comparison, quite insubstantial. They are, we say, "abstract," or "conceptual," for they do not seem to have the same resistance to physical touch and movement as does a house or a mule or an electric shaver. They cannot be seen or touched, or at least not as easily seen or touched, for they are not material things at all.

Aside from being less concrete and more abstract, however, objects like "love" and "happiness" have the same qualities and the same relationship to human beings as more tangible things. These conceptual objects both invite and impede action; an individual may seek "freedom" and yet be constrained by the requirements of "work" or "family" and thus feel caught between "duty" and "desire." Conceptual objects, like material ones, present people with inviting textures and hard surfaces, pulling us in one direction or another, interfering with or facilitating our conduct. They are, no less than the world of things, a part of the environment, of the obdurate world into which we are born and that confronts us at every turn, urging or compelling us to travel in certain directions or to see matters in a certain light.

Culture *is* the world of objects in which human beings live.[3] It is the environment within which conduct occurs—a landscape of tangible and conceptual objects that are created and sustained as human beings act in their everyday worlds and that subsequently constrain conduct. The everyday actions of people furnish and refurnish the world with objects that then attract, repel, or even puzzle them. These objects are abstract as well as concrete: love, truth, respect, duty, freedom, individuality, cooperation, work, play, as well as the tangible things people encounter or make. These objects are an inherited world, for they come to us in the language we learn as children and in its associated symbol systems. Yet the cultural environment is also one that remains firm and obdurate because human beings continue to act toward the objects it contains. By acting toward and talking about objects of all kinds human beings sustain their reality. My house invites so long as I and others continue to accept its invitations; "duty" calls as long as someone listens to its call.

This view of culture makes it external to human beings. Properly speaking, therefore, we do not "learn" or "acquire" culture, any more than animals "learn" or "acquire" the environments in which they live. Human beings experience culture, they live amidst its objects, they use it, they find that it assists or impedes them as they try to achieve their objectives. But they do not learn or possess it, except in the sense that any living thing must, if it is to survive, learn about its world and regard a part of it as its own special territory. Culture is not behavior, nor is it anything as abstract as "values," "knowledge," or "meanings." It is an external, obdurate, constraining environment filled with objects of significance to human life.

Two additions to this conception of culture as the human object environment will aid in applying it to the analysis of American culture. The first has to do with the nature of motivation: Culture invites and impedes action, and so any attempt to grasp the motivation of human conduct must take culture into account, for the dispositions human beings have to act in various ways are to an important degree derived from culture and its objects. However, culture does not completely account for motivation: human objectives are created by individuals for themselves and do not simply derive from the way objects invite them to behave.

A concept of culture is crucial to any discussion of human motivation because it is both the variety of goals posed by culture and the range of means it affords for attaining them that account for the characteristic direction and force of conduct that we find in a given society. Symbols and the objects for which they stand—duty, success, happiness—are magnets of meaning, attracting human efforts to reach them. If one engages in "hard work" in order to attain "success" and thereby justify one's "worth," it is in large part because culture is a massive field of objects that "suggests," by the sheer force of its presence, the way life ought to be conducted and what it is for, much as water "suggests" the nature of the life of a fish.

But culture does not dictate conduct. It is the world, but it is a world in which human beings must construct their own actions, for they are not automatons programmed by "the culture," nor are the various plans and models "the culture" affords for the living of life complete or exhaustive or always reliable. Culture is simply the environment, albeit one that is more abstract and less tangible because of its symbolic nature. Like any environment, it rewards and punishes the actions of organisms that confront it, providing means for the satisfaction of needs and wants, but also obstacles to their fulfillment. It is the source of learned impulses to act in certain ways, but also of barriers to the completion of some acts.

The relationship between the culture, as environment, and the humans who inhabit it is one of mutual determination.[4] The wants, needs, desires, and inclinations of individual human beings are shaped by their experience in a given culture. In this sense, the cultural environment "determines" the makeup of the individual. But cultural objects are of interest and importance to human beings because of their wants, needs, and desires, and, in this sense, human beings "determine" their culture. If the members of a given culture want and need "love," for example, it is because they have learned to regard this object as a very important one. The individual's need for "love" is thus shaped—"determined"—by the environment, in which love is a constantly stressed, always visible object. But, in another sense, "love" remains an important and visible object precisely because of widely socialized impulses. It commends itself to human attention because of the learned expectations of those for whom it is an important object, and in this sense it is a product of those expectations.

The cultural environment is something that exists before the individual and depends for its continuation on public and cooperative actions and not simply on the individual's acceptance of it, but it is nevertheless something about which individuals feel possessive. If "duty" and "desire" loom as large objects on the cultural horizon, for example, I am likely to learn to want to do my duty and control my desire—but they are *my* duty and *my* desire. Individuals do not merely accept or learn cultural objects, for they come to own them, to possess them, and to feel that they are entitled to take at least some liberties with them. The culture of the Puritans, for example, invited them to be deeply concerned with their state of grace, to worry about salvation and the depraved condition of human nature. Once accepted, the object became theirs to pursue, to worry about, to interpret, to devise ways of detecting or even evading.

Cultural objects thus contain the seeds of their own transformation, both because they fall under the control of individuals who may interpret and use them to their own ends and because they rarely encompass a fully consistent, final, perfectly systematic set of "designs for living." Culture does provide objects and visible paths for moving toward them, and in this sense it "provides" models of conduct. But it also "provides" things to worry about, to be anxious about, and thus also reasons for discourse, for efforts to interpret the meaning of the world and of their place in it.

The second addition to the concept of culture involves the degree of consistency or harmony among the various objects of a culture. Like the environment inhabited by the members of any species, the cultural environment inhabited by human beings is complex, not simple. It is a tangled and not an orderly web of meaning. Or, to shift metaphors, the cultural landscape is filled with rocks and hard places, for it is littered with objects left over from the past as well as newly discovered ones, and thus confronts people with contradictory objects that issue competing invitations. It is not an environment encountered or traversed easily, for it tempts and pushes the person in a variety of opposite directions.

As Kai Erikson has pointed out, we need not limit the concept of culture to those societies with a seemingly stable and well-integrated way of life, nor must we suppose that culture consists only "of those forces that promote uniformity of action." Culture shapes thought, action, and feeling, not only by emphasizing certain tendencies but also by permitting people to imagine their opposites.

> The mind that imagines a cultural form also imagines (which is to say "creates") its reverse, and to that extent, at least, a good measure of diversity and contrast is built into the very text of a culture. Whenever people devote a good deal of emotional energy to celebrating a given virtue, say, or honoring a certain ideal, they are sure to give thought to its counterpart.[5]

If, for example, "duty" is an important object, people will not only talk about it and devote their energies to it, but they will worry about its opposite, however they conceive it—as "selfishness," as "sloth," or as "desire." They are likely to be anxious about whether they are doing their duty, daydream about being released from duty, talk about duty, write plays that explore issues surrounding duty, and be on the lookout to punish those who stray too far from its demands.

Erikson suggests that cultural ideas—what I call objects—*and* their opposites are crucial to grasping a culture, for "the identifying motifs of a culture are not just the *core values* to which people pay homage but also the *lines of point and counterpoint* along which they diverge."[6] The array of cultural objects thus does not consist simply of directives and models for conduct that channel human activity along certain lines to which members are expected to conform, for it also consists of ways in which the culture induces tension and organizes diversity. Culture is filled with competing principles, competing meanings, and competing objects.

The individual response to cultural contradiction, according to Erikson, is *ambivalence,* an inner conflict in which the person is pulled in two directions. To resolve this ambivalence requires that one choose one object to the exclusion of the other or that one find some way of combining them. One must, for example, fix one's eye so firmly on "duty" that "desire" can be kept in the far periphery of one's vision where it cannot easily intrude; or one must, in a similar way, make "desire" central and "duty" peripheral; or one must balance the two, finding ways to honor both cultural commitments. Cultural contradictions thus supply an additional tissue of motivation, for the person must resolve inconsistencies as well as respond to the culture's invitation to act in certain ways.

The societal response to cultural contradictions is *differentiation* and *specialization*. Those who share a culture tend to sort themselves into segments that reflect the tensions and conflicts embedded in the culture and thus create a kind of "division of labor" in which the diverse and opposite emphases of the culture are embodied in a variety of groups, categories, and collectivities. Under some conditions, the division of cultural labor may lead to conflict between groups, each of which, emphasizing an extreme position on a given value, virtue, or way of life, finds itself threatened as well as offended by the other. It is not implausible to interpret the current controversy over abortion in this light, for it is arguable that the abortion issue symbolizes a deeper division in American culture over the nature and importance of family, traditional piety, and individual freedom. Some array themselves on the side of freedom, individuality, and privacy, while others emphasize the authority of traditional definitions of family life and gender roles and stress that the public good is more important than the private. The key point is that the culture itself is divided on these issues and that conflict over the abortion issue is one current expression of this cultural division.[7]

Under other conditions, cultural contradictions may find expression in a less conflict-laden form, where there develops "an implicit agreement to apportion the work of the culture as well as its rewards on the basis of the contrasting qualities that each group represents"[8] and there is, accordingly, a complementary relationship between the various groups that, taken together, embody the culture and its opposite concerns. With one major reservation, the sexual division of labor can be viewed in this light. The assignment of "masculine" and "feminine" traits and the belief that they are biologically fixed and inevitable can be seen as a way of dividing the cultural labor and thereby simultaneously honoring opposing conceptions of the person. If men are seen as "strong" and women as "nurturing," for example, one may read from this assignment of traits that both virtues are valued in a culture and that it is given to each sex to express one of them. The reservation has to do with the way in which this and other aspects of the cultural division of labor are created, for it assumes too much to define such arrangements as matters of "implicit agreement." Sometimes they are, but at other times they are more the outcome of conflict or of the imposition of definitions by one group upon another.

The perspective that emerges from combining Kai Erikson's analysis of cultural tension with a concept of culture as a field of objects can supply a powerful purchase on American life and the personal experiences of

Americans. It commends to our attention the objects Americans pursue and avoid, the ways in which they resolve ambivalence at an individual level and engage in cultural conflict or create a cultural division of labor at a societal level. The first step in applying this perspective is to propose a description of American culture and to make some assessment of how it came to be what it is.

This is no simple or easy task. It is not a matter of consulting the best authorities or marshalling quantitative evidence, nor of surveying a literature that has explicitly studied "American culture." The best authorities offer interpretations of the culture, not "facts" about it, and these interpretations are extraordinarily diverse. There is no standard arithmetic of cultural analysis, no algorithm that permits one to count, add, multiply, and divide objects and their meanings, nor does it seem likely that, even if there were, one could inductively arrive at a convincing view of American culture. Moreover, assumptions about American culture are so deeply embedded in sociological and other studies that they rarely are themselves matters of explicit analysis.[9]

Accordingly, my effort to essay a theory of American culture will depend as much upon my own membership and participation as upon reputable scholarly sources or a carefully marshalled body of evidence. There is no point in coating this effort with a false legitimacy of method by portraying it as "participant observation," for that implies a much more considered and diligent program of observation than I have carried out. What I offer in the following pages is a biographically, theoretically, historically, and sociologically grounded interpretation of American culture, together with selected illustrations to support it.[10]

The Travails of Adolescence as a Cultural Paradigm

Human beings come to know their world—their familiar, object-strewn, cultural environment—in part through the problematic circumstances with which it confronts them. Their interpretations of life, what they know or believe to be true, and the goals they hold important are formulated in word and deed as they attempt to act and as they encounter obstacles. Thus, it is useful to begin a portrait of American culture by examining a few of the ways in which it creates problems, focusing specifically on the ways it engenders ambivalence.

The problems parents and children have with one another, particularly during the phase of the life cycle when the children are going through adolescence and preparing to leave home, provide not only a useful beginning point but also what amounts to a paradigm for the analysis of American culture. The upheavals of adolescence are a key part of the lore of American culture. Parents often dread, or are thought to dread, the onset of puberty, not only because of the awakening of sexual life in their children but, perhaps more fundamentally, because they perceive the outlines of contests that lie ahead. They anticipate that the child will seek increasing degrees of freedom from parental control, look to peers rather than home for approval and guidance, and attempt to increase the emotional and social distance between self and family. They know that their efforts to retain influence over the child and to blunt what they regard as excessive "peer pressure" will in the end fail, but many will nevertheless persist in these efforts.

For parent and child alike, adolescence, adolescent rebellion, peer group pressure, the promised land of adult freedom, the unfairness of parental control, the arrogance and impatience of youth, and the authority of parents and other adults are as much a part of the American cultural landscape as the Grand Canyon or major league baseball. They are eagerly anticipated or dreaded events, feared and envied experiences, awesome or awful sights, exciting or boring, filled with pitfalls or opportunities. In a variety of ways they illustrate the objects in American culture that invite and offend, produce both ambivalent and extreme attitudes, and occasion discourse that seeks to make sense, to explain, and to generate hope.

Consider, for example, freedom as a key object of adolescents. Freedom has a variety of meanings: to go places without parental supervision or even knowledge; to dress as he or she sees fit (or, as parents fear is really the case, as peers or advertisers see fit); to form ideas and beliefs independently of parents, choosing religious, social, political, or philosophical convictions without interference; to have a place, a room, where others come only when invited, which can be as messy as the young person wants, on the theory that slovenliness is the flag of independence; to explore developing sexuality; to do things "my own way" and "myself" without the constant tutelage of parents; to imagine one's future without the weight of commitments to parents, grandparents, aunts and uncles, little brothers, ethnic and religious ties, or anything else that might bind one not only to the enclosing community with which one has grown up but also, and more important, to one's dependent, controlled, and established place in it.

At the same time that they want or are believed to want increasing degrees of freedom, however, adolescents are also said to want guidance and limits. It is commonplace in American life to view the adolescent as someone who is both testing the limits of his or her own freedom and seeking some limits within which to live. The good parent is often portrayed as one who wisely recognizes that a considerable measure of adolescent rebellion is bluff, and who is able to establish reasonable limits without engendering hostility and thereby stimulating even more serious rebellion. Similarly, the adolescent is often seen as relieved that parents resist efforts to secure more freedom and that they are, in fact, capable of asserting their authority in order to set rules.[11]

Images of adolescents are thus mixed, for they are thought to want to escape the restrictions of their parents but also to retain the security they provide, to be free but not too free, to choose but within limits, to move toward the future but not too fast. Whether in their actual behavior or in the way this behavior is conceived and interpreted in the culture, adolescents seem to live amidst a landscape of objects that pull them in contrary directions: toward the excitement of the future but also the security of childhood; toward the freedom of choice but also the security of authority; toward a world in which they will be the adults but also a world of adults in which they have an established place. The innermost world of the adolescent seems to be one in which "I'm not a child anymore!" and "I don't want to grow up!" are competing slogans, shouted or whispered, each seeking to dominate.

The parents of adolescents likewise often have an ambivalent, conflicted view of their children. There are, to be sure, parents who avoid ambivalence. Some are prepared to push their children from the nest at the earliest opportunity, to tolerate or at least not seek to change whatever choices their children make, or to ask as few questions as possible about where their children go or what they do. Others cling, continue to apply to their sixteen-year-old daughters and sons the same detailed scrutiny they applied to them when they were ten, or strenuously resist the child's efforts to reach such cultural milestones as a first unsupervised date or a driver's license (is there any object more magnetic to the adolescent or more feared by the parents of adolescents?).

A great many parents, however, experience ambivalence about their children's inexorable maturation and find adolescence a frustrating, sometimes rewarding, often bittersweet stage in the family life cycle. Indeed, that is how adolescence is interpreted in American culture, as occasion for both joy and sorrow, anticipation and regret, excitement and dread.

Unless one is committed either to the repression of every sexual impulse or to its unrestricted expression, one contemplates the onrushing sexual development of one's children with mixed emotions, feeling a sense of joy about their discovery of sexuality (and perhaps even an envious desire to relive one's own first sexual awakening) but also of foreboding about the lesser and greater pain this facet of human life will cause them. A parent sitting alongside a child-driver as the car lurches down the pavement in the first trials of gear shifting, or watching the family car disappear around the corner on the first solo performance, cannot help feel both pride and dread, remembering one's own first taste of the glorious freedom of wheels and the predicaments in which, as a result, one found oneself.

Many images of adolescence seem to recognize, and in some sense to resolve, these mixed, conflicting views of what adolescents are and of where they might end up. A common image, for example, has the adolescent both as a rebel—serious or playful—against parental standards and authority and as a slavish conformist who will do whatever the peer group demands or seems to demand. On the one hand, this image expresses fear (or celebration) of the adolescent quest for freedom. The parents of adolescents are apt to fear or resist rebelliousness in their own children, for it is their authority that is under challenge, at the same time that they may admire someone else's child who survives an excessively restrictive upbringing to achieve independence in spite of parental efforts to thwart it. On the other hand, this image also expresses fear, and in some ways also celebration of conformity. Americans spend a great deal of time worrying, in conversations with one another, with teachers, with psychologists, about the dangers of the peer group as a mechanism of excessive social influence on their children. At the same time, however, many parents also worry lest their children not be "popular" with other children.

Although this mixture of images highlights the ambivalence Americans seem to feel about adolescence, it also, in a curious way, provides an interpretive frame for understanding this "stage" of the life cycle. The cultural fact seems to be that conformity and rebellion are both viewed with ambivalence, both to be feared and welcomed. Discourse about the dangers of peer group influence is a way of separating acceptable and unacceptable forms of conformity, of defining the limits within which conformity is expected and the possible dangers of exceeding those limits. Thus, for example, parents joke about the latest fashion in footwear (is it Reeboks this week?) while they worry about peer pressures for drug use. The rebellious, secretive, conspiratorial solidarity of peers is acceptable when it is expressed in the conventionalized routines of adolescent fashion, for it allows what, from the wiser perspectives of parents (who exchange knowing smiles behind their adolescent child's back), is a rebellion that is no real rebellion and a conformity that is of no significance. If peer pressure seems to favor "substance abuse," however, then there is something serious about which to be concerned. Even for the vast majority of adolescents and their parents who are not caught up in the trauma of drugs, discourse about this problem serves to define some of the limits of rebellion and conformity, to establish boundaries within which both must be contained.

Likewise, the social construction of adolescence as a stage or phase of the growth and development of the person during which problems of rebellion and conformity are to be expected provides a mode of discourse and an interpretive theme that makes sense of and recognizes competing cultural objects. Adolescence is constructed as temporary, not as a permanent condition of the person but as a difficult period of life through which most people are able to pass with only small injuries and few scars. Sooner or later, the rebellious, moody, difficult, uncommunicative, secretive, peer-swayed adolescent will "settle down," for no matter how problematic he or she now is, it's "only a phase" of development. Parents cite with approval some version of Mark Twain's observation about how little his father knew when he, Twain, was eighteen and how much he had learned by the time Twain had turned twenty-one. Teachers and counselors opine that adolescence is a difficult time, and social critics and social scientists offer reasons as to why it should be so traumatic a phase in modern life.

A view of adolescence as a temporary phase that heralds the necessary and inevitable transformation of the child into the adult has a variety of functions. From the standpoint of sometimes desperate parents it is grounds for hope and optimism that the present miserable circumstances of their and their children's lives will grow steadily less miserable with no more effort than it takes to wait. But this interpretation is also a way for people to make sense of the conflicting meanings of their culture. The trauma of parents and children pulled this way and that by conflicting desires and goals becomes not only more tolerable but also understandable if it can be interpreted in the framework of change. Differing kinds and expressions of conformity and rebellion, of the quest for freedom as well as security, can be assigned to different stages of the life cycle, to different age roles, and thus conflicting cultural meanings and urges can be given their proper place and honor.

As the child moves closer to the day when he or she leaves home and officially becomes an adult we see some of the same conflicting urges and interpretations that mark adolescence. The grounds for conflict change from issues of adolescent "freedom" and parental "control" to those of "staying" and "leaving." But the underlying condition is similar, for parents and children alike seem pulled in conflicting directions by their culture.

At some point—typically at or shortly after graduation from high school or college—American parents are ready, even eager for their children to leave home and to start lives of their own so that the parents can resume theirs, regaining the freedom and independence they have put aside in raising children. As the rabbi says when asked "When does life begin?" in the punch line of the familiar joke, "Life begins when the last child graduates from college and the dog dies." American parents begin life as a couple and, as their children grow toward adulthood, many of them talk about the day when they will once again be a couple, free from the demands and the supervision of their children.

Yet the event of the departure itself, as distinct from the idea of it, is frequently resisted by parents and a matter of contention between them and their children. Parents worry that their children are not yet secure enough financially to make it on their own, or that they have made the wrong choice of mates or careers, or that they are not old enough or mature enough. Such resistance does not always occur, of course, for a great many parents manage to send their children on their way without much concern. And bitter scenes between children anxious to strike out on their own and parents determined to keep them at home at any cost are probably far less common than lesser experiences of ambivalence and anxiety in which a parental sense of excitement and pride at the child's leaving is mingled with regret and worry.

However absent or severe the ambivalence, anxiety, or conflict, it does seem clear that "leaving home" and "staying home" represent inevitable but still potentially difficult choices for children as well as eagerly or reluctantly anticipated events for their parents. Freedom and independence may be sought by adolescents in the rebellion of cluttered rooms and peer culture, but at some point they must be sought in the territories of adulthood. And for the young no less than their parents, striking out into this new territory can seem a perilous as well as an exciting journey, for along with the "freedom" and "independence" of adult life, the young also perceive at least some of its problems: the possible difficulty of finding a "career" and establishing economic "security," the likelihood that the "authority" of employers will replace that of parents and teachers, and the need to accept "responsibility" for themselves rather than accepting the care of parents. Thus, the young may feel ambivalent and want to postpone leaving, if not by remaining in their parents' household then perhaps by maintaining the symbolic tie of a bedroom that remains the child's property and thus a psychological link to home.

The concrete experiences and adjustments of children and their parents in this phase of the life cycle are, of course, quite diverse and are in no sense simply determined by culture. One can find in all social classes young people who cling steadfastly to home, and parents who fear their children will never cut the apron strings. There are lower middle-class (and upper-class) sons and daughters who work for a family business and whose orbits, even in adulthood, are defined by a nuclear or perhaps more extended family, but who chafe under the restrictions and feel a profound regret or anger that they have never declared independence. There are young people who leave home and are never heard from again or who cut ties of emotion and belief and sustain only the strained ties of telephone calls and yearly visits. There are some young whose anxiousness to leave home leads them to interpret every parental act as an effort to force or seduce them into staying, and parents who interpret every act of the child as a gesture of rejection. And there are individuals whose transition into the territories of adulthood seems smooth and uncomplicated and who express either a sense of relief about the fact or surprise that others encounter such difficulties.

What does this diversity of experience mean? One way of explaining it is by arguing that there are diverse subcultures in American society, established on such grounds as social class, race, ethnicity, religion, region, community, and neighborhood, and that individual experience reflects subcultural preferences. This position has some validity, for the problems of conformity and rebellion for adolescents and of staying or leaving for young adults do seem influenced by family patterns that are anchored in ethnicity, by the different prospects and values of the college-bound as compared with those who seek employment immediately after high school, or by the differences between life in the city and life in the small town. Another explanation emphasizes the process of individual adjustment within the family or school, and explains variation in psychological terms. Again, explanations of differential experience that emphasize psychodynamic factors are partially valid, for it is not uncommon for children of similar background, even from the same family, to respond quite differently to these issues. One child may find adolescence and young adulthood a painful and perhaps intolerable journey while another in the same family seems to experience no difficulty whatever.

My interest, however, is not in explaining the various forms of adjustment to these problems, but in emphasizing that this diversity is itself a key part of American culture. If we focus simply on explaining in sociological or psychological terms why people adjust differently, we lose sight of the robust cultural objects that form the ground on which this variation lies. The adolescent who engages in no extreme rebellion or slavish conformity to the perceived demands of a peer group nevertheless experiences this phase of life in the company of, or at least aware of, those who do. The young person who, during adolescence and later, becomes embroiled in conflict with parents and interprets their actions as efforts to maintain control and postpone independence does so in a social context where others seem to grow up more smoothly and to have more relaxed or tolerant parents. Standing outside the variety of experiences with conformity and rebellion, staying and leaving, we can perceive a cultural environment that shapes, though it does not determine, the experiences of all.

Key Objects in American Culture

What is that cultural environment? What are the main objects that attract and repel the interest and action of those who encounter them, facilitate and restrict their conduct, and occasion discourse and interpretation? We can begin to sketch some of the major features of the American cultural landscape by examining the objects that are brought into relief by the life cycle events just considered and by considering how people talk about them. My thesis is that these events and modes of discourse reveal not just the problems of adjustment of American adolescents, young people, and their parents, but an important part of the cultural environment—its main objects and webs of meaning.

The words I have used to describe some of the anxieties and conflicts of children and parents—many of them common, everyday words that do not originate in the technical discourse of the sociologist but in the common sense understandings of Americans—are also words that designate some of the core objects in American culture. Freedom. Responsibility. Independence. Choice. Security. Limits. Authority. Happiness. The future. These are visible and central objects that invite typical forms of action, impede other acts, and take their meaning through mutual opposition. They are environmental landmarks as much for those who have little difficulty reaching or avoiding them as for those who do.

It would be impossible to catalogue all of the objects of American culture or to chart the complex relationships among them. Accordingly, I will focus on a few objects, and do so by emphasizing the centrality of one of them, freedom. By examining this major cultural object we can see the variety of other objects that are related to it and that stand in opposition to it, as well as the dilemmas of choice that these opposing objects create.

Freedom. Like the others, this is an abstract object that takes on a variety of concrete shapes depending on the circumstances in which it is encountered or sought, and sometimes remains formless and elusive. It is a magnet toward which every American is drawn, and the experiences of growing up and leaving home are but one manifestation of its attraction. More elusively, but no less important, freedom seems to be a quality of the person, for Americans are enjoined by their culture not only to act freely, but to *be* free persons. Americans wish to be free in so many ways that it is impossible to catalog them. Free: to go where one pleases, to do what one wants, to live and believe as one sees fit, to think what one will, to say what one wants, to associate with others or not, to wear any costume, to espouse any cause, to choose one's friends, to adopt any calling for which one is qualified, to be what one wants to be.

It has been tempting for intellectuals to debunk the idea of freedom as mere political ideology or to point out the many ways in which Americans either carry the idea of freedom to excess or are less free than they imagine. There is truth in what they say, for "freedom" is a potent political symbol used to rouse the support of Americans for hot and cold wars, and it is hard to deny that it is composed of as much illusion as reality. But this mode of interpretation of the culture conceals more than it reveals, for it fails to recognize the many subtleties and contradictions associated with the idea of freedom. In particular, it does not grasp the extent to which "freedom" takes on significance through its opposition to other objects, nor the ambivalence Americans feel about it.

What does it mean to Americans, in the most general sense, to be "free"? To the adolescent it means, as much as anything else, escaping the authority and control of parents or teachers. Whatever concrete activities or experiences the adolescent may imagine or construct to symbolize or embody freedom, a considerable part of the meaning of the object is derived by the contemplation of what it is not. It is not parents and teachers telling you what to do, imposing demands whose sense you do not understand;

it is not having others choose for you; it is not living within the limits set by other people. It is, in the positive sense, an object difficult to render concretely—as difficult for the social analyst as for the individual. But, in the negative sense, its magnetic pull is enhanced by the opposing force of authority, limits, security, and related objects. To be free is to escape authority, go beyond the limits, risk established security.

But freedom is not an object of adolescence alone, for it appears and reappears in diverse contexts. The demands of work and marriage, of politics, of civic involvement, of religious and ethnic ties, of local community, of extended family—all represent forms of authority, limits, and security that give particular shape to freedom at any given time. "Freedom" thus means coming and going at work or in the home as one pleases, being one's own boss, escaping political commitments, completing civic duties and retiring to private life, changing one's religious affiliation or resigning from an ethnic group, moving to a city where one can enjoy an autonomy not found in the small town, resisting the demands of distant kin on one's time and energies.

Although freedom exerts a magnetic pull, it is also an object to be feared and, under some circumstances, resisted; and the very objects that, by opposition, give freedom its meaning also attract as well as repel the individual. This is a crucial point, for unless it is forcefully made and clearly understood, the central realities of American culture are distorted into that commonplace caricature that sees it as excessively individualistic, materialistic, success-driven, and preoccupied with the rights of individuals to the exclusion of a concern with their responsibilities.

It is clear when we look at the young that even when the independence, freedom, and possibility of choice that adulthood seems to promise are coming closer into view, security, limits, and authority continue to hold an appeal. The world of childhood, particularly for those who are eating regularly and live in some emotional and social stability, is a solid and secure place, a comforting place, a known place. And when the time grows closer to withdraw from it, it is not surprising that children look back wistfully at it and, in some ways, do not want to leave. Who can blame them? Indeed, it is not only the children who may not wish to grow up, but their parents who may worry lest they grow up too fast. The world of childhood is warmly perceived because it has a more or less stable structure of authority, because it sets clear limits, because it is secure.

One is tempted to psychologize and say that it is in the nature of childhood to want this kind of stability, but in the nature of adulthood to seek a freer, more independent, autonomous mode of adjustment. But the roots of the adolescent's—and the adult's—nostalgia for the absolutes of childhood are cultural and not psychological. Authority, limits, and security are appealing objects not because of the nature of the child's psyche but because they are objects in the culture every bit as important as the opposing objects of freedom, independence, and choice. Indeed, psychological accounts of the transition from the security and dependence of childhood to the autonomy and independence of adulthood are a form of discourse in which we make sense of the conflicting and confusing cultural landscape by assigning some traits to children and others to adults. It is, in other words, a way of elaborating and rationalizing a particular form of the cultural division of labor.

Just as authority, limits, and security are important objects to the adolescent and young adult, though conceived in the specific shape of the childhood past, they are also important objects in the adult world. Indeed, it appears that, for adults, their importance looms larger and that of their opposites smaller. Reaching middle age, we are told, adults become more conservative, concerned with the upbringing of their children, protective of an established way of life. Popular psychologists describe a "mid-life crisis," a period of self-assessment (sometimes accompanied by a frenzied effort to recapture lost youth through sexual and other exploits) in which the lofty ambitions of youth must adjust to the mundane accomplishments —or lack of accomplishment—of the middle years. More "realistic" goals have to be set, the self accepted for what it is, the limits and circumstances of one's life accepted as inevitable.

This process of adjustment is often interpreted by linking it to the powerful American emphasis on occupational or financial "success," for in a society where people are encouraged to aim their hopes as high as possible, it is clear that most must learn to live with the fact that they have missed the target. For the vast majority who fail to reach the pinnacles of success, there are abundant cultural resources for adjustment: family, leisure pursuits, hobbies, community involvements, and a variety of alternative satisfactions can readily be substituted for success. Some men and women evidently make the substitution, rejecting the continued pursuit of the "bitch-goddess" success and replacing it with other cultural objects. Others may wish to do so, but cannot, for they are drawn toward the continued avid pursuit of success even while the object itself becomes increasingly elusive and other objects more appealing. By the same token, if the freedom to construct a life, to be independent, to choose for oneself

seems increasingly hemmed in by the commitments that have accumu-
lated by middle age, there are available cultural resources for inverting the
meaning of one's situation, taking comfort in the security of one's position, in the firm authority of the community in whose bosom one resides,
in the solidity of choices that need never be confronted again.

Middle-aged adults presumably respond as diversely to the problems of
being middle-aged as do adolescents to the problems of youth. Faced with
the inexorably narrowing canyon walls of time, they may try desperately to
climb out and set their sights again on freedom and independence. Sexual
adventure, career changes, middle-aged dropping out, and psychotherapy
provide alternative routes for the climb: an affair may express rebellion
against the sexual exclusivity of marriage, a career change provide the
basis for seeking a fresh kind of independence, or psychotherapy or some
other form of counseling help define the inner reaches of the psyche as the
territory where freedom is sought and won. Or they may stay within the
walls and find excitement—a sense of adventure, independence, freedom
—by coping with whatever challenge lies unseen around the next bend of
time.[12]

But in all this variety of response, the cultural landscape seems to remain remarkably constant. The various opposing objects are like a major
uplift in the geology of culture, distant peaks that now appear within
reach, now obscured as one's vantage point changes or as their features
are obscured by clouds or by nearby foothills. Freedom is close to independence and choice, and as the individual strives to move toward these
objects, first one and then another seems closest or most important. The
adolescent is at one moment adamant about the right to choose his or her
friends, but accepts limits on freedom of movement. Later, the freedom
to dissent from religious doctrine may seem the most important thing in
life. Reaching middle age, individuals look around themselves and find
that they have almost reached security, but that independence has receded
somewhere in the clouds, or that they have nearly, but not fully, attained
success. There is no simple marked trail, to the top or to anywhere else,
only a variety of interesting and compelling alternative paths that cross
and diverge, appear and disappear.

In the image of American culture I have been sketching, two interpretive themes can be perceived, both of which involve dilemmas of choice
in the face of opposing cultural objects. The first can be expressed (and
often is described) as an issue of conforming versus rebelling. Should one
go along with the constraints and demands imposed by others, or should

one rebel against them, marching to the beat of one's own drummer. The second can be expressed as an issue of staying versus leaving. Should one flee from or remain defensively attached to a situation or social context in which one is faced with the need to choose between equally appealing or difficult objects. "Conforming" versus "rebelling" and "staying" versus "leaving" are dilemmas of choice because life often seems to confront Americans with the need to choose between one orientation or the other in order to cope with ambivalence and interpersonal conflict. They are interpretive themes as well, for they are among the standard ways Americans perceive not only the choices that lie open to them but the essential nature of the relationship between the person and society.

In a culture that confronts its members with objects that stand in varying relationships of mutual opposition and that, taken one at a time, are apt to be both attractive and repulsive, ambivalence is a common psychological state. Any contemplated act represents a choice of one object and denial of some other, and often necessitates taking the good with the bad. The adolescent girl who, opposing the more conservative ideas of her parents about fashion and following the lead of her peers, wears clothes they consider too revealing or suggestive chooses independence from parental standards and acceptance of the limits of the peer culture. The choice has the potential for generating a great deal of ambivalence, for parental limits and authority are comforting as well as irritating, and peers are demanding as well as liberating. And if the girl is ambivalent, so are her parents likely to be also, for her assertion of independence is a source both of concern and pride, of irritation and satisfaction.

The counterpart of ambivalence in the person is apt to be a feeling of rejection or betrayal in the others who witness or seek to influence the choices that have produced this ambivalence. Even in American culture, allegedly so individualistic, culture does not exert its magnetic influence in a social vacuum, but in concretely bounded situations and groups where people have interpersonal relationships of varying intensity. If all of these individuals are made ambivalent about many of the choices they must make, they are also all prone to interpret one another's choices as rejection of themselves as well as of their advice and as betrayal of the relationship as well as a departure from expected modes of conduct.

Thus, for example, the adolescent is pulled toward independence by peers and toward continued dependence by parents, for those objects do not appear on the landscape by themselves but are brought within view as people interact with one another and talk about life. Young people in their private circles talk about themselves and their plans, reassuring one another about what they must do if they are to gain their sought independence from parents. Adolescents and their parents discuss or dispute rules and limits, the young reminding their parents how mature and competent they are, the latter emphasizing their own duties and responsibilities. In such conversations, attention is focused on the objects participants seek, but it is also focused on the participants themselves and on the relationships between and among them. Parents remind their adolescent children not just of their responsibilities for one who is still, whatever the child thinks, a dependent person but also of their investment of time and effort in the child, their emotional attachment, their hopes and expectations. The child's quest for independence thus becomes colored by a parental sense of personal rejection or betrayal of family. Similarly, adolescents in their own world invest the behavior of members with significance for interpersonal relations and the solidarity of the group as well as for the independence and freedom of the individual. What the adolescent boy does to secure his own independence he does as well to show loyalty and support for the efforts of his peers, so that, whatever doubts he may express or backsliding into dependence on adults he may reveal takes on a similar coloration of rejection and betrayal.

Feelings of interpersonal rejection or of the betrayal of group solidarity are articulated in many ways, but chief among them is the assertion and defense of norms and values. What sociologists call "norms" and "values" may provide guides and directives for conduct, but they are equally (if not more) ways of defending and buttressing those established patterns of conduct and feelings of mutual obligation that develop as people interact with one another repeatedly over long periods of time. An adolescent's assertion of independence is typically the occasion on which the previously unarticulated expectations of parents assume the more concrete shape of rules, norms, or values. His or her doubts about or even a hint of departure from the previously ambiguous expectations of the peer group precipitate the laying down of more rigid rules of fashion or behavior.

The result of this linkage between personal ambivalence, interpersonal conflict, and articulated norms is a perception of "conforming" and "rebelling" and "staying" and "leaving" as important issues for the individual. The individual is not merely faced with a choice of objects or of acts that will advance him or her toward already chosen objects, but with a choice of "conforming" to or "rebelling" against the formulated normative demands of one group or another, or of remaining a part of that group or not—of "staying" or "leaving." In other words, from the vantage point of the ambivalent person, faced with charges of rejection and the assertion of rules, the choice seems to be either to "conform," by accepting the limits that are being imposed and maintaining commitment to those who impose them, or to "rebel," by rejecting both the limits and their sponsors. It seems to be difficult to occupy a middle ground in which there is a more relaxed give and take between parents and their children—or, for that matter, between husbands and wives, or employers and employees.

Adolescents, for example, seem to be drawn toward extremes of rebellion and conformity. For some, ambivalence is resolved by a seemingly complete rejection of parental values, guidance, and authority and an equally complete acceptance of the authority of their peers. Others adopt a reverse strategy, in which peers are largely irrelevant and over-conformity seems to be their dominant orientation to adults. And even when parents and children manage to work out some kind of *modus vivendi* that permits them to steer clear of either of these extremes, conflict easily takes an extreme turn in which accusations of disloyalty are hurled by parents and rebellious acts are contemplated by their children. The center, when it holds, does so only at the cost of great effort.

In much the same way, ambivalence seems to foster a perception that one must either make a clean break from the group, collectivity, or social situation with which one is currently engaged in order to escape its restraints, or that one must remain a member or participant and give one's full loyalty. An angrily shouted, "I can't stand it here anymore, I'm leaving," a slammed door, a child storming down the street are familiar experiences in most American families. Some leave and come back, some leave and don't, some only threaten. Indeed, the same scene, with appropriate modifications of props and dialogue, occurs everywhere: spouses, employees, children, friends, members of organizations, and a great many others play out the cultural drama of leaving or threatening to leave.

American culture thus seems to foster an extremist outlook on life. Two paths across the cultural landscape seem well worn and therefore inviting: One main trail leads toward various forms of rebelling or leaving, the other toward conforming and staying. The perception seems to be that the middle way is difficult, that one often must choose between extremes. This centrifugal tendency appears in countless situations of everyday life in which individuals fear that they will conform too much, or not enough; in which adolescent children and grown men and women storm out of houses and offices; in which parents fear that their children are rebelling against their authority; in which people stay defensively close to the communities where they are born or doggedly pursue careers they dislike.

This extremism is linked to the contrasting ideas about the relationship between the person and the society in American culture. In one view, the society is paramount and the individual secondary; in the other, their position and importance are reversed. Now we see these opposing views linked more clearly to the ambivalence fostered by American culture. It is as if there can be no easy relationship between individual and society, no middle ground in which the person recognizes the importance and constraints of "society" (whether represented by a community in which the person resides or a group of which he or she is a member) and yet also retains a sense of individual autonomy. Instead of perceiving this middle ground, Americans seem inclined either to elevate the free, choosing, autonomous person to an idealized position and view any social constraints or attachments with fear and suspicion, or they make the society all and the person nothing.

A Historical Perspective

The full significance of conformity versus rebellion and staying versus leaving as metaphors by which American culture is interpreted and lived can be grasped more clearly if we shift focus away from the everyday situations in which these dilemmas and interpretive themes appear and begin to examine them in a broader and more historical light. I begin with the latter metaphor, "staying" and "leaving," for it is a dilemma of historical origins as well as contemporary relevance.

American society was born in the departure of men and women from Europe and their arrival in North America to seek a variety of religious, social, economic, and personal goals. It was shaped by them and their descendants, as well as by successive (and continuing) waves of voluntary and involuntary immigrants, who left the communities in which they were born to migrate across the oceans and across the continent and settled a land that, in spite of its native population, seemed empty and virgin. And it continues to be formed by individuals and families on the move, migrating from the industrial Northeast to the Sunbelt, from the rural South to northern urban ghettos, from suburbs to newly "gentrified" central cities, from farm to city, or from city to country. Physical mobility from a place of origin to some new location is a recurrent fact of American life.

The English Puritans, for example, sought to leave behind what they regarded as a corrupt and religiously unsatisfying world and create a new commonwealth, a "City on a Hill," in the wilderness of North America. Others left other kinds of pasts and sought economic opportunity, freedom, or, perhaps, just adventure in the New World. Nineteenth-century immigrants—fleeing religious persecution, population pressure, or social injustice, or perhaps seeking the golden cities of America—found themselves in the coal fields of Pennsylvania, the steel mills of Gary, the prairies of Minnesota, the tenements of Boston, or the ranches of Montana. The world they built subsequently became a point of departure in its own right. Vermont farmers faced with a harsh climate and depleted soil that grew rocks better than crops looked to the more fertile lands of western New York or Ohio. The children of Pennsylvania farmers, searching for fertile new land, moved down the valleys of the Allegheny Mountains until their descendants ended up in the poor and isolated hollows of the Blue Ridge or the mountains of West Virginia, or, later still, headed further west and embarked on the Oregon trail. During the 1930s, defeated dust-bowl farmers headed for California and ultimately found themselves in her orchards, fields, and defense plants. The children of Detroit automobile workers and other displaced victims of declining smokestack industries in the 1970s looked to Texas or California to find jobs and perhaps even fulfill the American dream.

American society has always been a society of considerable actual, potential, or imagined mobility, not only in a geographic sense but also in terms of social status and social class. This mobility is not merely an observable social fact, however, for it has had and continues to have a formative influence on American culture. The idea that people are free to leave or stay as they see fit—or that, under some circumstances, one has no choice but to leave—is as significant as the fact that a considerable amount of both leaving and staying can be observed throughout American history. To grasp the origins and importance of the idea, we must examine both American history and the social psychology of migration. By doing so we can understand how a culture whose origins and development have been dependent on mobility continues to offer "staying" and "leaving" as an important and necessary choice in most of the situations of life.

We can grasp this aspect of the culture by formulating two general principles. First, when people pick up stakes and move, whether from the shtetls of eastern Europe or the tenant farms of the rural South, they carry a good part of their culture with them and they retain a relationship to established and familiar ways of life. For the migrant, the past always remains as a force to be reckoned with, whether as something that tugs on the heartstrings or as a reminder of all that one was trying to escape. Memories of that past thus may serve as a reference point for one's new life, as a source of solidarity with others of like origins, as a mark of one's origins and perhaps inferiority to those who hold power in one's new place, or more simply as a reminder that things could be a great deal worse than they currently seem to be. Whatever its specific message, the past exerts a hold. Moreover, as American immigrants have found, it exerts a hold on their children as well, who may seek to shed any manner of dress, behavior, or speech that would identify them as the children of immigrants or who, in later generations, may seek to recover what their parents had discarded.

The second principle is that when people find themselves in a particular place, whether it is the anthracite coal-mining region of eastern Pennsylvania, an immigrant neighborhood on the lower east side of New York, or the prairie farming community of Blue Earth in southern Minnesota, they tend to build a more or less settled way of life and to seek to defend it and to pass it on to their children. The New England Puritans sought to build a community that would contain their religious quest and permit the expression of those degrees of individual freedom their conceptions of God and duty permitted. Other immigrants to colonial America sought to build on these shores a society that would very much resemble the one they had left behind, although allowing them the opportunity to achieve a station they could not have achieved had they remained at home.

Wherever we look at people who have moved from one place to another, we see them building, at least for a time, a way of life that they think of as potentially permanent. The New England Congregationalists who found themselves in the "Western Reserve" of Ohio built towns with squares and churches that even now resemble the town commons they left behind in Vermont or New Hampshire. The Slovaks who settled in Chicago and its near suburbs built solid homes to contain a way of life they would defend against the blacks they perceived as intruders during the 1960s. Walking through either the town square of Oberlin, Ohio or the residential streets off Cermak Road in suburban Chicago, one has the impression of a way of life that was meant to last. The white Congregational church on the green of the former and the rows of narrow yellow brick homes of the latter seem to have been put there by people who expected their children and their children's children to use and enjoy them, and to maintain the way of life they represent.

But the very same life choices that were open to—or forced upon—one generation of Americans have always been open to, forced upon, or at least dreamed of by the next, and therein lies the crux of a problem for individuals as well as an important part of American culture. Once the settlements on the eastern seaboard were established in the seventeenth century, for example, the frontier beckoned—first the Appalachians, then the prairies, finally the mountains and the West—although it took a century for movement to get seriously under way and another for that movement to explode westward. Even as early settlers were forming an established agrarian way of life, their children were contemplating a more industrial and commercial future, visualizing the opportunities that might lie open to them. The grip that the old were able to maintain on the young loosened, for a son whose father sought to retain traditional modes of supervision and inheritance had the alternative of leaving home and seeking his fortune elsewhere.[13] Although traditional notions of hierarchy and social deference remained, the more equal distribution of wealth in colonial America, together with the fact that a man controlled his labor (which was then scarce and therefore valuable) and could aspire to own land, meant that superiors found it more difficult to coerce or control their inferiors, who could elect to go elsewhere once their period of indenture, if any, was over.[14] Colonial farmers developed a more commercial, speculative attitude toward their land and toward the future. In short, those who had migrated from the Old World to the New, even in colonial America, were rooted in established communities, yet at the same time on the lookout for the future and what it might offer. That future often lay elsewhere than in the community of one's birth.

For subsequent generations of Americans, under a variety of different conditions, opportunity frequently lay somewhere else—in "the West," the city, California, the Sunbelt, anywhere other than the place where one was born, where one's parents lived, where one had friends and an established place. As a result, a common American experience has pitted the established customs, the social commitments, and the ties of kinship and friendship of the place of one's birth against the unknown but enticing possibilities of another town, another region, another way of life.

It does an injustice to the intricacies of American culture, however, to conclude simply that Americans are "restless" or "mobile," for that way of describing the culture overlooks the extent to which an established way of life continues to appeal even to those who must abandon it. The New Englanders who abandoned their stony fields for what was then the West must have looked wistfully back over their shoulders, and their desire to get on to the future must have been tempered with at least some anxiety about what it would bring. Similarly, those who embarked on the great transcontinental migrations of the nineteenth century could not have done so blind to the dangers that lay ahead or unmindful of the way of life they were leaving behind. Lewis O. Saum's account of the mood of the Americans before the Civil War suggests that all was not the unbridled optimism of Emersonian self-reliance or robust individualism, for there was much somberness, a lingering belief that providence would determine what became of the individual, and an attachment to "society" as well as the recognition that a move west meant the abandonment of the company of familiar and cherished others.[15] If there was a belief that a person could make a new life elsewhere, there was also a sense of the difficulty and the cost associated with doing so.

It is probably not much different for contemporary Americans who respond to the inner impulse to move or who are forced by corporate edict or economic necessity to go elsewhere. Whatever sense of excitement may be generated from the anticipation of starting fresh someplace else, of having another chance to make a go of it, there is also a sense of reluctance to leave one's home and family and of anxiety about what a new life will be like. Movers worry about how their children will adapt to a new school, or how the aging parents they are leaving behind will fare, or whether they will find a community to replace the one they have abandoned.

The problems associated with leaving one place and going to another frequently have generational overtones, a fact of no small significance in light of the earlier discussion of staying and leaving in adolescence. It is generally the young who leave and the old who stay; the young who are urged toward a happy future that lies elsewhere and the old who urge them to seek contentment where they are. Those who have lived in a place for a good part of their lives and built a way of life tend to become attached to it and to wish that their children will one day share in it. This is true even—and perhaps especially—when parents have themselves come from somewhere else and then face the possibility that their children will, as they did, seek their fortunes elsewhere. Those who are committed to life in the American small town, for example, think of themselves as having deep roots there and frequently view the prospect of leaving with considerable alarm. But the roots are often shallower than they seem, for there is something in the ferocity with which the small-town way of life is defended that suggests an anxiety about it. Perhaps this anxiety reflects the knowledge that, however much the small town is thought to reflect an ancient way of life, there are really few communities in America whose residents can trace their ancestry back for many generations. Or perhaps, it reflects the recognition that the small-town way of life is venerated, even in small towns, by a great many people whose roots, and perhaps even preferences, lie somewhere else.

It is the young, for the most part, who leave, and the old who stay; it is parents who raise their children to accept the moral and geographical boundaries of the way of life they have forged, but who recognize that their children are likely at some point to feel the urge to go. Erik Erikson caught this dilemma in his analysis of the role of the mother in the American frontier community, an analysis that has far broader applicability because it depicts a more general dilemma fostered by American culture. The frontier, as Erikson depicted it, was competitive and rugged, and the frontier woman saw in her children

> future men and women who would face contrasts of rigid sedentary and shifting migratory life. They must be prepared for any number of extreme opposites in milieu, and always ready to seek new goals and to fight for them in merciless competition. For, after all, worse than a sinner was a sucker.

Frontier American women, Erikson claims, developed methods of child-rearing that would avoid maternal over-protection and thus keep from weakening potential frontiersmen. These women sought on the one hand to build stable and durable communities whose members were committed to their way of life, and on the other to train young people who would be able to accept the call of the frontier and to move on. Erikson writes that

> the same families, the same mothers, were forced to prepare men and women who would take root in the community life and the gradual class stratification of the new villages and towns and at the same time to prepare these children for the possible physical hardships of homesteading on the frontiers. Towns, too, developed their sedentary existence and oriented their inward life to work bench and writing desk, fireplace and altar, while through them, on the roads and rails, strangers passed bragging of God knows what greener pastures. You had either to follow—or to stay behind and brag louder.[16]

God knows what greener pastures! The call of elsewhere is not heard only in the mind's ear but in the talk of men and women, in the rumors they spread, in the knowledge they bring back from afar. As Erikson argues, there were two possible responses to that call—either heed it or loudly and defensively ignore it by remaining in place, for

> the call of the frontier, the temptation to move on, forced those who stayed to become defensively sedentary, and defensively proud. In a world which developed the slogan, "If you can see your neighbor's chimney, it is time to move on," mothers had to raise sons and daughters who would be determined to ignore the call of the frontier—but who would go with equal determination once they were forced or chose to go.[17]

Thus, in essence, staying and leaving were choices that early shaped the culture by shaping the perceptions of families raising their children. To "stay" or to "leave" was not simply a dilemma individual Americans faced, but one that became built into their views of the world and how to live in it.

Erikson's formulation helps us understand why American culture seems to foster both an aggressive mobility and a defensive commitment to place. "Boosterism"—the confident, Babbitt-voiced praise of some particular piece of American real estate toward which all of Western civilization has led—is one example of this cultural contradiction, for it contains more than a hint of anxiety. The booster is convinced that fate has had "this place" in mind all along, that it is truly "God's country," that there could not possibly be a better place to be. Yet there are other boosters in other places claiming the same thing, and one is always prey to the suspicion that the decision to stay attached to this place may mean that life passes one by. "Talk it up" is thus a slogan used by men and women who prefer to subdue anxiety with the sounds of confidence.

"Staying" and "leaving" must be understood in part as interpretive metaphors by means of which we can grasp the way American culture channels thought and action. Although a great many people throughout American history have, of course, faced a literal dilemma of staying in one place or leaving to go to another, others have faced it in a more abstract way. A great many Americans have felt the need to decide not whether to stay in one geographical place or depart for another, but whether to shed or retain ethnic, religious, and other group identities. Although the latter entails a different kind of mobility than the former, the dilemma is much the same in either case.

Irish, Germans, Italians, Swedes, Jews, Poles, and many other immigrant groups in this nation of immigrants each developed a collective sense of ethnic loyalty and identification, building on the cultures they brought with them to the New World and adapting them to its exigencies. Each ethnic group—whether Jews in the lower east side of New York or Swedes in the prairie farming communities of Minnesota—thus struggled to build a sense of place for itself, not only through demographic concentration but by the elaboration of a way of life that would somehow fit within the larger mosaic of American society. And each participated to one degree or another in a struggle with the surrounding society—for the right to maintain distinctive cultural and linguistic practices and, crucially, for the loyalty of their children. This struggle is not just of interest to the members of particular ethnic groups, however, for it has been as influential in the formation of American culture as the larger dilemma of mobility of which it is a part.

Whatever its culture (and however distinctive it is in fact from that of the surrounding society) the ethnic group represents a more or less settled way of life to its adult members—to the old who have raised their children and to those currently doing so. First-generation immigrants rely on previously learned skills and cultural understandings to gain a footing in the New World, and as they do so, adapting old patterns to new realities, they forge a way of life to which they become committed and to which they expect their children to remain loyal. Subsequent generations both inherit and modify the culture their parents and grandparents have forged, perhaps changing some of its emphases, abandoning some traditions even as they create others to take their place.

As it undergoes a change in boundaries or cultural contents, however, the ethnic group remains a distinctive kind of *place* in American society, a place that is defined less by the concrete geography of urban neighborhood or rural community and more by an abstract social geography in which people identify with a variety of groups, organizations, communities, and collectivities that are as apt to be dispersed as compact. Still, as a place, the ethnic group is even today "home" to a great many people engaged in the tasks of earning a living and raising families, and in the past it was home to even more. As such, it presented (and continues to present) its members, particularly its children, with the familiar dilemma of staying or leaving.

Just as strangers have, since the beginning, roamed American trails and highways "bragging of God knows what greener pastures," enticing others to follow them and engendering a defensive commitment to place on the part of those who stayed behind, so, too, the surrounding society has been an enticing greener pasture to the members of ethnic groups. If the settled way of life inherited from one's parents offers a security of place and purpose, the world outside promises the chance to be free and independent, to make of oneself whatever one can. The ethnic enclave offers tradition and its limits, while the wider society offers the freedom to express one's talents and to transcend those limits. The ethnic group, through the ideological support of an exclusive religious tradition, offers a final word on what is good, right, and true; the larger society offers the chance to think free of traditional limits, to escape the constraints of conventional piety.

The ethnic group member is thus faced with a familiar dilemma, whether to "stay" attached to the group or to "leave" for greener social pastures. The movement in question does not involve the distances of space but of identification and loyalty, but it is nevertheless a matter of compelling ambivalence. To pursue or to respond to the call of opportunity has often seemed to require a diminution of ethnic loyalty and identification. One must learn a different way of speaking English and to suppress the dialect of the ethnic enclave, whether this entails shunning the Yiddish accents of Brooklyn for the models offered by WASP high school teachers or the drawl of Appalachia for the dialect of the midwestern city. One must learn to measure one's aspirations and conduct by a more universalistic yardstick than the traditional expectations of "our people." [18]

The ethnic group member who elects to leave (completely or partially) does not do so without engendering considerable ambivalence both in self and others. Learning to speak "correctly," for example, entails a constant self-conscious watchfulness, and every self-corrective act in some degree thus symbolizes a rejection of one's ethnic and linguistic background. Adopting the behavior and beliefs of outsiders or attempting to restrict their knowledge of or access to one's ethnic origins and community similarly requires a form of self-scrutiny and caution that is likely to engender at least some guilt, even in those who wish to move as far as possible from their ethnic origins. For even when the bonds of belief and world-view have been loosened and the person feels a new sense of allegiance to a wider, more universalistic set of norms and values, there are still bonds of friendship and kinship. As often as not, the rejection of more particularistic ethnic beliefs or behavioral styles is read by others (and perhaps by the mobile individual as well) as a rejection of those ties, and such rejection provides occasion for both remorse and reproach. Leavers may thus feel ambivalent, for they want what society has to offer, but they may also want what their ethnic group provides. And even if they feel no sense of conviction about the group itself, they are likely to feel attached to some of its members. Stayers are also likely to feel some ambivalence, for many of them have been tempted by the world outside the ethnic enclave, and even those who have not are apt to want their children to have access to its opportunities.

The result is the familiar aggressive mobility and defensive commitment to place. The ethnic group member who elects to leave must do so determinedly, resisting the call of those ideas, familiar patterns of life, or persons left behind. Often this requires a certain callousness, a gruff, angry rejection of ethnicity and all that it stands for, just as those in every generation who leave American small towns or who renounce the religion of their parents often seem to find it necessary to display an exaggerated rejection of their background, forever pointing out the provincialism and narrow-mindedness of their origins. Those who elect to stay are often tempted to remain defensively proud, to resist the call to move or to subdue their own doubts about staying by talking loudly about the virtues of their place.

Ethnicity has thus had a powerful impact upon American culture, although for reasons that have not been readily apparent. The conventional view is that the immense variety of immigrant cultures has contributed particular bits and pieces to the totality of American culture. Although it is indisputably the case that this has occurred—Americans have drawn on diverse sources for their ideas, material culture, dress fashions, music, food, and other cultural objects—there is a more fundamental way in which ethnicity has shaped American culture, and that is through its reinforcement of (and additions to) both the contradictory objects and the behavioral dilemmas that confront Americans.

Early patterns of settlement and migration established geographical movement as a major pattern of behavior, a typical, but also very problematic way of responding to and confronting a cultural environment filled with competing objects. One could stay or leave, and by doing either obtain some important cultural objects (or avoid some) while also denying oneself others. One could leave the place of one's birth and set out for the West, thereby escaping the past and building a future for oneself; or one could reject the call of the frontier and remain defensively attached to one's origins. The widespread and continuing arrival of immigrants in American society reinforced this pattern, not only because immigrants were themselves movers, but also because membership in an immigrant community or an ethnic group would become, in its own way, as important a measure of place as would geographical location. An eastern farming village of the eighteenth century was an organic community; the ethnic group of the twentieth century is a more abstract social unit. Both, however, provide a sense of place for their members; both promise a way of securing some of the objects Americans learn to seek; both also stand as obstacles in the way of Americans pursuing other valued objects. Ethnicity thus reinforces a culture that was, in the first place, built out of a sense of contrast between the Old World and the New and between staying in one place and leaving it for another.

"This place," "here," whether defined simply in terms of a community or neighborhood or in the more abstract terms of ethnic group or religious group membership, thus exerts a hold on the minds of Americans, but so does "elsewhere," whether defined as the next county, a place halfway across the country, or membership in a society in which ethnic or religious particularism has no significance. "Here" and "elsewhere" are both appealing because each offers both a path toward important cultural objects and a retreat from others, a way of securing what one wants or avoiding what one does not want but also a path that forces one to give up some of the things one wants. Moreover, "here" and "elsewhere" seem to be distinct, different, calling for a hard, perhaps irrevocable choice between extreme paths rather than an effort to follow some middle way. Those who responded to the call of the American frontier often did face such a choice; those who venture away from ethnicity often perceive that they face it.

Other Dilemmas

A variety of other dilemmas can be perceived in American life, each an offshoot of the contradictory objects of American culture and its fundamental dilemma of staying or leaving. Rebelling versus conforming and going it alone versus seeking the aid of others are the two major dilemmas of interest here.

The conviction that life imposes difficult choices of leaving and staying supports the related idea that there are no options in one's relations to others save conformity and rebellion. For conformity to and rebellion against the goals and practices of the community or ethnic group of one's birth are ways of symbolizing one's psychological or physical presence or absence. Just as the culture fosters aggressive mobility and defensive commitments, so too it fosters aggressive rebellion and defensive conformity, and engenders considerable ambivalence no matter what choices the individual makes.

In American society, to "stay"—to remain attached to the community or ethnic traditions of one's parents—is also to conform. Not only are those who remain behind likely to reproduce the lives of their parents in significant ways, conforming to the same standards and values, but they are also apt to experience their decision to stay as a kind of conformity. Some will chafe under the restrictions they have accepted for themselves, whereas others will accept them more cheerfully. For both, however, staying means conforming to what others expect.

Even if one gladly remains while others leave, the knowledge that they have done so colors one's view of self and requires some rationalization, for in a culture that confronts the individual with choice, one is never far from reminders that others have chosen differently. The intentional stayer must be cheerful about conformity, making it a virtue and perhaps pointing to the flaws of those who have been unable to accept themselves for what they are. One of the ways this is done, of course, is through a defensive conformity in which a wall of absolute commitments and beliefs is erected to shield the person from doubt. If small towns and ethnic groups are filled with talk about their virtues, the result for the individual is apt to be a willingness to absorb this talk and to repeat it so as to subdue doubt. The pressure to conform is also a collective response to doubt, a tendency to squelch the words and deeds of those whose voices seek to rise above the roar of approval of established ways. Thus, for some stayers, conformity is simply a natural result of the decision to remain, whereas for others it becomes an intentional symbol of that decision.

Not all of those who choose to stay—or who have no option but to stay—will successfully immerse themselves in the cheerful sounds of conformity. The young man who remains at home to take over the family business while a younger sibling goes off to the city, the woman who dutifully marries within the fold and thus abandons ambitions that would have taken her elsewhere, or the middle-aged man who looks back and regrets that he felt so constrained to accept what seemed to be his lot all chafe under the restrictions of the places in which they find themselves. This would be so under any circumstances, for each encounters a great many reminders that things could have been otherwise. But a sense of oppressive conformity is often created precisely because of the constant babble of the voices of others reminding themselves just how much they like who and what they are.

The insistent voice of conformity incites the urge to rebel, for if one cannot leave, if it is too late to go west or to change one's name and take leave of ethnicity or religion, one can do other things. One can drink, cultivate eccentricities, espouse contrary political opinions, take up unpopular causes, play the fool, go philandering, and in a variety of other ways demonstrate simultaneously one's commitment to and contempt for the place in which one has remained and the kind of life it encourages or exacts. Time wears life's ruts deeper and saps the strength it takes to escape them, but it does not easily assuage the anger of those who recognize too late their eventual destination, especially when other voices, through excessive praise of ruts, remind them of how deeply and unalterably they are cut.

Those who leave are in many ways no freer of the contest between conformity and rebellion than those who stay. In a culture in which there are powerful voices of conformity, leaving may itself be as much a means of rebellion as a way of attaining important cultural objects. For the American small-town dweller or ethnic group member, for example, the climate of conformity has often seemed to be so heavy that there was no choice but to get out. Not only has the society outside seemed to beckon as a place where other important cultural objects could be attained, but the place where one started provided a powerful push. Its message has been that, however much one may value some features of life in a settled community, there is no way that one can get away with certain socially disapproved actions and beliefs. This town, this group, this way of life, America itself: Love it or leave it!

Those who do leave are frequently ambivalent about having done so, for they perceive that departure may be taken as a sign of their rejection of and rebellion against valued others whom they have left behind. The ethnic group member is apt to miss the warmth and sense of being at ease among similar people as much as he or she enjoys breathing the air of freedom and being away from close scrutiny. The expatriate from the small-town or urban neighborhood alike may miss similar kinds of warmth, or perhaps just the security of place and position that such locales can provide, even while appreciating the loosening of the bonds of conformity.

The ambivalence of leavers, no less than of stayers, is a social force of some consequence. It promotes an exaggerated sense of the oppressiveness of the small town or the ethnic neighborhood and of the view that one must make a clean break or even rebel. One way of subduing the doubts one has about having left one's origins is to imagine them as more restrictive than they ever were and to paint parents, kin, and other authority figures from one's past in far darker colors than they deserve. The same ambivalence may also lead to the excessive romanticization of small-town and community life. There is a form of nostalgia for the past in American life that takes a great variety of forms, one of which is the nineteenth-century agrarian myth that lives on in twentieth-century idealizations of life before industrialization and urbanization. No small part of the impetus for this nostalgia comes from the ambivalence of those who have, throughout American history, been moving from one place, ethnic group, and community to another.

The dilemma of conformity and rebellion is central to American culture in another way that is somewhat independent of the issue of staying or leaving. Just as freedom is an important cultural object that is secured, in part, through leaving and rebellion, so authority is also an important object. Americans perceive themselves faced with the necessity of choice between staying and leaving, and especially between conforming and rebelling, because both freedom and authority loom significantly on the cultural landscape.

The roots of freedom as a cultural object lie in the American revolution as well as in the economic conditions of the New World, both of which loosened the grip of the past on the lives of ordinary people and turned their gaze toward a future in which some degree of freedom could be sought. The former provided an ideological base for the incorporation of this object into the culture, for it promised that "life, liberty, and the pursuit of happiness" were inalienable human rights. The latter made it possible for men and women who in the Old World would have remained in a fixed social and economic position to aspire to mobility.

It is a mistake to suppose, however, that Americans simply make freedom their cherished object and ignore authority. It is evident from the way contemporary Americans talk about freedom and authority that the latter holds considerable appeal. And there are, in fact, several reasons to expect that a culture that was forged in an effort to break the grip of the past and create a new, free human being will continue to have a place for the idea of authority, and will be divided in its attitude toward authority. Social life everywhere spawns both the use of power and efforts to legitimize its use, even in societies that emphasize equality and democracy. And there is a more particular reason why a turn toward authority is a recurrent part of American life even as authority is feared and resisted.

A culture that trains the eye toward the future and toward freedom makes use of the past and of authority as devices of contrast. The "future" is not only an abstract object, but one that is yet to be encountered, one whose shape must be imagined. "Freedom" is likewise an object of uncertain meaning, for one does not have contact with it in the same way one does with a building or a tool. How is one to know when the sought future has arrived or when one is free? Part of the meaning of the future is acquired by contrasting an imagined future with a known past, and freedom takes on a more concrete shape by contrast with authority. Indeed, in American culture, the past is deeply associated with authority and the future with freedom, for the ontogeny of the individual from childhood subservience to adult freedom metaphorically recapitulates the phylogeny of the culture from European authority to American freedom.

The idea of freedom thus seems to require the idea of authority, for to be free in American culture is to be free *from* something, and typically it is to be free from authority, whether of the legal system, the church, tradition, or even the charismatic leader. One knows one is free when one can "question authority," as the contemporary bumper sticker urges, when one can get away with the occasional antinomian gesture, when one can say "no" to the boss or spouse and experience the thrill of rebellion. The Boston Tea Party is an important tale in American culture because it gives historical sanction to a recurrent urge to overthrow, get back at, undermine, and otherwise resist established authority.

The presence of so strong a contrast conception suggests a fascination with both sides of the contrast, an interest in and preoccupation with authority that is as strong or nearly as strong as the preoccupation with freedom. The idea of "freedom" seems to require the idea of "authority," and, indeed, the exercise of freedom seems to require the presence of some kind of authority. But in a culture where the quest for freedom is conceived in large part as an escape from authority, the latter necessarily becomes an important and often a sought cultural object. For the very definition of freedom in relation to authority breathes life into the idea of authority and makes it, under certain conditions, a desirable object in its own right. In combination with certain native traditions of authority, this process makes for considerable ambivalence and, often, conflict.

American society was not founded solely by people who wanted to remake the world, nor have the recurrent infusions of new people and ideas through immigration brought only those interested in becoming the "New Adam." Rather, from its inception and throughout its history, the United States has contained significant numbers of people with roots in a more traditional past who wanted to maintain at least a part of that past, including its conceptions of authority. The earliest settlers took European society as their model—to some extent as a model of what they did not want to create, but to a great extent also as a model of the world they wanted. Some of their descendants sought to maintain the way of life that had been forged for them even as others sought to change it or to move on to places where they could create a new way of life. When the sources of immigration became increasingly non-Protestant during the nineteenth century, the old rural and small-town, Protestant middle class sought to retain its sense of moral ownership of American society, defending its way of life.[19] And immigrants themselves have both brought traditional patterns from the Old World and created new traditions in America and, having stabilized these traditions, sought to defend and preserve them.

In a culture that makes authority nearly as visible an object as freedom, cultural divisions between the past and the future, between established ways and new ways, and between the preservation and the abandonment of tradition readily become linked to the contrast between authority and freedom. Authority becomes a valued object because it is perceived as a part of the valued past, as representing stability and certainty in a society where everything seems to change, where the young always seem to be slipping or running away from their parents or their parents' way of life, where nothing remains the same for very long. If for some people authority is a necessary part of the cultural landscape because it gives shape to their vague conception of freedom, for others it is necessary because it can be used as a landmark in an otherwise constantly shifting landscape.

The dilemmas of staying versus leaving and conforming versus rebelling focus attention on the relationship between the individual and others. To stay or to conform is to be with others, to accept mutual dependence, to live, whether cooperatively or competitively, in the midst of a family, ethnic community, neighborhood, or other collectivity and to accept its moral authority. To leave or to rebel is to go it alone, to declare independence, to live either psychologically or physically apart from other people and to stress reliance on self rather than on the aid or the moral codes of other people. And it is the individual who must decide, choosing to leave or stay, rebel or conform, go it alone or seek a supportive social milieu.

There is, then, another dilemma posed by American culture: whether to seek and accept dependence upon others or to go it alone as an independent being who has no need of others. Cultural objects like "freedom" and "choice" draw the person toward the path of independence, for to be free and to exercise choice is to be free of the claims of others and to make choices without regard to their choices. Because of its essential ambiguity, freedom becomes palpable only through contrast, and part of this contrast is provided by the capacity to resist the claims of other people, to limit one's sense of obligation to them. The adolescent typically wants to lighten the heavy sense of obligation to parents, just as the adult often wants to retreat into the private world of the household, where the claims of citizenship can be set aside or ignored. For both, retreat and occasional rebellion symbolize one part of the meaning of independence, which is a sense of not being depended upon by others.

The other side of independence is the feeling of not depending upon others, for part of what makes freedom palpable is the refusal to become entangled in relationships that would make one's actions contingent on the actions of others. The child who asserts the right to "do it myself" and the adult who doggedly works at a problem without seeking aid that would be readily available are both demonstrating this aspect of independence. A task performed independently and without help becomes a tangible sign not just of competence but of the independence that competence certifies. To be independent thus means to be "not dependent" as well as "not depended upon."

At the same time as the culture fosters independence, it also fosters dependence. If, as I have suggested, Americans seek the security of place and authority as well as freedom of movement and action, it follows that they are drawn toward dependence as well as independence. Here, as before, the issue is what will make security and authority palpable and thus serve as evidence of contact with these important cultural objects. Just as resisting the claims of others is a way of making freedom palpable, so accepting those claims and making claims upon others is a way of making security a solid thing. Devoted parents who will "do anything" for their children, or energetic individuals who are the "pillars" of their communities or of numerous voluntary organizations, seem to accept more than their share of claims upon their time and energy. In doing so, they realize one of the significant objects of their culture—to be someone upon whom others can depend and who is willing to depend upon others.

Like the other dilemmas discussed above, independence and dependence stand in a relationship of mutual opposition and tension, for the experience of one depends on its contrast with the other. The choice of "independence" is made self-consciously, with "dependence" lurking in the background both as something feared and as something desired. And, similarly, "dependence" takes on meaning for the individual partly through contrast with "independence," toward which there is also at least some ambivalence. The result is that American culture fosters the same kinds of aggressiveness and defensiveness with respect to independence and dependence as it does in the case of conformity and rebellion or staying and leaving.

American declarations of independence thus seem to protest not only abuses and usurpations of the authority of employer, family, or state but also the possibility that the individual might actually need the aid or company of others. Many Americans say they would rather be their own bosses, for example, than work for others, and this preference expresses a fear not only of subservience to the control of others but also of any form of dependence upon them. This is an aggressive form of independence that hints at an underlying ambivalence, for it suggests that the contest between the desire for contact and the desire to go it alone is resolved by exaggerating one's attachment to independence. If freedom and security both appeal and thus cause ambivalence, one way to abolish doubt is by an aggressive independence that tries to push from consciousness any lingering wish for dependence.

By the same token, one can find evidence of a strong American desire for dependence that hints at an underlying ambivalence with respect to independence. Much of the literature of the 1960s counter-culture, as well as of popular psychology, makes a great deal of the ways in which American society frustrates the simple human desire to live in contact and mutual dependence. There is an edge to this criticism, an attachment of very great sentiment to words like "community," a bitterness in the condemnation of the interpersonal relationships supposedly fostered by American society. The sharpness of this discourse suggests that it is not simply an assertion of the value of dependence in a culture that emphasizes independence, but rather an extreme statement of the value of dependence formulated by those attempting to resolve their ambivalence about this aspect of the culture.[20]

It is, in fact, difficult to account for the near hysteria with which American intellectuals and social critics sometimes condemn individualism unless one views their attacks as a part of the discourse through which

Americans deal with their inherently contradictory attitudes toward the relationship between individual and society. The shrillness with which individualism is condemned as a source of all kinds of social ills, along with the aggressive communitarianism of many social critics, suggests that they are struggling with their own ambivalence as much as with their conceptions of the culture. And, in the same way, the ferocity with which individualism is sometimes advanced or defended and the evils of communitarianism (of which "communism" may be our most potent cultural symbol) condemned likewise suggests ambivalence in the critic.

Shrill intellectual battles over individualism and communitarianism externalize not simply the ambivalence of those who do battle but, more fundamentally, the internal contradictions of the culture that give rise to ambivalence. These battles thus reveal the same cultural terrain as do, for example, the experiences of adolescents. The quest for independence from parents and the simultaneous acceptance of dependence upon peers reveal the presence of ambivalence and of the cultural conflicts that engender it. To be simultaneously free of claims made by and upon parents and enmeshed in claims made by and upon peers is to resolve ambivalence by being both independent and dependent at the same time. Parents who worry about their children's dependence on peers or their exaggerated quest for independence from family commitments likewise give voice to this cultural dilemma.

American culture thus seems to foster opposition between independence and dependence, much as it fosters opposition between conformity and rebellion and between staying and leaving. There is a readiness to think that one must choose, that there is no middle ground, and that one must become either independent or dependent, just as one must choose between the extremes of conformity and rebellion or of staying and leaving. The choice of an independent path often seems to produce an exaggerated fear of the dangers of dependence upon others, and the choice of dependence leads to intense condemnation of the problems of independence. Here, as elsewhere in American life, the middle path seems difficult to find and follow.

Next . . .

In this chapter I have sought to develop an analysis of culture as the environment within which conduct takes place, and to depict some of the main objects of American culture. Freedom, responsibility, independence, choice, security, limits, authority, happiness, and the future are among the objects that surround Americans, that serve as the goals of their conduct, and that, because they stand in various forms of opposition to one another, have the potential to generate considerable ambivalence. The individual response to this ambivalence seems to take the form of a characteristic way of looking at life in which the person feels caught on the horns of three important dilemmas: whether to stay or leave, whether to conform or rebel, and whether to be independent or become dependent.

Although American culture has its own history and generates its own forms of ambivalence, it is also an example of a more general phenomenon of modernity. American culture coexists with a particularly modern form of social organization that must be understood if we are to grasp the processes and forms of self-construction. Modernity and its relation to society and community is the topic of Chapter IV.

CHAPTER IV

Modernity, Society, and Community

If we are to grasp the full impact of American culture upon the self, we must understand it as a particular expression, perhaps the epitome, of a more general phenomenon of modernity. American culture was formed and continues to be formed from a particular set of historical conditions and experiences, but in a more general sense America is a modern society, and it is this characteristic that has shaped its culture and in terms of which it must be understood. In this chapter I explore the meaning of modernity, paying particular attention to the concept of community.[1]

The Essence of Modernity

The phrase "modern society" is pregnant with implications about the nature of contemporary life and its relationship with the past, and it plays a significant role in popular as well as intellectual discourse. Its meaning and use are related to a transformation that has taken place over the past several hundred years and that encompasses such momentous developments as the decline of feudalism, the Protestant Reformation, the Enlightenment, the rise of capitalism, and similar landmarks in the rise of "modern society." Sociologists have described this transformation in many ways, but for all practical purposes their image of modernity has emphasized a straightforward change from communal to societal modes of organization. Here I will argue that this image is fundamentally incorrect—that instead of unidirectional change from community to society, we must understand the modern world as one in which community and society are locked in tenacious and perpetual tension.[2]

We may begin to develop this view by seeing modernity as changing the way people regard themselves in relation to the social world. Human beings are reflexive creatures, objects of their own attitudes and actions as much as they are thinking, feeling, and acting subjects. Reflexivity requires a perspective, some platform on which the person can imaginatively stand and from which the self as object can be apprehended. In the immediate situations of everyday life, a platform is given by our grasp of the situation as a whole and of its structure of roles; by imaginatively "taking the roles" of others we can adopt their attitudes toward ourselves and thus experience ourselves. Beyond the immediate contexts of interaction, we gain a platform from which to view self by constructing a sense of social order —a vision of society and its constituent groups, organizations, and institutions. This sense of social order not only constitutes an important part of social reality, but provides a necessary basis for a sense of an orderly self.[3]

Prior to the advent of "modern society," a sense of social order was sustained by more concrete and immediate boundaries than is now the case. Where people lived for generations in the same places doing the same things, a sense of social order was provided for by *organic community*, an enclosed and largely self-sufficient social entity whose boundaries of membership and cultural meaning were confirmed by language and by physical space.[4] Religion, with its division of the world into sacred and profane realms and its explicit ideology, also cemented a sense of organic community as the proper boundary of the social order. This social order and images of it were also profoundly shaped by those with the power to define it, control it, and guarantee it. Organic community, with its shared culture and clear boundaries, provided for the sense of social placement on which personal order depended.

The history of European society and its derivatives since the Middle Ages has been a history of changes in the human vision of the social order and of corresponding changes in the self. This statement may seem to reduce to a formula an immense amount of human experience, including wars, revolutions, alterations in family structure, industrialization, the growth of cities, and other momentous developments that transformed the social world as well as its inhabitants' images and experiences of it. This is not, however, a reductionist effort to explain this vast history, but merely an observation about how things might look from the perspective of ordinary human beings if we were to focus on the way social life has appeared to them at various times during their recent history.

Over the past several centuries, the "boundaries" of social life—those conceptual limits within which people exist and that enclose and give shape to the immediate social contexts of everyday life—have been enlarged to encompass *society* in addition to *community*. Once, social life was coordinated largely within organic communities that sustained culture and contained and guided individual lives. But trade, exploration, religious change, technological innovation, the rise of nationalism, and secularization made the individual less secure within the stable boundaries of an orderly and dependable organic community and engendered new forms of social organization. At first, the *nation* became the relevant container of social life, and its boundaries provided the ultimate frame of reference within which social order and individual selves were constructed. The more recent trend in the shifting construction of social order is suggested by the word and the concept of society.

The organic communities of the past provided encompassing worlds for their members. Although such communities engaged in various social, economic, and political relations with other communities, they sustained the everyday round of life for their members, who seldom had cause to look beyond local boundaries. Organic communities were key units in which individuals (or families) held membership, and their boundaries of territory and culture were also the boundaries of the self.

The essence of modernity lies in its transformation of the boundaries of social order and individual existence. An early and dramatic form of this transformation was the incorporation of numerous organic communities into a larger entity, the modern nation-state. One of the principal effects of nations is their alteration of the psychological horizons of ordinary people. Nations invite and sometimes force people to look beyond the immediate boundaries of community. They invite because they hold out the prospect of opportunities that lie beyond the home community. They force because they exact various requirements from their citizens— taxes and military service, for example—that they may well not wish to yield. Nations, in a social psychological sense, provide new horizons, new and wider visions of social order that extend beyond the confines of the organic community.

These effects of the development of nation-states have occurred very unevenly throughout history, just as the development of nations themselves has been uneven. Even in contemporary nations there are many individuals whose images of social order are formed mainly by the locale in which they reside or the tribe to which they belong and have little to do with a sense of inclusion in a nation. And in the course of European history, as in the contemporary developing world, the process of nation-building has been stimulated by a variety of social, economic, and political conditions in which individuals have participated out of diverse motives. In general terms, however, the trend in human affairs has been toward the psychological incorporation of larger numbers of individuals into larger social units.

The nation is such a larger unit, one whose contemporary relevance remains considerable even as the psychological container it provides begins to yield to another. For, although nationalism is far from dead—and, indeed, in some ways seems at its most ferocious peak—the longer-term trend is toward an image of social order provided by the word "society." Where "nation" is a concrete container of discrete and largely territorial communities, "society" is a more abstract container of communities that are themselves more abstract. And, as I will attempt to show, the communities it contains may include towns and cities but also encompass a variety of other collectivities whose membership is likewise more abstractly defined and often defies easy description. Indeed, "community" in "modern society" is frequently invisible to the naked eye of the sociological observer and even to many members of society.

The word "society" has, over the past two centuries, gradually acquired a connotation that makes it a "container" of a plurality of communities. When modern people speak of "society," they do not mean "nation" or "state," nor do they use the word merely as a synonym for the company of others. "American society" may in fact be coterminous with the United States of America, for example, but when its members speak of "society" or of "American society" it is not the political unit they have in mind. Rather, their attention is fixed on another kind of object, a bounding and containing social entity that is the largest enclosure of significance in their lives. This social entity, "society," encompasses communities and provides the larger context in which they exist.

A clue to the contemporary meaning of "society" can be found in the way it is reified in everyday usage. Society is no neutral sociological term describing a configuration of social institutions or other social parts. "Society" is spoken of as if it were coercive, an external and constraining entity whose existence is real and solid. Reification is, of course, an inherent part of social life. As human beings talk about the social worlds they inhabit they necessarily act toward them as objects, endowing with solidity and an almost material existence that which in fact consists of their own activities and imaginings. What is interesting about "society" is that a relatively abstract conception has come to seem as solid as the more concrete entities of community and nation. Although such palpable social entities as groups, associations, organizations, cities, towns, neighborhoods, states, and nations continue to have salience, it is the more abstract entity "society" that has become the most general construction of social order and platform for the self.

Just as "society" has become an abstract concept that provides useful images of the contemporary social order, the social construction of community has also changed. Although human beings continue to be unavoidably and passionately oriented to communities, these modern communities are less tied to concrete locale, more abstract in boundaries, and more diverse in their foundations. A conception of society, especially one embodied in reified speech and legitimated by social scientists, has in the modern consciousness become juxtaposed to a conception of community as a basis of social and personal order. Modern human beings use the word "society" to designate that which contains their ever shifting, fading, emerging, and dissolving communities. Some of these communities, we shall see, are essentially territorial—based upon the fact that people live and work in the same places for significant portions of their lives. But many, perhaps the majority, are built on less visible and concrete foundations, for it is the essence of modern life that within the larger container we call "society" men and women may find community in an astonishing variety of ways.

"Society" and "community" are, of course, key terms in the imagery sociologists have constructed to portray the modern world. As Raymond Williams has pointed out, Ferdinand Toennies' distinction between *Gemeinschaft* and *Gesellschaft* and its subsequent widespread adoption by social scientists had the effect of ratifying the direction in which the meanings of these terms had been drifting for centuries.[5] "Society," a word that originally referred to relationships among people, began to take on the more abstract meaning it has today as a cover term for the institutions and arrangements that govern those relationships. And "community" began in the seventeenth century to take on a meaning formerly associated with society, namely those more immediate and surrounding social relationships.

The imagery of community and society used by sociologists both reflects and feeds a more widespread folk conception of social life. *Gemeinschaft* and *Gesellschaft* are not merely terms that capture what sociologists believe to be an objective social reality, for they also capture the essence of how most people themselves construct images of social order. The average person, unconcerned with sociological abstraction, nevertheless has an awareness of community and society and of the problematic linkage between the two. "Community" is not just that place where everyday life is conducted, but is more or less explicitly viewed as that warm and supportive place where the individual may find refuge from the more extensive and frightening reaches of society, the latter a place where opportunities and temptations abound but also where there are risks and frustrations. "Society" is not just the word we use to designate the container of communities as well as another stage on which the person may perform, but carries an often negative connotation as a source of causality, of influence, of trouble and oppression. As Williams points out, "community" connotes warmth and positive feelings, and one of its more common meanings, from the nineteenth century to the present, has been a designation of "alternative" social arrangements—alternative, that is, to the cold impersonality and large scale of "society."[6]

Although an image of *transition* is entrenched in the standard sociological image of modernity, we need a different, even a radically different interpretation in order to capture the impact of the modern world upon the person. "Modernity," I will argue, does not consist of a transition from one kind of social order, *Gemeinschaft,* to another kind of order, *Gesellschaft,* but rather a continuing and unavoidable sense of contrast between them. The person in modern society continues, as he or she must, to be attracted to and shaped by community, but it is a new kind of community, which exists within the context of society and poses new problems as well as new opportunities for the individual.

When society *was* community, the latter supplied a natural enclosure not only for social order but for the self. The boundaries of community surrounded its individual members and gave them a sense of place, an idea of where they stood in relation to others and why they stood there. Although it was perhaps seldom just or benign, this sense of place nevertheless lent continuity to daily life and conveniently arranged its disparate activities into a whole.

But as the outer boundaries of life have expanded, first to the more concrete level of "nation" and then to the more abstract "society," their capacity to sustain the person has diminished. The organic community with its familiar faces and repetitive round of activities provided a place of human scale in which people could locate themselves. It had known horizons, and they were physical as well as symbolic. Buildings, fields, mountains, streams, roads, walls, and other works of humankind and nature provided a substantial and immediate field within which human activity was located. They were landmarks that could be seen, and the field they constituted was sufficient to contain the greater part of everyday life.

As human beings come to live in society, the scale of things is transformed. The field of human activity extends beyond the geographical horizon, for the imaginations people have of one another (to invoke Charles Horton Cooley's notion of society) encompass individuals who will never see one another nor interact directly.[7] The scope of possible social relationships widens, which is partly why modern people have found it necessary to differentiate community from society, seeing the latter as the wider field in which they operate and the former as a sheltering home. And social structure becomes more conceptual, more abstract, and less directly tied to material landmarks.

It is the contrast between community and society that marks the experience of modernity and works a transformation of the person by the modern world. For as the field of modern imagination has widened to a societal scope, modern people nevertheless continue to have many expectations geared toward the smaller dimensions of social life designated by the term "community." Humans are social creatures whose "natural" propensities are to live in contact with other human beings, to socialize with them, to base their images of self on a sense of membership in and attachment to such organic communities as they can find or construct. They are drawn, in other words, toward the comfort and security of community. But people are also drawn toward the freedom of modern society, toward the construction of selves whose sphere is the society and its more abstract and dispersed communities. One reason is that organic communities make claims upon individuals. They confer a sense of place and purpose, but they also impose obligations. Under modern conditions, where the individual can survey a multiplicity of communities within the wider field of society, there is a constant temptation to escape the obligations of more compact and concrete communities, embodied by specific persons and their claims, and to construct the self instead by claiming membership in more diffuse and abstract communities whose members are more distant and whose claims on the individual are thus heard more faintly.

The Impulse to Community

The nature and significance of the contrast between the appeal of society and its freedoms and the tendency of human beings to construct community can be clarified by an examination of sociological discourse itself, especially the concept of *role*. Although this pivotal concept is so widely employed that it scarcely seems to require definition, its very ubiquity conceals the fact that it both reflects and expresses the experience of modern life. Here is another instance where scholarly discourse illuminates culture and society in unexpected ways.[8]

Roles are generally defined by sociologists as clusters of behavioral expectations attached to "positions." There is, for example, a position called "professor" located within a larger network of differentiated occupational positions. To this position there attach certain "rights, duties, and obligations," and those who occupy the position and are charged with this role are rewarded or punished depending in part upon how successfully they carry out their duties. A slightly more sophisticated conception of role would point out that the "rights, duties, and obligations" provide a framework within which individuals construct and interpret their actions, and not a set of rigid guidelines for conduct.

One of the latent effects of the sociological concept of role is to reinforce the more common idea, which is both affirmed and resisted in the modern consciousness, that the individual is separate from the role. Undergraduates are taught that sociologists are less interested in behavior than in the "structures"—including roles—that support and constrain that behavior. Especially during the heyday of sociological structural-functionalism, sociologists were keen to stress their interest in the systematic relationships among patterns of behavior rather than in the behavior itself or in those whose behavior it was. The intent was to stress the importance of social and cultural patterns; the result was often to reinforce an idea that is itself often expressed in contemporary life that the person is "real" and the role is "artificial."

This greater interest of sociologists in the role than in the person is a predictable form that a sociology of modern society might take. Modern life is in many respects impersonal, emphasizing the requirements of roles rather than the characteristics of those who are to perform them. Life in a modern society is characterized not only by a complex division of labor but also by a tendency to make human beings interchangeable parts, to emphasize the ways in which their roles function externally to constrain and channel their conduct. It seems quite natural, then, that sociologists would elaborate a role theory suited to the analysis of life in modern society.[9]

Having elaborated this concept of role, sociologists encountered its limitations. Students of formal organizations discovered "bureaucracy's other face," its informal structures—including its informal roles—that complemented and sometimes contradicted its formal ones.[10] All that a professor does, even as professor, evidently cannot be explained by reference to the professor role or the patterned relationships of authority and communication in which this role is implicated. Symbolic interactionists likewise challenged the rigidity of the sociological conception of role, arguing that it would be more profitable to emphasize the fluid process of role-making than conformity to role demands.[11] Indeed, the symbolic interactionists argued that *conventional* roles—those formally defined, well-known, standard roles such as "professor" or "mother" or "president"—on which sociologists focused were only one category of role. Alongside them, they argued, must be set another kind of role, the *interpersonal* role, which consists of a patterned and repetitive set of relationships between individuals who have a history of interaction and whose roles are a product of their interaction rather than of prior social definitions.[12] And even structural-functionalists discovered such phenomena as role strain and sociological ambivalence, the consideration of which forced major revisions in the sociological theory of roles.[13]

Much of this controversy among sociologists about the proper way to define the concept "role" and about how to analyze behavior using the concept reflects more than simply scientific concerns. For, in fact, this disciplinary tension can be seen as a reflection of the inherent tensions of social life, and particularly of modern social life. Just as we saw earlier that sociological discourse about the self seems to reflect cultural tensions about the self, so, here, sociological debates about what roles really are seem to mirror underlying polarities. For there does seem to be a separation between "person" and "role" that is inherent in all social life and that is widened in modern society. On one side there is the flawed, imperfectly socialized, sometimes rebellious or confused human being, and on the other side there is a socially standardized set of expected performances. Human beings develop ideas about what "professors" should be and do, and these ideas constrain the way real, flesh and blood professors behave. At the same time, however, real human beings seem regularly to fall short of the demands placed upon them, to think of alternative ways of doing things, and—very crucially—to pay attention not just to those patterns of conduct that they have learned to enact but also to those patterns that they have invented as they have interacted with specific others over months and years. Human beings do not seem to interact only as standard roles, but also as real and, to some extent, unique persons who shape their roles even as their roles shape them.

Modern society places special emphasis on standardized role performances, for its division of labor is complex and the movement of persons between roles is not only tolerated but, in many circumstances, encouraged or demanded. As a result, there is also a heightened sense of contrast between the standard role and the actual performance, between the formal prescriptions people learn and the actual patterns of conduct they forge and solidify as they interact. In driving hard toward standardization, modern society engenders a "natural," spontaneous resistance. The reasons are plain when we look more closely at the way roles have been defined—or attempts made to define them—in the development of modern society. Some stock ideas of the sociological functionalists will help in this analysis.

In one of the most important images of modern life constructed by sociologists, social roles have become more sharply and precisely defined, with mutual obligations of narrow reach tending to replace those of broad scope. In the modern "contractual" social order, individuals stand in very precise relationship to one another, their mutual rights and duties very closely defined, their interaction closely coordinated in relation to their position in an organization, and the claims they may make on one another strictly limited. Role relationships are, in other terms, *specific* rather than *diffuse*.[14] In the specific role relationships encouraged in modern society, the burden of proof typically falls on the person making a disputed claim to show that it is legitimate. If a professor, for example, resists a student's efforts to get extensive individual tutoring, claiming that such a commitment falls outside the range of professorial responsibility, the burden is on the student to show that it does not. In a more diffuse role relationship where the scope of mutual obligations is both broader and less well defined, such as the husband-wife relationship or the friendship relationship, the burden of proof falls on the one who resists the other's claim. Couples tend to assume that any request made by a partner has to be given serious consideration, whereas those in more specific role relationships assume that anything not specifically covered in their mutual role definitions can be disregarded unless a convincing case to the contrary is made.

There can be little question that modernity gives more emphasis to the specific role relationship and less to the diffuse. It is not the case, however, that specific roles have simply replaced more diffuse roles, for there is good reason to argue that they cannot do so. Wherever human beings interact with one another repeatedly, they begin to adapt formal role definitions to individual peculiarities and, crucially, they begin to develop feelings of mutual obligation that are more extensive than their roles may require. Although people may in the beginning interact as segments defined by their narrow social roles rather than as "whole" human beings, repeated interaction tends to create deeper feelings of obligation, feelings that are in some sense "free floating," for they pertain not to contractually specified obligations, but to more general feelings of indebtedness that inevitably arise. When human beings interact they do not merely perform the requirements set forth in their respective roles, for they also reward (and punish) one another in more personal and individual ways. The praise that a teacher offers in performance of the teacher role reinforces the self-esteem of the student just as much as it rewards good student role behavior; the student's appreciation likewise is something taken personally, and not merely contractually, by the teacher.

Human beings interacting within the framework of roles that are limited in scope meet one another's needs in ways that are not relevant to those roles, and so their relationships begin to extend beyond those roles. They are likely to feel obligations that are broader and more diffuse than they are supposed to feel; they are apt to invest the role relationship with more affect than it is supposed to carry; they may well come to regard their interaction as important and worthwhile in its own right and not simply as a means of discharging role obligations. Moreover, they may often feel caught between their inclination to respond to others in ways that are strictly defined by roles and a wish to respond to their more diffuse and affect-laden claims. Part of the experience of modern life seems to involve the conflicting attractions of self-interest versus altruism, strict contractualism versus attention to status, and emotional neutrality versus emotional investment.

The social roles modern people perform and the social units within which they do so thus often tend to take on greater value than they are supposed to. The very organizing principles of modern life, which stress rationality, contracts, and limited affect seem to be resisted by the social psychology of human beings, who have a tendency to value what they have learned to do and the way they have learned to do it for its own sake, who develop relationships with and a sense of obligation to the whole person and not just to the social role, and who invest emotion in the others with whom they interact.

To put these same points in a slightly different way, modern society has disrupted, transformed, and in many cases simply destroyed the organic communities of the past, but it has not eliminated those human tendencies that were satisfied within those communities. Organic communities provided places where traditional activities could be rewarded, where diffuse obligations could flourish, where a stable set of affective ties could develop between people who were linked to one another as whole, concrete, and particular persons and not only as social roles. Such organic communities are inherently difficult to sustain in the modern world, and in important respects they have simply vanished, but the human propensity to construct and to live in a world of concrete particularity, of contact with whole persons and not simply with roles, endures. It is a fundamental part of our being—not something that culture or society may capriciously discard.

The main implication of the foregoing analysis is that human beings are in some sense "naturally" inclined toward community—that is, they are disposed to develop cohesive relationships with other people, to prefer the company of familiar others, and to invest relationships with more value and affect than would be required simply by the performance of roles. There is another, closely related analysis that leads to the same conclusion: whatever the shape of the society in which human beings reside, they are initially formed within a context, that of some kind of family or its functional equivalent, that closely resembles the organic community in its support for and absorption of the person. The family, for all practical purposes, is a community, and it may be especially so in modern societies, where other kinds of communities have declined. Each of us is thus born into a functioning community that shapes our subsequent cognition of the social world. The family is not simply a place where people are taught the rules of society, or from which they are launched into society, for it is, even more fundamentally, a social unit that gives us a paradigm for experience, for our whole approach to social life.[15]

Human beings begin life by learning to define an interpersonal community as natural, and as they move through the life cycle and into a widening social circle, they use that very basic map of the social world established in childhood as a template for future expectations. Even when modern people seek the freedom of society, as opposed to the constraining warmth of the compact community, and attempt to form or imagine communities that, in their abstractness and narrowness, are more tailored to their individual demands, they measure their successes and failures by standards learned very early in the process of socialization. They seek the company and sanction of like-minded others.

Humans in the modern world are thus molded by tension between the familiarity and security of community, or community-like settings, and the novelty and opportunity of society; between the need for interpersonal relationships and the wish to escape them; between the obdurate social world and the possibility of flight from it. Community is thus of enduring relevance in modern society because it is an inescapable result of human activity, albeit a result that takes new forms in the contemporary world and brings with it a sharp sense of contrast and paradox.

What, then, is the nature of modernity? Sociological answers to this question have generally implied a straightforward transformation from one mode of social organization to another: from simple to complex, from community to society, from rootedness to rootlessness, from agriculture to industry, from the country to the city. The main implication of my analysis is to suggest the need to conceive of modernity as involving not simple transformations, but a deep sense of contrast between the organic communities that have historically sheltered (and oppressed) individuals and a new, larger world of society in which new forms of community, yet to be described, come into being. A major reason for the sharp sense of contrast is that human beings continue to need what the organic community once provided, namely a dependable world of concrete particularity.

But the sense of contrast inherent to modernity is not only one of the *loss* of a fondly remembered world of organic community. It is also a feeling of *liberation* from a tightly enclosing and restricting world in which individuals were bound to a place and not free to leave, in which roles were ascribed and not achieved. Community is not only a valued form of social organization sought by contemporary men and women but a form whose grip many of them are happy to have escaped or to be free of. And the past—history—is not only something modern people remember with a profound and constantly rekindled sense of a lost world, for it is also something we wish to forget, to put behind us, to escape, to abolish. Thus, in order fully to grasp the nature of modernity and its impact, we must give more consideration to its emphasis on the future and its wish to abolish the past.

Modernity as Liberation

A fundamental impulse of modern life is toward the future and away from history; indeed it is an impulse toward a future unrestrained by any past.

Because of my special focus on American society and culture—and because American culture seems to epitomize modernity—it seems fitting to explore this aspect of modernity by examining the work of a principal early critic and exponent of American culture, Ralph Waldo Emerson. His declaration of American intellectual independence, "The American Scholar," was written as a Phi Beta Kappa oration and delivered at Harvard on August 31, 1837.[16] Although it contains strong themes of literary nationalism and of individualism, it is essentially an expression of the central impulses of modernity.

Emerson sounds a theme of literary nationalism at the very beginning of his oration. "Perhaps the time is already come," he says,

> when the sluggard intellect of this continent will look from under its iron lids and fill the postponed expectation of the world with something better than the exertions of mechanical skill. Our day of dependence, our long apprenticeship to the learning of other lands, draws to a close. The millions that around us are rushing into life cannot always be fed on the sere remains of foreign harvests.[17]

What is necessary if the weight of received European thought is to be removed from the shoulders of American scholars is, first, that the alienation of humankind from itself be understood and overcome. A complex division of labor has parcelled out the many functions of humankind—producing, building, thinking—into specialized roles that prevent each human being from realizing a full humanity.

> The planter, who is Man sent out into the field to gather food, is seldom cheered by any idea of the true dignity of his ministry. He sees his bushel and his cart, and nothing beyond, and sinks into the farmer, instead of Man on the farm. The tradesman scarcely ever gives an ideal worth to his work, but is ridden by the routine of his craft, and the soul is subject to dollars. The priest becomes a form; the attorney, a statute-book; the mechanic, a machine; the sailor, a rope of a ship.[18]

The essay urges the American scholar to fulfill the role of "delegated intellect," of "Man Thinking," to eschew subservience to received thought, to be more than a parrot of the thoughts of others.

Yet to do so is inherently difficult, for the very act of thinking, of being "Man Thinking," creates thoughts, books, ideas that are the object of misplaced veneration.

The sacredness which attaches to the act of creation—the act of thought—is instantly transferred to the record. The poet chanting was thought to be a divine man. Henceforth the chant is divine also. The writer was a just and wise spirit. Henceforward it is settled, the book is perfect; as love of the hero corrupts into worship of his statue.[19]

Instead of producing active, creating, self-confident, thinking persons, therefore, the life of the mind readily deteriorates into the life of the "bookworm," the "book-learned class," the "bibliomaniacs of all degrees." "Meek young men grow up in libraries, believing it their duty to accept the views which Cicero, which Locke, which Bacon have given, forgetful that Cicero, Locke, and Bacon were only young men in libraries when they wrote these books. . . . This is bad," Emerson writes, "this is worse than it seems."[20] For the purpose of books is to inspire:

I had better never see a book than to be warped by its attraction clean out of my own orbit, and made a satellite instead of a system. . . . The book, the college, the school of art, the institution of any kind, stop with some past utterance of genius. This is good, say they,—let us hold by this. They pin me down. They look backward and not forward. But genius always looks forward. The eyes of man are set in his forehead, not in his hindhead.[21]

At each moment, then, as we engage in the act of creation—whether of thoughts or of things—we deposit results that will come to confine future generations. Each age must, therefore, "write its own books; or rather, each generation for the next succeeding."

The role of the scholar is to create, to inspire, to show "facts amidst appearances," and the fulfillment of this role requires "self-trust." The scholar must "hold by himself" and "defer never to the popular cry." The scholar must look forward, as indeed, for Emerson, all humankind must look forward. Emerson's vision is, of course, one of individualism, of a "new importance given to the single person," and the scholar partakes in this vision. "We have listened too long," Emerson warns, "to the courtly muses of Europe."

The spirit of the American freeman is already suspected to be timid, imitative, tame. Public and private avarice make the air we breathe thick and fat. The scholar is decent, indolent, complaisant. . . . What is the remedy? . . . If the single man plant himself indomitably on his

instincts, and there abide, the huge world will come round to him.
. . . Is it not the chief disgrace in the world, not to be an unit—not to
be reckoned one character—not to yield that particular fruit which
each man was created to bear, but to be reckoned in the gross, in
the hundred, or the thousand, of the party, the section, to which we
belong; and our opinion predicted geographically, as the north, or
the south. Not so, brothers and friends,—please God, ours shall not
be so. We will walk on our own feet; we will work with our own
hands; we will speak our own minds.[22]

In the person, cheerful, self-confident, self-reliant, lies the capacity and
the duty to think the world fresh, to create the world anew.

Emerson's topic was the life and responsibilities of the American scholar,
but his oration is a text of modernity. The past, enshrined in the world
of books, is to be absorbed and respected, perhaps, but not given more
than its due. We should, in scholarship, but, more broadly, in life itself,
value the doing, the creating, the thinking, more than the results, whether
thoughts or things, of what we do. Our eyes should be directed toward the
future, for that is where life is, and not toward the past. We must, crucially,
not be contained, bound, warped, restricted, chained, limited, distorted,
confined by the past. Informed by it, yes, but not controlled. Life is in the
living, in the present, and to the extent that it is merely a reproduction of
the past we do not achieve our human potential, our capacity, as Emerson
put it, to be "Man" in some specific form, as "Man Thinking" or "Man
Farming," and not simply and more narrowly "thinker" or "farmer."

Emerson's vision of modernity is, of course, an "individualistic" one,
not in the sense that it wants to make the person isolated from others and
thrown back only on such resources as the individual can muster, but in
the sense of "self-reliance" for the direction of one's conduct and life. One
ought to speak one's own mind, to trust oneself rather than the opinion of
the past or of the contemporary mass. Emerson sounded a powerful note
of warning against *conformity*, not only to the knowledge and ways of life
received from the past but also to the opinions of one's fellows. This seems
to me to be the heart of his individualism, and also of the individualism
of modernity more generally.

The sociological critique of individualism has stressed the ideological
uses of individualism as a belief system that supports the social status
quo, and it has condemned the tendency of this doctrine to isolate one
person from another and to make individuals feel responsible for every-

thing, good or bad, that occurs to them. Although such pathologies of individualism certainly exist, there is a great deal more to individualism than this critique grants, for at the heart of modern individualism lies a desire to enable the person against the power of society, whether "society" is represented by the past or by the social pressures of peers. Indeed, an emphasis on the worth and value of the individual, and, indeed, on the greater importance of the individual than of society, is inherent to modernity itself. If the modern impulse is to overthrow or to forget the past, it is also to make the person the ultimate source of judgment as to what shall be put in its place.

"Modern" and "modernity" are thus not simply terms we apply to the present in order to distinguish it from the past, nor are they adjectives that capture some simple sociological qualities like "structural complexity" or "openness to innovation." When "modern" people talk about what it means to be modern, they sometimes have "the past" in mind as something gladly to be abandoned. To be modern is to escape this past, to be free of its influence, to have loosed the social chains that make the free, individual person merely a thrall of society. To be modern is to be empowered to rely on one's own judgment, to be free to walk with one's own feet and to speak one's own mind and not to be chained to outmoded conveyances or ideas.

But if one of the driving impulses of modernity is to escape the past and seek the future, and to subvert the community or the society to the individual, the experience of modern life is more nearly one of ambivalence. It engenders a feeling of liberation from history on the one hand, but frequently also a sense of the loss of some of what the past represented. It engenders a fear of conformity, but also a wish for the security of organic community. Hence in America, which is a paradigm of modern society, we find numerous examples of this ambivalence. The past is romanticized, on the one hand, as we are continually reminded of the virtues of the extended family that once was, or of the simpler and less hectic lives of our grandparents, or of a bygone world of home remedies and a closer and more honest confrontation of the experience of death. And it is rejected, on the other hand, as we look forward to the "best America [that is] yet to come," emphasize the ubiquity and certainty of social change, and speculate about life in the twenty-first century. Likewise, Americans celebrate the virtues of community and worry that they are too individualistic, but they also celebrate freedom and fear conformity.[23]

The impulse toward freedom, the future, and society thus runs counter to an impulse toward the boundedness and support of community and its established ways of living. The result is that human beings seek to overthrow traditions even as they create them, for as they interact, even within the narrowly and specifically defined roles of a complex division of labor, they become attached to one another, they come to feel a sense of identification with one another, and they come to value established ways of doing things. Modern people, therefore, are always involved in seeking to destroy what they have just created, to escape from the very communities they construct, to shed the very identities that are so important to them.

Although modernity thus clashes with our natural human proclivities, it is not thereby diminished in its force. For, against the "natural" quest for order, for membership, and for the assurance of place and purpose, one must set an equally "natural" quest for freedom. If we were to stress only the wish for community, there would be every reason to think that modernity would be a short-lived phase of the human experience. For it is, in some respects, hard to understand why and how the modern impulse to individualism and the overthrow of the past can endure in the face of such powerful tendencies toward community. Why is the modern impulse so pervasive and powerful?

The impulse to modernity reflects a part of our "human nature" that is every bit as fundamental as the impulse to community. Our symbol-using, culture-forming nature imbues the individual, who is a creation of community and culture, with the capacity and often the inclination to resist community and culture. The capacity for negation, for resistance to social control, for self-direction, and for innovation is inherent in a human creature who depends upon symbols and meanings.

The issue of how and why human beings are in natural tension with community and culture as well as dependent upon and attracted to them is complex and will receive more detailed treatment in Chapter V. The view I want to propose is not a Freudian image of a human organism whose biological instincts are pitted against civilization, but a pragmatic conception of a symbolic creature who, in gaining a self, also acquires a taste for freedom. It is a delicious paradox of humankind that the very acquisition of a self through participation in social life both ties the person to and frees the person from culture and community. For, on the one hand, we only acquire the capacity for self-direction through membership in a community and through our residence in the same cultural world as the other members. But, on the other hand, that capacity for self-control is also a capacity for self-direction, for the conception of self-interest as against the interest of the community, and for the positing of private worlds as against the shared cultural world.

Modern society has brought this "other side" of our human nature, what we might call a quest for the individual, far closer to the surface than at any previous time in the human experience. The sway of organic community has been reduced to the point where the impulse to autonomy and privacy is more often expressed and more widely felt. Throughout human history the power of organic community and its shared culture has been such that the errant, resistive impulses of individuals could be readily subdued, controlled, or channeled. That has changed, for with the gradual solidification of the idea of the individual, of the notion that people have the right to create their own futures, of the conception of human beings as having inalienable rights to "life, liberty, and the pursuit of happiness," the power of the person and of private visions of the good and the true has grown and that of the organic community has shrunk.

What makes us modern, then, is not that we have abandoned the past and its traditions of organic community, but that we are constantly engaged in doing so, always with either a profound sense of regret or a keen sense of relief, so that we long for and flee from the past almost as vigorously and regretfully as we rush toward the future. Although the memory of the past and its organic communities is now kept alive more by memories of childhood community, the hope for interpersonal contact, and collective myths than by the lived experience of contemporary people, it is nonetheless a memory that helps define the very essence of modernity.

This view of modernity implies a very different way of looking at the experience of self in modern life. It is thus imperative to examine community in more detail, for unless we grasp this key aspect of social structure we will fail to develop an adequate theory of the person in American society. Accordingly, the remainder of this chapter will provide a fuller portrayal of the relationship between modernity and community.

The Essence of Modern Community

We may begin to grasp the essence of community in modern life by noting how diverse are the social units to which the term is applied. Contemporary people speak of "community" far more often than one might expect, given the near disappearance of organic community, and when they do use the term they apply it to almost anything. Sometimes the word conveys no clear designation of the social unit to which it refers, as when people speak of "our community" or "the community." At other times, the group, organization, association, or collectivity they have in mind is spelled out: the "Black Community," "Jewish Community," "Gay Community," "Medical Community," "Peace Community," "local community," and so the list could be extended almost indefinitely. It appears that "community" can be or mean almost anything.

The sociologist is apt to respond to the contemporary usage of the term community by dismissing it as inappropriate or misplaced. "True" community, in the traditional lexicon of sociology, is organic community, and nearly all of the social units to which contemporary people apply the term fall short of this venerated and probably mythical social form. These social units are narrow in scope, homogeneous in composition, specific in purpose, and often transient in membership. Hence, they do not provide a full round of everyday life but only contain the person for a part of the day. They do not enclose diverse individuals united by their common participation in a division of labor, but rather similar individuals brought together for limited purposes. Their function is not to provide sustenance or meaning to life, but to address specific goals, whether they involve making a product or advancing the interests of an ethnic group. Their members do not associate with one another from birth to death, but come together and depart as their goals and interests dictate.

Under these circumstances, it seems only natural for sociologists to eschew the contemporary vocabulary of community. Yet by doing so they neglect the contemporary meaning of community as it is understood by ordinary people, and their analysis amounts to little more than moralizing. Organic community is an important moral ideal in modern life, but we do not contribute to an understanding of that life by refusing to accept contemporary usage. Instead, what we must do is to examine why that usage has come to be as it is and to grasp what it designates.

In contemporary usage, "community" designates both specific units of social organization and an ideal mode of social participation, a mode that is understood by the lay person at least vaguely in terms of the moral ideal of organic community, but also a mode that is felt may be episodically duplicated in a variety of social units that are not themselves and can never be organic communities. When people speak of "community" or of their particular communities they employ the vocabulary of community both to designate specific social units as communities and to convey an attitude toward themselves and toward social life. The attitude of community consists of a readiness to think, feel, and act in a particular way—to participate in social life in a communal mode—and it is this attitude with which our analysis must begin.

What is the communal mode of social participation? First, it entails both identification with the community and a willingness to regard the self from its vantage point. In contemporary language, to speak of community is to identify with those who are members of this community—to express one's sense of likeness and oneness with them. Moreover, to speak of community is to constitute what Mead called the "generalized other," that more general perspective from which the person may have an experience of self. When people use the language of community—which they would not have to do in an organic community, but must do in a world where organic community is a moral ideal that expresses one valued mode of social participation—they identify, at least temporarily, with the social unit they call a community and they agree, at least temporarily, to make that social unit the generalized other.

The contemporary language of community is thus partly a language of identification, a way of indicating important facts about oneself to self and to others by stressing the characteristics that are shared by the other members of a social unit and by taking the perspective of that unit toward oneself. Modern people use the word community when they wish to announce their identification, and to remind themselves and others that at least for the time being they are acting from the perspective or vantage point of this particular group, organization, association, category, social class, ethnic group, or other social unit.

Second, a communal mode of participation at least temporarily locates the person in the larger society of which the particular social unit is a part. To invoke the word community is to establish a relationship between oneself and the larger society. It is both to place oneself within this society and, for the time being, to suspend any claim of participation in it except as a member of this community. There is also a societal mode of participation in which the person constitutes the larger society as the social unit of significance and refuses to be confined within any particular group, organization, or class. But when the language of community is used, it is a signal that the communal mode is being invoked and that location within the larger society is being established on the basis of identification with a community.

The communal mode of social participation may occur in diverse social units and contexts, which explains why the term community is so widely applied. Almost any social unit can support a sense of likeness with others, constitute a generalized other, and locate the person within the larger society. This mode of social participation is one that is in principle both open and attractive to all members of modern society, and one that may find expression almost anywhere.

Contemporary American society, for example, treats the ethnic group as an important social context for the communal mode of participation. When people identify with their ethnic communities they feel a powerful sense of likeness with their fellow ethnics. To be a Jew in the company of other Jews, or a black in the company of blacks, is to feel a comforting sense of similarity. This feeling exists not only at the level of discourse or in relation to the cultural objects that are significant to members of the group but also at the level of impulse itself. The experience of comfort ethnic group members feel in one another's presence owes in part to the fact that they share unspoken assumptions about life, that their very reflexes are the same. The ethnic group—whether experienced in a nearly full round of everyday life, the formal setting of a religious holiday, the relaxed occasion of a street festival, or simply the inner world of the imagination—thus provides a social context in which the person may experience a sense of likeness, regard the self from the vantage point of a more or less homogeneous group of others, and feel a sense of place in the larger society.

But other groups, organizations, and social categories also provide such contexts. The communal mode of social participation often seeks the comfort of concrete social relationships and the security of a shared culture within territorially defined social units—small towns or urban neighborhoods, for example—that have clear boundaries and provide a reasonable expectation that people will be like one another. But community may also be found elsewhere. The family, for example, provides a frequently chosen arena for the communal mode of social participation. One shares experiences with the members of one's family—indeed, one may share a particular version of the culture with them—and the family provides the requisite sense of comfort and security. It can be an object of identification, a generalized other, and a way of locating oneself in the larger social world. Likewise, schools, work places, social classes, social movements, gender, age, novel experiences can all provide contexts for the communal mode. Indeed, any ecological location, group or category membership, shared experience, social status or role, or other sociological attribute may be the basis for the communal mode.

The critical feature of community in modern life, then, is that it is a desired mode of social participation that may be socially grounded in a great variety of ways and assume a great many different social forms. This mode of social participation often takes the organic community of the past as its moral ideal. The goal is sometimes to recreate or reproduce the organic community, but more commonly it is to evoke at least some of the positively valued sentiments thought to be associated with organic community. When people speak of community they seem to want the sense of attachment to and oneness with others that they associate with organic community, as well as access to the perspectives of others and the sure sense of self that such access affords. To be a member of an organic community is to be absolutely certain of the responses of others to common life situations, and thus to know exactly where one stands with them. It is this sense of certainty that the communal mode of social participation seeks to reproduce in modern life, and not the specific, historical social form of the organic community.[24]

We can explore this image of modern community in more detail by examining an issue often raised by critics of contemporary life, the alleged narrowness and homogeneity of contemporary communities. Among the standard critiques of American society, from Alexis de Tocqueville to Robert Bellah, is the fear that Americans too readily associate with and attach themselves only to similar others. The faintly derogatory concept used by Bellah and his associates to designate this phenomenon—"the lifestyle enclave"—aptly suggests the real nature of this fear: Americans are so individualistic and their capacity for community has so declined that they can find the company and social supports they need only from others who are essentially like them. The result is a decline of public life and a withdrawal into the company of like-minded others.

"Lifestyle," a term we are told was frequently used by those whom Bellah's group interviewed, is viewed as an "expression of private life" and "unrelated to the world of work": "It brings together those who are socially, economically, or culturally similar, and one of its chief aims is the enjoyment of being with those who 'share one's lifestyle.' "[25] The lifestyle enclave appears to Bellah and his associates as a form of social organization increasingly characteristic of American society, and in their minds it is to be contrasted with genuine community.

> Whereas a community attempts to be an inclusive whole, celebrating the interdependence of public and private life and of the different

callings of all, lifestyle is fundamentally segmental and celebrates the narcissism of similarity. It usually explicitly involves a contrast with others who "do not share one's lifestyle." For this reason, we speak not of lifestyle communities, though they are often called such in contemporary usage, but of lifestyle enclaves.[26]

These lifestyle enclaves are "segmental," for they involve only a part of the person—the private part—and they include only those with a common lifestyle.

The analysis of "lifestyle enclaves" set forth in *Habits of the Heart* thus bears a strong family resemblance to other works that are critical of American culture and society. Organic community, with its "celebration" of the "interdependence of public and private life," has declined; people are self-absorbed and have only segmental contact with one another; work has lost its central place in the definition of both self and community. Bellah and his associates do admit that lifestyle enclaves may be better than nothing, for they perhaps embody some elements of community and do provide some basis for identity. But they are apparently not much better than nothing for this purpose.

Bellah's analysis fundamentally misreads the nature of community and the communal mode of participation in modern American life. Although it is true that the contemporary grounds of community have become both narrower and more abstract, the range of community forms is wider than Bellah and company understand, and "lifestyle enclaves" are far less isolating and privatizing than they imagine.

We can see where their analysis goes astray by considering the social movement as a form of community, one that indeed combines elements of private and public. The social movement *is* a community of like-minded others; its members mutually identify because they are like one another in their vision of what the society could be. It may be true that some social movements, particularly the "expressive" as opposed to the "instrumental" movements, celebrate the "narcissism of similarity." But a large share of social movements in American society—the Civil Rights Movement, Environmental Movement, Women's Movement, and even Anti-abortion Movement—are explicitly and fully public even while they provide focus and energy for individual lives.

Although Bellah and his associates might not label the Environmental Movement, for example, as a "lifestyle enclave" (perhaps because the pejorative intent that lurks beneath the surface of this term discourages them from doing so), it seems to have some of the characteristics of such enclaves. The Environmental Movement does consist of those who share similar purposes and who may also be similar to one another in economic, social, and cultural ways. Its members associate with one another, and participation in common activities and mutual identification provide a sense of social identity as well as a place for social support and a sense of membership.

But there is more to the matter than this. It is worth noting, first, that the members of the movement are in some ways quite similar to one another, but in other ways rather different. They are alike in their commitment to environmental quality, to the protection of a specific environmental feature from harm, or (in the case of some opposition movements, such as the organized opposition to nuclear power) to the prevention or elimination of environmental hazards. Yet, at the same time, the members of such movements may very well be diverse in class, ethnic, religious, and ideological characteristics. There is, indeed, often a "celebration of diversity" rather than of the "narcissism of similarity" in such movements, for it does not escape the attention of movement participants that otherwise different people are brought together by their shared commitments.

Second, the members of social movements, as well as of "lifestyle enclaves," are probably no more homogeneous than the members of classic organic communities, and they may well be less so. Critics of contemporary life all too conveniently forget that this "real" form of community was sustained by a considerable degree of cultural homogeneity. Their sense of likeness—and of difference from outsiders—was powerful, as was their sense of commitment to a common way of life.

Moreover, movement participation is inherently a public act for a considerable portion of the membership, although by no means for all. Movement leaders, those who attend protest meetings or write letters, and those who put their bodies in front of bulldozers are participating in a very active public life. Theirs is not a narcissism of similarity, but often a selfless devotion to what they perceive as the common good—the good not only of fellow movement members but of the public as a whole. And even those whose participation in a social movement takes more private forms —donating money, reading movement books and periodicals, silently approving as television news shows rallies, or merely wearing the same clothing as environmentalists wear—are thereby connected to a public life.

We do not need to confine attention to the social movement in order to demonstrate that "lifestyle enclaves" are less private and isolating than they are alleged to be. The same is true of those communities founded on age, specifically retirement communities, which are often criticized because they isolate the old among themselves and reduce the age diversity of the communities in which all live. It is questionable whether these communities are nearly as isolating as they are made out to be, for there is ample evidence that the old, in fact, create "genuine" communities where people interact, where they care about and take care of one another, where there is a sense of being in a place where one can enjoy life.[27] The communities formed by the old may be "unexpected" from a sociological perspective— the sociologist wants to find alienation and despair in such homogeneous communities, perhaps, because the conventional wisdom disapproves of them—but I doubt they are unexpected from the vantage point of the old themselves. Jewish old people who retire to Florida, for example, are doubly homogeneous, for they are alike both in their ethnicity and stage in the life cycle. Yet this deep similarity seems to be the basis for solid feelings of membership and participation in community life.

Moreover, Bellah and his associates do not seem to understand that contemporary forms of community can be as functional for contemporary people as older, more organic forms of community once were functional. As more people survive into very old age, for example, the typical length of life remaining to individuals and married couples after their children are grown has increased. Two centuries ago not that many married couples lived much beyond their children's own maturation, but now the vast majority do. People live not only to see their children mature but to see their grandchildren mature. There is a life after the child-rearing years, an extended period of time when people can, in fact, begin to "enjoy life," having met their responsibilities to bear, raise, and launch their young into the world.

It is not clear why communities of the old—free of crying babies and marauding adolescents—should earn the disapproval of social scientists and social critics, unless it is because the critics of such social arrangements have their eyes fixed on a romantic vision of the past rather than on the real lives of real people. Judged against the standard of organic community, contemporary retirement communities do indeed show great homogeneity, and they do not celebrate diverse callings. There is only the calling of being old and enjoying life. Yet, in fact, the old seem to keep in touch with their families as much or as little as they wish, they vote, they join social movements, they are active in religious organizations. Such communities meet with disapproval not because of the realities of life within them, but because they contradict the moral assumptions of the critics. If Bellah and his associates fear the privatization and isolation of lifestyle enclaves, it is not because they grasp the reality of these places, but because they dislike them. But a great many old people, it would appear, are delighted at last to be free of a calling—to be free of the demands of children and of work—and to be able merely "to enjoy life."

The communal mode of participation—and the contexts within which this participation occurs—is open to choice, a fact that itself profoundly affects the nature of this participation and of modern communities. Contemporary Americans assume as a matter of course that they may choose whether and when and how to identify with others. This attitude of choice profoundly affects the nature of participation itself and the power of communities relative to that of individuals.

Choice is significant, first, because it means that communal participation is itself regarded as an option, as something the individual chooses to do and not as something he or she must do. To be sure, there is a widespread impulse toward communal participation, for people want to feel the sense of identification with others and participation in common goals that the communal mode entails. But the person feels under no automatic obligation to identify with a particular community, for he or she is apt to reserve the right to identify or not, and how strongly to identify, and to feel that whatever identification he or she feels has been freely chosen.

The most fundamental form of choice is whether to be in the communal or the societal mode of involvement and identification. To have a choice about community is, first of all, to have a choice about whether one will, for any period of time, identify with *any* social unit and thus make it one's community. There are a great many times in modern life when the person elects to identify with others, to feel bound to their purposes and at one with their definitions of situations. But there are also times when the person does not identify with any social unit, electing not only to resist identification with a particular community, but to eschew the communal mode altogether, to be an autonomous member of society at large rather than of one of its particular communities.

The result of this attitude of choice is that the taken-for-granted sense of obligation that we think of as characterizing the organic community is replaced by an oxymoronic "voluntary obligation." Once the communal mode of participation is chosen—as it will be by nearly all members of modern society from time to time—powerful feelings of obligation and attachment to others are apt to develop. To identify with one's neighbors, professional associates, fellow ethnics, or classmates is to feel bound to them and to collective purposes. But in modern life one typically *chooses* to be obligated; the individual decides whether to identify with a particular set of others and, having made the decision to identify, then feels attached and obliged.

I do not mean that people necessarily think of themselves as choosing a communal mode of participation or as choosing to feel identified, attached, or obliged. Indeed, it is probably rare to experience such decisions so self-consciously. Instead, people choose the communal mode of participation as they make decisions about particular lines of conduct: whether or not to attend an event of potential communal significance, such as a funeral, a retirement dinner, or a neighborhood picnic, whether and how to celebrate a religious or an ethnic holiday, or whether to become active in a social movement organization. The need to make such decisions is common, for acquaintances die, colleagues retire, Fourth of July picnics are held, family and friends expect us to celebrate ethnic and religious holidays, and we are frequently implored to support causes with our participation, or at least with our checkbooks.

These decision points—whether, for example, to attend a funeral for a close relative of an acquaintance or work associate—are really points at which we decide on a mode of social participation. To decide that one really ought to attend the funeral of a colleague's parent, for example, is to choose to be obligated to a particular community for a period of time. Indeed, it is to participate in the *creation* of a more or less impermanent community. The decision to attend is a decision to feel obligated, and thus also to feel attached, for the time being, by participating in rituals of status passage and social reintegration. The funeral is a specific social occasion that creates and regulates emotional feeling and expression by those present, and in so doing it creates a temporary community. It provides, in effect, a concrete social context that permits a communal mode of social participation. One attends the funeral and does the "emotion work" that produces identification with the others who are there: we feel sad, and in feeling sad we feel joined to others who are also sad. Death is an experience that affects us all, we are apt to say; it is the human condition; and so we are joined in recognition of this fact and in remembrance of the life recently ended.[28]

In the organic community of the past, events like funerals were the concrete manifestations of a more constant communal life in which there was little question of the individual's choosing whether or not to participate.

But in the modern world, such events are not manifestations of community but ephemeral communities in themselves. People are assembled and transformed into a community for the time being, a community that they have elected to join but that, once joined, acquires some influence over their conduct. The occasion provides for the expression and experience of a communal mode of social participation, but it is a chosen occasion and a chosen obligation, rather than a mandatory form of social participation.

One of the most important consequences of the attitude of choice is a weakening of the claims that any social unit can make on the individual. Any particular group, category, organization, or assembly has relatively weaker claims over the identification and loyalty of the individual than does the organic community. The claims any social unit can make on its members obviously reflect its control of resources and thus its power over the person. But, this aside, claims are a function of the strength of the individual's identification: the stronger the sense of identification with the social unit, the greater the individual's feeling of obligation to its purposes and willingness to accede to its demands.

Where identification is a matter of choice, the strength of claims is reduced, for although a voluntary sense of obligation may be powerful for a brief period of time, it is not apt to be enduring. One always has the option of withdrawing one's identification—of choosing to be less fervently Jewish, less visibly ethnic, less loyal to the organization, a peripheral rather than a key participant in the temporary community of the funeral or the community celebration. I do not mean, of course, that the communal mode of participation is always under a cloud or that the person is conscious of choice at every moment. Not only is there an urge toward the communal mode of participation in modern life, but it satisfies important needs that would otherwise not be met. Rather, there is a capacity and a readiness to choose, and so the claims of any social unit are reduced because there are so many circumstances in which alternative contexts of communal identification present themselves and because a societal mode of participation is a constant possibility.

The ethnic group member, for example, is attracted by the rich concreteness and warmth of interaction within the fold of the ethnic group, and particularly by its capacity to provide an automatic sense of being at ease, and therefore at one, with others. But other social units compete to provide a context for the enactment of communal sentiments. The ethnic group member is also conscious of similarity with others on the basis of neighborhood residence, political belief or affiliation, gender, occupation, and other criteria. One may thus feel at home within the ethnic group, but one may also feel at home and identified with neighbors, fellow Democrats, women, or professors.

The question here is not which of these other bases of identification will come to prevail in any individual case, but rather how the existence of competing bases of identification affects any given social unit. The ethnic group must contend with the fact that its members are tempted to identify with other social units, and that the visible presence of other possible communities occasionally puts its members in the position of weighing alternatives and making choices. The psychology of identification is shaped by the open possibilities of identification, and where there are many possibilities and where people approach life with the basic attitude that they have the right to choose, the strength of any particular social unit's claims are reduced.

Furthermore, the possibility of choice pertains not only to which social unit will be chosen as the basis for communal identification but whether any unit will be chosen. A neighborhood, an ethnic group, and an occupation each provides a safe haven for the person, a social unit with which to identify and one that repays the individual in the currency of familiarity, a retreat from the constant need to make choices, and a secure place within the larger reaches of society. But if a communal mode of social life is appealing, so is a societal mode in which the individual is tied to no particular community and seeks to carve out a place and a life based on autonomy. Society is an attractive as well as a frightening place, and so any community must contend with the fact that its members are tempted not only by other communal possibilities but also by no communal attachments whatever. The Jew may be tempted away from Jewish identification by another religion or by the appeals of occupation, but also by a more secular and open form of social life in which the claims of any particular community are rejected in favor of more autonomous social participation. The point, then, is that every community in modern society faces the problem of attracting and retaining members, for membership in the social units of modern society is separate from identification with them. This image of community deserves further exploration in its own right.

Membership and Identification

Most individuals in modern society are members of many social units. Some of these units are sharply defined and the individual is clearly known to self and others as a member, whereas others have more ambiguous boundaries and more tenuous definitions of membership. A nuclear family, for example, has clear definitions of membership, and sharp and consensual boundaries separate those who belong from those who do not. The same is true of the variety of organizations and associations within which daily activities occur: schools, work places, professions, clubs, and similar social units know who belongs and who does not, as does the individual member or aspirant. Yet, of course, the members of these units are also aware that there are many degrees of membership and involvement. One may be formally a member of a family and yet participate very little in its social and emotional life, and one may be a committed worker or a "nine-to-fiver."

There are also many social units whose membership is not nearly as clearly defined. Viewed as a social unit defined by the subjective perceptions of its members, social class has this character: there are no clear definitions by which people sort themselves into classes, so that the broad categories of "working class" and "middle class" are available to be claimed and used by individuals with a wide range of occupations and incomes. Similarly, membership in a "generation" or in a social category such as "Yuppies" is ambiguous; there are no truly definitive criteria that mark an individual as a member of the "Sixties Generation" or as a "Yuppy." Thus, the individual may well be uncertain about his or her class or generation, and, as with more sharply delineated social units, feel very involved, indifferent, or alienated from any particular social unit of which one may or may not be a member.

A large part of the complexity and uncertainty of group membership in modern life owes to the separation of membership and identification. One may be a member of a particular social unit—that is, one may meet whatever criteria exist for membership in this unit—without the fact of membership determining the kind or degree of identification with the unit. Thus one may belong to a family or occupational group, but feel no profound sense of likeness with other members; or one may belong and feel either a strong sense of likeness or a wish to identify. And by the same token, one may identify with a given social unit, whether it is a profession, a social class, a generation, or a circle of friends, and yet not meet formal criteria of membership. This latter situation is the familiar phenomenon of the "reference group," a social unit to which the individual does not belong but that nonetheless provides standards of conduct and models for the self.[29]

The first consequence of the separation of membership and identification is to make any social unit a potential locus of the communal mode of social participation. In the world of the organic community, only the community functions as a community for its members. To be sure, a variety of social units within the community command a portion of the loyalty and identification of community members. The family, for example, is still a unit of identification within the organic community, for its members identify with one another and pursue family as well as community goals. But the family is contained within and regulated by the community, and the identification of family members is tempered by their identification with the community, which is the larger container of significance in their lives.

Where membership and identification are separate—where individuals can choose to withhold identification from any social unit to which they belong or to bestow it on any unit they choose—all social units become available as places in which to experience the communal mode of social participation. That is, any social unit in principle can provide others with whom the individual can feel a sense of likeness and oneness, and thus identify; any social unit can provide clear-cut and unquestionably legitimate goals that bestow upon the person a sense of purpose; and any social unit can provide a stable set of members who are available for the formation of the concrete and durable social ties that are so much a part of the experience of community. In short, whereas organic community seems to require a specific kind of social structure, the communal mode of social participation can adapt itself to a variety of structures. Within the larger container of society, a great variety of social units can serve as communities.

Social units in modern society ordinarily convert member identification to their own purposes. Members who identify with a family, an ethnic group, a social class, a neighborhood, or a work organization are available for its collective purposes. The unit's goals become theirs, and their energies become mobilized to its purposes. For the social unit, member identification becomes a sustaining resource; for members, the social unit becomes a way of living, at least for a time, in the communal mode, and warmth, security, and identity become the main rewards of participation. That is, the social unit becomes the source of others in whose company one can feel a sense of purpose and wholeness, as well as a sense of certified placement in the larger society.

The conversion of almost any social unit into a potential locus for the communal mode of social participation has a transforming effect on the life of these social units. This transformation occurs because the separation of membership and identification makes it more difficult for social units to regulate identification and membership. Any social unit has both criteria of membership and means of regulating the identification of members. In the world of organic community, it is the community itself that is the main object of identification and assigns membership in subsidiary units where the scope and intensity of the individual's identification is typically predetermined. But where membership does not carry with it a taken-for-granted degree of identification, the social unit faces the more difficult task of ensuring that enough members identify sufficiently with the unit that its purposes can be achieved, while also keeping the identification of members within reasonable bounds.

On the one hand, social units in the modern world cannot take for granted the identification of their members. Children are born into families and readily identify with their purposes until they enter the larger world of school and peers, at which point the family enters a competition for their loyalty, energy, and identification. Once enrolled in school, the child acquires increasing degrees of freedom to identify with peers, and to use identification with them and their purposes as leverage within the nuclear family. Similarly, the organization hires an employee, and seeks to induce and to reward identification with it and with its goals, but it is handicapped because the individual can take his or her identification elsewhere. Even if jobs are scarce and the individual thus feels compelled to follow the organization's dictates, it is often possible to withhold full identification. This problem is exacerbated in American society, where conformity versus rebellion and staying versus leaving are themselves so salient as choices the individual can or must make.

On the other hand, there is another problem faced by contemporary social units, one caused by excessive rather than too little identification. Where any social unit can provide a locus of the communal mode of social participation, there is always the possibility that the organization may become the *primary* object of identification for some of its members. A family, organization, or social movement may become not merely a place where the individual temporarily or intermittently experiences the communal mode but a place where community is exclusively sought. In the family context, some members of a nuclear family become over-identified with it, making it fully the center of their lives and their mark of place in the world. Some children, for example, refuse to leave home and create their own families; spouses become encapsulated within the nuclear family and make it exclusively their world, regarding no other social units as worthy of their identification. In work organizations, some employees make the company the sole object of their identification, putting its purposes before all others and finding no community except within the corporate walls. And members sometimes become committed to social movements to the exclusion of all other forms of social participation and identification.

Strong identification has positive consequences for a social unit, but over-identification presents problems. The individual who identifies exclusively with a nuclear or extended family, for example, may well become crucial to this unit's success, for identification carries with it a willingness to service other members of the family, to do what other members will not, to assume the burdens of caring for elderly members or providing a source of financial or emotional support. The professor who so strongly identifies with the local college or university that the rewards of the discipline shrink to insignificance is often a key organizational resource, for this is the individual who is willing to undertake tasks that others regard as insufficiently rewarding or important.

But strong identification also has its costs for the social unit, which finds itself in the position of having to "service" the over-identified member. The child who never leaves home must be absorbed into the daily round of his or her parents' lives, even though they might well prefer to empty their nests and rebuild the sense of themselves as a couple that they had before their children were born. The college must not only reward the identification of its "locals," but often finds itself in the position of finding a place for their energies and skills even when they have become obsolete from the organization's perspective. Even in a society not committed to traditional patterns of behavior, the strongly identified member is typically a force that favors tradition and resists change, for familiar ways of doing things become embedded in the person who is so strongly identified with the organization that there is no ready way to dislodge him or her.

Social units are thus sometimes hostage to the loyalty and identification of their members. Families must find ways to cope with children who won't leave home and other members who want to make the family the center of their world. Organizations must find ways of using the energies and skills of those who, by virtue of their strong identification, have come to exert significant control over the organization's destiny. Strong identification, which becomes possible in a world where individuals may choose the degree to which they will identify with any given social unit, thus introduces a serious asymmetry into the life of these units, which may receive more loyalty than they wish from some members and not enough from others.

Under some circumstances, identification may in fact transform a social unit into a kind of community. Where the unit attracts the nearly exclusive identification of a large number of its members, the salience of the particular goals of the unit may begin to decline and that of "community" as an object of the unit may increase. If this occurs, the social unit then begins to function as a community, in the sense that it becomes the principal or even the exclusive focus of identification for enough members that it becomes the locus of a culture and the maintenance of an identity becomes its main social function.

Organizations, for example, must capture enough identification from members to convert individual energies to organizational purposes, for identification provides the motive force for individual acts to secure organizational goals. But, ironically, where the organization becomes an exclusive object of identification for a great many members, its goals are apt to become secondary to the object of providing a community. As an organization becomes a community, it solidifies a culture and responses to it—ways of thinking, feeling, and acting that began as means to organizational ends, but that evolve into an organizational culture to be maintained as an end in itself. And, as a culture solidifies, identification with the organization and with its culture comes to be a primary criterion of membership. Those admitted—who are hired or permitted to join—are those who will "fit in," who can be expected to share in the organization's culture.

All social units in the modern world have the potential to be transformed into "communities" of this kind. Families may become rather exclusive social worlds that develop their own cultures and provide for the identities of their members, whose participation in other social units is always peripheral to their family involvements. Work organizations, neighborhoods, ethnic groups, social movement organizations, voluntary associations—indeed, social units of almost any description—may become "communities." The implications for the social structure of modern societies are striking.

First, we must begin to understand that "community" is no longer only a social structure that provides for or commands identification, but that it may also be a social structure that *results from* identification. The organic community, which was a largely self-sustaining world that existed before the individual and gave the individual a place and a culture, commanded the energy and loyalty of its members and thus not only provided for identification, but demanded it. In the modern world, where identification is portable, acts of identification become the basis on which community comes into being. If enough of its members identify strongly and exclusively with it, a family or an organization of almost any kind may, for all practical purposes, become a community within the larger society.

Second, community becomes a far more volatile, even invisible phenomenon than at any time in the past. The organic community was a social structure visible in the activities, mutual identification, and culture of its members, and made concrete by geographical place. Modern community is as apt to be a mode of social participation as a social structure. Where it is the former, it may be located, temporarily or permanently, within any of a great variety of social units. And even where it is a social structure, it may be anchored in ephemeral and transitory social units as well as in more durable and visible social units. In either case, the social structure of community is often not visible to the naked sociological eye, for one cannot as easily discern the presence of community that assumes such variegated forms.

If we examine any social unit, for example, we may well find individuals whose activities are virtually indistinguishable from those of their peers, but for whom this social unit effectively functions as a main locus and perhaps as the only locus of identification. For these individuals, the social unit in question effectively serves as a community, even though for others it commands only a fraction of their identification. Strength of identification is often not plainly visible, for similar organizational performances may be motivated by differing degrees and kinds of identification with and commitment to the organization.

The large social structure of community may also be largely invisible. There are few social units with many of the characteristics of organic communities, for the fully self-enclosed social world, anchored in one place and with a culture and criteria of membership that precede the individual, is largely a thing of the past. There are many social units that function as communities part of the time for some of their members, and some social units that have been converted into communities by the identifications of their members. Accordingly, the sociologist may see a few remnant or quasi-organic communities and a host of concrete social units, yet fail to see the shifting community life that is taking place in the interstices of these visible structures.

Community in the modern world thus becomes as much a phenomenon of collective as of institutional behavior, and we cannot grasp its essence without considering these contrasting ways human conduct is organized and directed. The concept of a *collectivity,* drawn from the study of collective behavior, is central to this understanding. A collectivity is the social entity within which collective behavior takes place. According to Ralph Turner and Lewis Killian, collectivities lack those defined procedures for selecting and identifying members and leaders that are ordinarily found in human groups and organizations.

> The members are those who happen to be participating, and the leaders are those who are being followed by the members. The collectivity is oriented toward an object of attention and arrives at some shared objective, but these are not defined in advance, and there are no formal procedures for reaching decisions.[30]

Collectivities, say Turner and Killian, are "not guided in a straightforward fashion by the culture of the society."[31] The behavior of members is co-ordinated, sometimes sheerly in a parallel fashion, as in panic flight, and sometimes through a newly created division of labor, but in any case the individual experiences a sense of social constraint in spite of the unfamiliar and often unconventional nature of the activity.

Collective behavior is characterized by its volatility, its shifting objects of attention, and its expanding and shrinking layers of leadership, membership, and participation. It is also marked to a great extent by frequent invisibility to the sociological observer. Outbursts of collective behavior —fads, crazes, panics, booms, and episodes of mass hysteria—occur unpredictably, and even the longer-lived phenomena of collective behavior we call social movements tend to escape the attention of observers until they are well underway. Moreover, collectivities of all kinds have a way of being both more and less than meets the sociological eye. On the one hand, social movements often prove in the long run to be more ephemeral and less consequential than they at first seem. But, on the other hand, they may inspire more loyalty than expected and attract a large following who identify with the movement but who are not visibly members of it.

In modern life, many (although by no means all) communities have many of the attributes of collectivities. Their membership is of more ambiguous and fluctuating composition, their lifetimes are more fleeting, and their shared objects of attention—that is, their cultures—are typically narrower and more abstract and lack the clarity and certainty we find in the organic communities of the past. Thus, like a collectivity, the community in which the person grounds his or her identity is sometimes a figment of the individual's imagination and a product of a will to believe that it exists. It is apt to be imagined and experienced not in relation to an organic round of everyday life but on the basis of more narrowly defined experiences, attributes, or group and category memberships.

To apply the metaphor of collective behavior to the analysis of modern forms of community we must see how institutional and collective behavior are both very different and closely linked. The social movement, for example, is a collectivity: it has an emergent quality, its objects of attention and leadership shift over time, and its membership shrinks and expands. Yet the movement relies on such organizational forms as the voluntary association, its activities are often connected with the affairs of government and politics, and it relies on and reflects the culture of its society even though it often seeks to change it. Even outbursts of collective hysteria or panic flight occur within the familiar settings of organized social life. And, by the same token, everyday, organized social life contains numerous small episodes of collective behavior, for leadership, objects of attention, and member selection and recruitment are not fully ordained by culture, even in the small group or organization.

We must therefore think not of a hard and fast distinction between institutional and collective forms, but of a continuum. At one end lie those formal organizations, bureaucracies, and institutions in which there is straightforward and clear guidance from cultural norms, definite procedures for selecting and identifying members and leaders, fixed and known objects of attention, and formal mechanisms of social coordination. At the other end lie pure collectivities, in which culture provides little guidance as interacting people strive to meet problematic situations, membership and leadership are relatively open and shifting, objects of attention vary over time, and social coordination is conducted on the run. Between these extremes lie social units in which there is a mixture of institutional and collective forms or in which the one form relies on or services the other.

The distinction between—and the interpenetration of—institutional and collective behavior is crucial to an understanding of modern social structure generally, and most particularly of the nature of community.[32] Collective behavior has more significance in the life of any society, I believe, than sociologists customarily grant it, and it has even more import in a modern society like the United States. Social movements have always been a significant mechanism of social change, but in American society they have taken on an important role not only in fostering change but also in conducting the routine business of the society. Although it is true that the democratic state often sustains the illusion but not the fact of citizen participation in decisions, social movements have become a key means through which citizen participation actually does take place. The environmental movement, for example, has in a variety of ways provided the organizational means through which citizens influence decisions about highways, waste sites, and nuclear power plants. Similarly, taxpayer rebellions, which have successfully promoted tax-limiting initiative legislation in several states, are social movements that connect average citizens with the democratic process. Such movements create social structures intermediate between the citizen and the state.

American society is one in which rather stable and fixed institutional forms of social organization are thus linked to more volatile collective forms in relationships of mutual dependence. The structures of government, religion, family, education, and other major institutions exist in a kind of symbiosis with a variety of collectivities, especially social movements and social movement organizations. This is no less true of community than of any other aspect of the society.

On one hand, it is possible to identify certain relatively stable and fixed communities, which we might call *institutional* communities, that fall well short of the mark of organic community but that nevertheless stand as institutional forms of social organization and provide contexts within which at least some people can experience and participate in social life in the communal mode. Whether based on ethnicity, locality, religion, or other criteria, these institutional communities have a relatively stable life, although, like other forms of social organization, they have many points of contact with and several forms of dependence upon collective behavior. On the other hand, we may also identify, although with much more difficulty and less certainty, communities of briefer duration, less stability, and more shifting focus and composition—*ephemeral* communities. These communities, which may be grounded in such longer-lived collectivities as social movements, but also in more sporadic episodes of community, provide additional contexts for social participation in the communal mode.

Next . . .

American culture—along with the broader culture of modernity that it epitomizes—thus creates distinctive constraints and opportunities for individuals as they develop and maintain a sense of place and purpose in the social world. It pulls the person backward and forward, toward other people and away from them, into conformity and toward rebellion. It makes available both communal and societal modes of social participation and drastically expands the grounds for forming and belonging to communities. If we are to understand how the person responds to American culture and modern society, we must have a coherent theory of the person. The statement of such a theory, one that transcends at least some of the limitations of existing scholarly discourse about the self, is the main task of Chapters V and VI.

CHAPTER V

A Theory of Identity

What coherent theory of the person can aid in reformulating our understanding of the person in American society? What body of theory is available from which to select? It is not surprising, in view of the degree to which modern culture fosters self-consciousness, that one has an almost limitless selection of theories of the person from which to choose. Sociologists, psychologists, and psychoanalysts have elaborated a variety of conceptual schemes, systems of analysis, perspectives, and theories that attempt to portray human beings and their relationships to others. Yet the best-known and most widely used theories seem inadequate to the job of analyzing the relationship between person and society in America. Freudian theory, through its concept of unconscious motivation, offers the possibility of a deep sociology of culture and its impact upon the person, but its worth is reduced by its theory of instincts and their inevitable collision with culture, a theory that does not seem to fit the contemporary experience.[1] Sociological theories of the self offer a potentially useful account of the various ways in which culture and social structure shape the person, but their crusade against individualism leads them to give the social dimension too much weight and to ignore the ways individuals act independently of and sometimes against social forces. And the humanistic psychologists express an attitude toward American society in their views of self-actualization, failing to see that what they think of as a scientific theory of the person is actually an ideological expression of American culture.

It is, of course, impossible to essay a theory of the person in America that is not, in one way or another, shaped by American culture. But, just as it seemed worthwhile to push toward the margins of American culture in order to construct an interpretation, so also it seems both necessary and fruitful to seek a theory of the person that, while it cannot be free of cultural influence, at least does more justice to the complexity of American culture. The basis of such a theory can be found in a philosophical tradition that is itself in many ways a profound expression of this culture: pragmatism. More specifically, the most fruitful source of insight for an understanding of the person in relation to American society is the pragmatist tradition as expressed in the work of George Herbert Mead. The pragmatist social psychology derived from Mead's work, symbolic interactionism, offers a sound basis for a theory that can show how person and society are related, how social change transforms the person, and how the nature and needs of persons constitute and shape the societies of which they are a part.

The fundamental task of such a theory is to explain how human conduct is socially energized and directed without making the person merely a thrall of society. The concept of *identity* developed within the symbolic interactionist tradition has provided an elegant but partial solution to this problem. Nelson Foote's analysis of identification as the basis of motivation, Gregory P. Stone's conception of identity as a coincidence of social placements and announcements, and the more recent analyses of identity by George McCall and Jerry L. Simmons, Sheldon Stryker, Peter Burke, and others all treat identity, or some version of it, as a pivotal concept in analyzing what people do and why they do it.[2]

The fundamental referent of identity is social location. In Gregory P. Stone's words, "When one has identity, he is situated, that is, cast in the shape of a social object by the acknowledgment of his participation or membership in social relations." Identity is a matter of objectification by others as well as self-objectification, for an identity is had when there is a "coincidence of placements and announcements," with a claim of participation or membership validated by others.[3] And most would agree with Nelson Foote's view that it is an identity that fills the empty container of a role with commitment and energy, making it possible for the situated individual to act with force and direction.

Yet the concept of identity that has emerged from the work of symbolic interactionists has three serious flaws. First, they have over-emphasized situated identity and neglected identity as a phenomenon relevant beyond the sphere of the immediate situation. There is little theoretical conception of the person as someone who endures beyond the audiences and appraisals of particular contexts of interaction. Indeed, there is a reluctance to theorize about persons, as if somehow to do so is to descend into hopeless psychologism. But if it is to be a fully useful concept, identity must be conceived as a sense of self that is not only produced within the situation but also brought to it.[4]

Second, social psychologists have sought to show how identity is anchored in social structure, but a truly sociological theory of identity has eluded them. Social structure is central in the work of Sheldon Stryker, for example, who emphasizes that the internal ordering of situated identities rests upon social structure and is not merely a product of unrestrained will. Identity is conceived as a sense of placement shaped largely by role, and his concept of "identity salience" recognizes that the various identities of the person are arranged in an orderly, hierarchical fashion rather than randomly.[5] But, in practice, his and other work in this tradition has been more interested and successful in measuring the ordering of role-identities than showing how social structure shapes the self.

This defect in identity theory arises partly through too much reliance on role, a concept that adequately depicts structure in the situation but that is overburdened beyond this microscopic level. In the concrete situations of everyday life, social roles provide perspectives from which individuals act as well as a basis for social placements. But, beyond the situation, placement occurs on the basis of membership in and identification with community, and not simply on the basis of an ordered sense of the individual's role preferences and obligations. Moreover, amidst the complexities and contradictions of modern culture, identity is formed on a larger societal stage as well as in forms of community infinitely more varied than those of the past.

Third, the quest for an account of the person beyond the immediate situation has also suffered from an excessively sociological conception of humankind. Although it is important to show how society creates the self, we must also recognize that there are limits to the control society exerts. Social life creates a person capable of resisting its constraints, able now and then to say "no" to its demands or at least to reinterpret them in a way that permits him or her to say "yes." Far from representing a "touching tendency to keep a part of the world safe from sociology," in the words of Erving Goffman, attention to the person and to individual resistance to the social order is necessary in order to grasp the nature of that order and its influence.[6]

Theoretical Foundations

The first task in reconstructing the theory of identity is to explore the concept of identity in more detail, revealing those dimensions of human experience that yield a sense of identity and showing the relationship between the self as it is experienced in the countless particular situations of everyday life and a more durable self that arises over time as the person encounters a variety of situations, social roles, and other persons. An appropriate beginning point is the word identity itself, for the term has several root meanings that can instruct us about its theoretical significance.

The dictionary is a good place to search for these meanings, for in seeking to determine how words are used and meant its authors do basic social research. The *Random House Dictionary* tells us that identity is

> 1. the state or fact of remaining the same one or ones, as under varying aspects or conditions. . . . 2. the condition of being oneself or itself, and not another. . . . 3. condition or character as to who a person or what a thing is. . . . 4. state or fact of being the same one. 5. exact likeness in nature or qualities. . . . 6. an instance or point of sameness or likeness.

The dictionary definition separates several images commonly evoked by the word "identity": continuity of the self in the face of external change; being a distinct and identifiable person and therefore differentiated from others; and being the same as or like others and thus identified with them. There is an additional and very contemporary meaning not captured explicitly by the lexicographer, but nonetheless implicit in the foregoing meanings: wholeness, which is to say, the quality of being a full, complete, integrated, and "together" person.

What does it mean to have "identity" in our contemporary, everyday usage of the term? It is to be like others and yet also to have qualities that make one different from them, so that one can have "Jewish identity," say, but also a more distinctive "personal identity" that is not defined in terms of group membership. It is to maintain a balance between similarity and difference in the face of individual development and changing social conditions, so that one can assimilate to the self demands for change or adjustment, but also fulfill an inner desire for constancy. It is to be a whole and complete person, and not fragmented into roles and ruled by scripts. It is to be connected with others and yet true to oneself. It is to participate in a variegated and often fragmented social life and yet to maintain continuity and integrity. Persons with identity, we are apt to say, know who they are, what they are doing, and where they are going.

These images reveal four elements—continuity, integration, identification, and differentiation—that are the essence of identity not only in the modern world but among human beings considered as a species. Each dimension consists of an objectification of self in relation to a specific aspect of human existence. *Continuity* is the feeling that one's experiences of self make temporal sense, that what one is doing, thinking, and feeling now is meaningfully related to what has gone before and to what will come later. It is the sense of being the same person in the face of external changes, or, if one has changed in some ways, of being a person who has undergone changes for which one can sensibly account. *Integration* is a feeling of wholeness, the sense that one's various activities, thoughts, and feelings fit together into some more or less coherent whole. It is a feeling of completeness and of fitness for a full social and personal life. *Identification* is a feeling of being like others, a sense of being at one with them in a common life. It is the perception that there is some community where one has a place with others who share thoughts, feelings, and actions. And, finally, *differentiation* entails a sense of boundaries between self and others, a feeling that although one is identified with others one is not absorbed by them. It is a sense of individuality that consists, at a minimum, of the capacity to perceive the difference between self and others.

These elements of identity are both conscious and unconscious. On the one hand, to have an identity characterized by strong elements of continuity, integration, identification, and differentiation is to be able to act without a high degree of self-consciousness. Those who seem to be "together" or to be "certain" of their identities appear free of worry about who they are and what they should do. They act decisively and firmly without having consciously to formulate a sense of identity. But, on the other hand, it is also true that the very phenomenon of identity requires some amount of self-consciousness. To characterize identity as a "sense" or a "feeling" about self is to suggest that even those with "strong" identities are sometimes conscious of having them. The mark of a well-established identity is that it is seldom problematic, but there is no person for whom identity is never problematic. Even those with sharply crystallized identities are sometimes conscious of or doubtful about them.

Identity is, therefore, like all other human meanings, compounded of impulsive responses and external objects. Internally, identity has motivational force. It is an organization of individual sensitivities to the external world; indeed, it is a requisite organization, for no activity can proceed without it. As individuals we have no direct consciousness of this aspect of identity, any more than we have direct consciousness of any other aspect of mental organization. Human beings can become conscious of identity only after their various acts get underway, when they become conscious of where their conduct is headed and attempt to steer themselves in one direction or another. In other words, people have explicit feelings of wholeness, continuity, identification, and differentiation only as they become conscious of themselves acting within a particular situation. Identity is a product of self-consciousness; it occurs as a conscious feeling only when the person is conscious of self.

Although a product of self-consciousness, identity is not equivalent to it. Not every human act evokes feelings of identity, for in many instances identity is non-problematic and the individual is conscious of self more or less within a taken-for-granted identity. The physician delivering an unfavorable prognosis to a seriously ill patient, for example, has consciousness of self, but not necessarily of identity. "Physician" is the non-problematic identity that shapes consciousness of self. It is from "within" this identity that the physician gauges how to deliver the bad news, what to disclose and what to conceal, how the patient will react, and how to react to the patient's reaction. In this illustration there is self-consciousness, for the physician has a view of self conveying news to a patient and it is in terms of an imagined view of alternative ways of the self doing so that a selection of means is made. But the identity—physician—is a mantle of which the individual has no need to be conscious unless this identity somehow becomes problematic.

Although it is taken for granted much of the time and thus does not constantly preoccupy us, identity is inherently problematic in human life. For although society and culture may make people variously aware of the ways in which they are like and unlike others and enhance or attenuate their sense of personal integration and continuity, these things are always problematic in some degree. That is, the maintenance of some balance between identification and differentiation and the nurturance of some feeling of personal wholeness and continuity are distinct and perpetual human problems.

The inherence of identity as a human problematic is a crucial point, and precisely because much popular as well as scholarly thinking about identity conceives it to be a problem faced only by modern people. The familiar contemporary story of the fall of humankind, which emphasizes the support and security provided by traditional communities and their loss in the modern world, treats problems of identity as peculiarly modern problems. Although the effects of modernity on identity are substantial, it is a serious mistake to assume that identity is therefore a problem of concern only to modern people. Identity is problematic in different ways in the modern world, and the self-consciousness of modern people is surely different from that of their ancestors, but there are a number of respects in which identity is problematic for all human beings. That is, there are problematics of identity that exist as a consequence of human existence and not of peculiarly modern social and cultural arrangements. Why is this so?

The meaning and significance of identity are revealed by examining the socialized human being acting within a single, defined social situation—a baseball game, a family dinner, or a meeting between student and professor. In such situations an identity is both a requisite to action and a product of the situation itself. In the single situation, the self is experienced as whole because it is more or less equivalent to a role; it is given continuity by the temporal flow of interaction in the situation as objects are sighted and achieved; it is given individuality by a role and the freedom it permits; and it is given leave to identify with others by virtue of common participation in an activity. In short, the single situation provides a microcosmic world that, for the duration of interaction, sustains an identity.

The key to situated identity is *role*—a familiar term that condenses several important insights into human conduct. Although often defined as the behavioral expectations attached to a social position (or status), a role is better defined as a *perspective* within a defined situation.[7] When people act within such situations as baseball games or meetings, each performs a set of actions that are intelligible to the others because they relate or contribute to the activity taking place in the situation. The pitcher throws baseballs toward the plate, but sometimes also to first base, engaging in an ongoing dialogue with the catcher, an exchange of signs designed to communicate intentions to one another but not the opposing batter. Sales representative and customer each perform a set of actions—turning in and filling orders, seeking and offering deals—oriented to the other and to their joint and individual purposes in coming together. Although social scientists often speak of such sets of actions (or the expectations on which they are based) as roles, it is more accurate to define the role as the social perspective on which such actions are based. The pitcher's role is not what the pitcher does or is expected to do, but rather the point from which the pitcher views the activities of the game of baseball and on the basis of which he calculates his own actions. The role of sales representative does not consist of the things the individual does, but of the vantage point she occupies relative to the customer, a perspective on which her actions are based.

To speak of a role as a perspective is thus to emphasize that a situation is a set of linked perspectives. The game of baseball, like all human situations, has an overall definition of the situation that conveys the object of the game and how it is to be played; and within the game there is a division of labor in which each player is given a perspective from which to act and contribute to the progress of the game. One's role in a game or in any situation is thus the perspective from which one views the situation and on the basis of which one constructs one's own conduct.

Frequently social interaction requires us to step outside our own perspective in order to view the situation from the perspective of another. The pitcher does this when he tries to imagine what pitch the batter is expecting. The sales representative does it when she guesses how much concession on price a customer will demand in order to close a deal. A common term used to capture this grasping of the situation from a perspective other than one's own is *role-taking*—so-called because to "take" the perspective of another is to view matters from the vantage point afforded by that person's role. Not infrequently, the perspective adopted is not that of a specific other person, but that of the situation as a whole. Any given player on a baseball team, for example, acts by taking into account not only his own perspective and that of others, but also the "perspective" of the game itself—its rules and etiquette as well as the particular situation of play.

When we think of people thoroughly absorbed in a situated activity such as a baseball game, several things immediately come to light that bear on the matter of identity. We may notice, for example, that a baseball player fully engaged in the game very nearly becomes identical to the position he is playing. To adopt a perspective in an activity—to look at the world for two hours or more through the eyes of a pitcher—is to become that perspective, to be captured by it and to have one's alertness to things dominated by it. A role makes its player whole, and it does so by excluding almost everything else from consideration. The person who is absorbed in an activity is, within the social reality constituted by that activity, a whole human being full of energy concentrated on being that person. Although we, from our perspective outside the game, might point out that "pitcher" is scarcely a basis for counting one as a whole human being, it is different when looked at from the inside. For a role is a unitary perspective that has the power to make human beings at least temporarily whole.

By the same token, a situation, with its activities and perspectives, also provides for a sense of continuity. The situated experience of personal continuity is essentially equivalent to a sense of emerging and ongoing *meaning* provided by orderly and expected events in which the person has a hand. Events in a defined situation occur and make sense in sequence, and they carry the person along, as it were, by their temporal logic. A baseball game, as any well-defined situation, is a more or less orderly progression of activities leading to some result. The progression is less orderly in the sense that things can and do go wrong—individuals play well or badly, they have greater or lesser skill, and the unexpected occurs. But the progression is more orderly—and more generally orderly—in the sense that there is widespread agreement on the object of the game, on the rules by which it should be played, and on the various markers of progress through it. Pitches, strikes, balls, hits, runs, outs, and innings are markers of a passage through time, markers that provide for a secure sense of continuity in the players. To say that the home team is down by one run in the bottom of the ninth inning with the tying run on first is to describe not only the situation of the game but the conditions that affect each player's continuing sense of self. Again, observers may think the sense of continuity created by the game is short-lived and incomplete. But from within the perspectives afforded by the game the progression of activities toward the game's object guarantees the continuity of self.

The game also provides for identification and differentiation. On one hand, each player is linked to all those present by various ties that derive from the game. At the most general level players identify with the game itself and so with all who partake of it. At other levels, they identify with fellow ball players, as against fans, and with the members of one's own team, as against members of other teams. It is the game—which we can think of as a microcosmic community with its own culture—that provides various bases for identification. Participants sense in one another a common set of responses to this situation in which they find themselves. They are united by those responses and by a crystallized set of objectified meanings surrounding the game of baseball.

On the other hand, the game provides for differentiation by the same means it provides for identification. Fans are different from players; one team is different from another; and at the level of play itself, one person differs from another because each approaches the play from a different perspective. Each player is like others in being a baseball player and yet different from them in being a pitcher, or a pitcher noted for getting a fast ball over the plate, or a pitcher who is making a successful comeback attempt. By virtue of its roles, the opportunities it provides for skill and virtuosity, and the constant necessity for the self-conscious control of behavior, the game sustains a sense of boundaries between self and others, lays the basis for seeing the difference between the interests of self and others, and makes possible individuality in the context of community.

It may seem that situated identity, because it is so closely linked to role and to socially standard definitions of situations, would so thoroughly organize the person's attention that there would be no room left for individual initiative or for any serious departures from the guidelines of a role. There are several reasons why such a picture is inaccurate. Definitions of situations provide objects toward which conduct is oriented, and roles provide perspectives from which to act, but their guidance is approximate and not exact. Moreover, although situations provide identity, they do so imperfectly and temporarily. Continuity, integration, identification, and differentiation are always problematic to some degree within the single situation. And when the person moves from one situation to another they become problematic in new ways.

Considered even within the microcosm of such situations as baseball games, human beings face problems related to their identities for at least three reasons. First, human conduct in any situation is inescapably subject to evaluation by self and by others, and so, short of perfection, identity is always subject to challenge. Second, there is an inherent tension between identification and differentiation, even in those situations where common goals are clear and all subscribe to them. And, third, no human situation is without problematic occurrences that interrupt ongoing activity and so also render less than perfect the identities of individuals. In each of these three instances, consciousness of self is transformed into consciousness of identity or of one of its dimensions.

Every situation forces human beings to evaluate one another's performances. There need be no elaborate system for evaluating performances nor a clearly articulated set of criteria by which they are evaluated. Nor must evaluation itself be a major preoccupation as people interact with one another. An activity such as a baseball game makes evaluation a salient matter, for the game has a clear object—winning—and fans, umpires, team managers, and fellow players express their evaluations unequivocally. But what occurs sharply and distinctly in baseball occurs less visibly, but with a similar result, in all human situations, even where comparative evaluation is frowned upon or norms prohibit the open expression of valuative judgments.

When human beings form conduct within situations, acting from the perspective of their roles to contribute to the situation as a whole, they face the inescapable risk of failure. In baseball, plays that should be made successfully sometimes are not, and they are scored as errors. Players who are expected to hit in the clutch are fanned and the team loses. More generally, people always run the risk of falling short of the mark, of doing less than their role requires or of not doing what they do well enough. Failure is inherent in the human condition, and it is one of the forces that makes identity problematic—which is to say not only that failure makes for self-consciousness but also that this self-consciousness sometimes calls identity into question. To fail at an assigned task or to perform it less well than one was expected to is to become conscious of that failure and to ask of one's self the same questions asked by others: Why did this individual fail? What went wrong? Can this person be relied upon to act as he or she should? And, most significantly and ominously, is this person who he or she claims to be? Failure, even minor and temporary failure, brings consciousness of the failed self and raises issues pertinent to identity: What happened to me that I couldn't do what I should have been able to do? Am I as good as my fellow players? Do I have the talent I thought I had? Am I really a baseball player?

Failure invites *doubt*, which is, ironically, an inescapable aspect of identity. If there were no failures, there would be no negative evaluations, no self-consciousness of failure, and therefore no concern about identity. But there would also be no identity under such conditions. For human beings do not have a consciousness of identity—they have no feelings of wholeness, continuity, identification, and differentiation—except insofar as these are laid open to doubt, which can then be laid to rest and identity asserted. Paradoxically, then, the specter of doubt lays siege to identity, making it less than complete and certain, and yet there can be no identity without failure and doubt.

A second way in which identity becomes problematic is through an inherent tension between identification and differentiation, a tension that is considerable in the world at large but one that is also to be found within the microscopic world of the situation. Human beings acquire identity through identification *and* differentiation. By participation with others in joint activities, inner impulses and objectified meanings are aroused and created, and these generate a sense of similarity. The fact that human beings are energized by a sense of contributing to common efforts is in part due to the capacity of such activities to crystallize and fuse individual and joint meanings. In an exciting moment of a ball game in which a team is playing well, each player feels at one with the others, as if his own impulses to act are precisely the right ones, and as if others can anticipate what to do before he even begins to do it. The sensation is one of effortless understanding and communication, of being a part of a well-oiled "machine" that is working just the way it is ideally supposed to work. There is a powerful human impulse to identify with the others with whom one is currently interacting and with the purposes toward which all are striving.

Yet there is also an inherent and powerful human impulse to resist full absorption in a role and full identification with group effort. Human energies seem most powerful when harnessed to a group effort with which there is powerful identification, yet full identification is almost always resisted. An explanation of why people resist full merger of identity and role can be found in the methods human beings use to exert self-control.

Human beings are able to control what they do—they have the capacity to consider alternative courses of action and to select one in preference to another—through self-consciousness. That is, the human being gets control over conduct through role-taking, examining impulses and possible lines of conduct by adopting the perspectives of others. But self-consciousness requires that a sense of boundaries between self and others be maintained. For to exert self-control—to inhibit one impulse and put another in its place—the person must be able to differentiate self from others, imaginatively to occupy their perspectives and visualize the self acting in various ways. This differentiation of self and others requires that full identification with them and with the role to which one is assigned be resisted.

In other words, it is impossible for human beings to act without identifying with others and with the common purposes in which they are engaged, for only through such identification do persons gain a sure footing and a sure basis for organizing their own impulses. But at the same time it is impossible for human beings to act without differentiating self from the perspectives and purposes of the group as a whole, for it is ultimately the consideration of alternative actions that the individual might take in relation to others that is the basis for cooperation with them. Identification and differentiation are thus in a natural state of tension. If the group and its activity often seem to demand more and more identification, the person has to resist full identification in order to retain control over conduct. And if the individual now and then demands more differentiation than the group can tolerate, the latter finds ways to assert its interest in identification.

The view that identification and differentiation are in natural tension amounts to an assertion of natural tension between individual and society. It is social experience that gives human beings selves and makes them capable of self-control, for without identification with others and acceptance of the roles accorded by them, individuals would have no basis for consciousness of self. But it is also the capacity for self-control that makes possible the organized complexity of human society, for human activities depend upon forms of coordination that are too complex for instinct and that require self-consciousness. This tension need not be conceived, however, as a battle between anti-social biological impulse and social restrictions. Human impulses, whether they relate to such fundamental biological conditions as sex and food or to matters of more social than bodily import, are social in their origins, social in the means by which control over them is attained, and social in the tensions they arouse within the self and between self and others.

It would be too much to say that the individual is a battleground on which are arrayed forces of identification and differentiation or self-interest and group interest. It would be more accurate to say that the individual needs to identify with others and yet also remain separate from them, and that the group both requires this differentiation and resists it. The basic point is that this inherent tension makes the person conscious of having an identity and yet also makes that identity potentially problematic. Excessive identification threatens to dissolve the person's capacity to exert self-control; excessive differentiation threatens the group's influence over the person. Both render identity problematic, for the sense of wholeness requires at once a social group or context to which it can be attached and a sense of separateness from that context, a sense of being a distinct part of it.

There is an additional reason for the inherent tension between the person and society, a reason implicit in the foregoing analysis. Consciousness of self is what enables human beings to inhibit one incipient act and to put another in its place. This amounts to a generalized capacity for negation, for refusing to adopt even those lines of conduct that are socially approved and expected. An organism that is conscious of self and that can say "no" to whatever impulse strikes it has the ability to conceive of self-interest as opposed to the interest of the group, and it thereby also has the most important part of the wherewithal actually to pursue what it conceives as self-interest.

Finally, identity is always rendered problematic because all human situations contain problematic elements. No situation is fully routine. No joint activity runs without a hitch to its conclusion. No baseball game, nor any other human activity, is free of obstacles that render meaning problematic and require human beings to detour, invent new solutions, find alternative paths. And to the extent that all human situations are in some fashion problematic, so too identity is always problematic.

Situated identity is tied to the maintenance of a defined situation in its usual and routine course. As long as participants are able to act from their perspectives and sustain the situation, their identities are not in question. But just as individual failure calls individual identity into question, so too a failed definition of a situation calls into question the established identities of all who are present. This is difficult to see in relation to such situations as baseball games, for it is seldom that their definitions are fundamentally challenged. Many such situations run quite routinely, and the problematic events that occur take place *within* the framework established by their definitions. But, on some occasions, definitions of situations themselves become problematic: soccer matches become transformed into riots; everyday routines are disrupted by natural disasters and accidents; people encounter situations they cannot define and make sense of.

When a situation becomes problematic, so do the identities it contains. A riot at a sports match turns fans or players into combatants. A disaster or accident demands that people assume new perspectives and take unfamiliar actions, often eliciting behavior people are surprised to find within their capabilities. In these examples, as the definition of a situation is first disrupted and then reconstituted, people carve out new roles for themselves, and in locating themselves within these new perspectives they acquire new identities. What transforms a definition of a situation and its roles also transforms the self, for a new role makes the person whole in a new way, changes the basis on which continuity is felt, and redefines the differentiation of self from others. And an altered situation is a new social world that reconstitutes the basis of identification with others.

The problematic situation, in transforming identities, also makes its participants conscious of identity. It is impossible to shift from one role to another without becoming conscious of the shift. At one moment people have the identity of fans caught up in the excitement of a close match. At the next moment they have more diverse identities within the context of a riot: some are active participants and instigators, some are peacemakers, some merely want to escape. At one moment, one is an ordinary person going about his business, at the next a hero called upon to rescue a drowning child or a good citizen who calls an ambulance and helps the victims of an automobile accident. Whatever it is that renders a situation problematic, the important result for identity is that participants become conscious of their roles. They become aware of movement from one perspective to a very different one. If the transition from one situational definition to another is swift—as it may be in such drastic transformations as riots and disasters—then consciousness of identity transformation is short-lived. If the transition is slower—as it may be when people cannot figure out precisely what is happening or when they have such experiences as falling into or out of love—then consciousness of role and identity is more prolonged.

However prolonged this awareness of identity and its transformation, it adds a new dimension to identity. Problematic definitions of situations serve as reminders to people that they have other identities than the currently operative one. Thus, integration is brought to the fore as an issue, for we are reminded that the role that makes us whole in this situation is not all there is to us. Continuity is momentarily challenged, for we are conscious of ourselves shifting from one line of action to another. And identification and differentiation are reconstituted, for there are new others to be like and unlike.

The very nature of human action and social interaction thus generates consciousness not only of self but of identity. The control of conduct through role-taking guarantees that individuals will be conscious of themselves in their roles. By imagining their appearance and possible actions through the eyes of others, people objectify themselves—and the objects they are to themselves are largely shaped by their roles. And because individuals may fail in their role performances, because there is an inevitable tension between identification with others and differentiation from them, and because situational definitions can fail or be transformed, self-consciousness is sometimes focused on issues of personal integration, continuity, identification, and differentiation.

When we look beyond the isolated situation we find even more reasons why identity is a naturally problematic state. Social life involves many different situations and a variety of roles, and thus new issues of identity are created as the individual moves from one situation to another. In societies of even modest complexity the individual is apt to hold membership in groups or categories that are differentiated from others. Not all roles are voluntary, nor is social life free of coercion, individual and group conflict, or distinctions between the interests of the individual and those of the group. Each of these conditions renders individual identity problematic and fosters consciousness of identity.

Role differentiation is an inherent part of social life. The baseball player is also a man, husband, father, citizen, patient, client, student, team captain, Sunday school teacher, consumer, voter. The professor is also a woman, daughter, committee member, union president, environmental activist, customer. The round of everyday life requires movement from one situation to the next, from one role to the next, and from one identity to the next. Each such transition is an occasion on which the person is momentarily conscious of identity, for one perspective must be shed in favor of another. And as individuals move from perspective to perspective they become at least momentarily aware of who and where they are.

Mobility from situation to situation (and from role to role) is inherently problematic for identity, although it is also the primary condition that gives rise to an identity that is larger in scope and longer in duration than that supported by the situation. In each situation, memories of previous engagements and thoughts of future obligations tend to reduce engrossment in the current perspective. The pitcher on the mound remembers that he has forgotten his wife's birthday and thinks of what he might say to her. The professor in the classroom is distracted by thoughts of committee responsibilities. From the perspective of such individuals the issue can be formulated in different ways. The pitcher worries about his concentration and tries to rule extraneous thoughts out of order. The professor worries about how she can manage her time more effectively. However formulated, such matters tend to make integration and continuity problematic. If the role of the moment creates an integrated and continuous self, the remembered and anticipated roles of other moments momentarily disrupt this sense of continuity and wholeness and lead people to make announcements to themselves and others: "I have to work on my concentration at the plate." "I won't accept any more idiotic committee tasks."

Such experiences are instances of role conflict and role strain, which are inherent and ubiquitous in social life, and are both problematic for and generative of identity.[8] They are problematic because they challenge an established sense of integration and continuity. But they are generative, in the manner of all such problematic occurrences, because they provide the occasions on which identity is consciously formulated. When individuals have to fit their assorted roles together, learning to allocate time and energy to each, their identities are called into question, but the opportunity arises also for their identities to be reformulated.

Role differentiation also has an impact upon identification and differentiation. A differentiated social structure of roles provides useful materials for individuation, and the more complex the structure the greater the opportunities for differentiating self from others. In a complex society, possible combinations of roles multiply enormously. But even the simple society, with role differentiation largely on the basis of age, sex, and kinship, provides for the minimum sense of difference and distinction from others. And each differentiated role is also a basis for identification, for those who perform a given role have in common a set of experiences and an outlook that render them alike. The finer the division of labor, the narrower is the ground on which individuals who perform a given role are potentially like one another, for their similarity may well be limited to that role and its perspective. Thus, in the simplest societies lacking a very complex division of labor, any given category of people are apt to resemble one another more than will a similar category in a complex society.

There is another kind of role differentiation that contributes to the problematics of identity. The concept "role" usually designates those relatively stable and highly patterned roles found in the major institutional spheres of a society. Within the family, for example, one finds such conventional roles as husband and wife, parent and child, brother and sister. And in other spheres, one finds lawyers, customers, bricklayers, presidents, managers, laborers, and the like, all roles whose dimensions and requirements are widely known to the members of a society. To label these roles "conventional" is to acknowledge that they *are* conventions—that, within their relevant situations, such roles offer a set of familiar perspectives for behavior.

But the scope of contact between people often extends beyond their assigned roles. Human beings interact on the basis of their conventional role assignments, but they also interact on the basis of broader and more extensive knowledge of one another, and their perspectives are informed by past experiences as well as mutual affection, loyalty, enmity, suspicion, and other attitudes not necessarily fostered by their conventional roles. To put the matter conceptually, human beings adopt the perspectives of *interpersonal* as well as conventional roles.[9]

Where conventional roles are directly the product of culture, interpersonal roles are the product of a history of interaction between unique human beings. Doctor and patient interact within a framework established by their conventional roles, "doctor" and "patient." But they will find their view of one another sometimes strays from strictly professional matters, even though they may try to avoid personal involvements and generally succeed in doing so. Where they interact repeatedly, their conventional roles will become molded to fit a more personal shape. And in some instances they will develop role relationships—that is, perspectives for dealing with one another—that are highly specific to themselves. The patient may become highly dependent upon the physician; they may become friends; they may become partners in some outside business enterprise. In short, they may develop an interpersonal relationship that overlays and colors the professional one.[10]

Such interpersonal relationships—friendship, rivalry, partnerships—have effects like those of conventional roles, for they provide a common framework of perspectives for the mutual interpretation and adjustment of conduct. And, like conventional roles, they create a basis for identity even as they make problems for it. Where an interpersonal role overlays a conventional role there is a potential for conflict, for the perspectives afforded by the one may call for different actions than those afforded by the other. In relationships between professionals and their clients the issue is often conceived in terms of the necessity of avoiding emotional entanglements. A physician or lawyer cannot, it is felt, make judgments with the same objectivity where close friends are involved. In other role relationships, the conflict may be experienced in terms of the contradictory requirements of two roles. One's role as a subordinate may require a demeanor that one's role as a friend makes difficult to sustain. Wherever such conflicts are experienced, identity comes to the fore, since individuals become acutely conscious of who they are in relation to one another.

The effect of role differentiation, like that of the various processes that operate within single situations, is to render identity problematic. But even more than in the isolated situation, role differentiation forces us to ask how individuals manage to deal with the problematics of identity. If various roles must be integrated and sequenced, how do people do this? If there are multiple grounds of similarity and difference between people, how is a balance struck between identification and differentiation? And, very crucially, what assumptions about human motivation are necessary in order to account for the dynamics of identity? The last question is the most important, for an answer to it makes possible answers to the others.

Identity has motivational import within the situation because it organizes the person's sensitivity to events and thus shapes the impulses that arise. To have a situated identity is to have an organized set of impulsive responses within a defined situation, responses that are more or less shared with others and that are brought under conscious control as people utilize their own and others' perspectives to form conduct. Identity is thus a crucial concept for an understanding of motivation. But identity also functions at a verbal level, for self-conscious assertions of identity are also assertions of *motive*—that is, of verbalized reasons for conduct that are offered by the individual to self or others and that subsequently affect the course of conduct. When identity becomes problematic within a situation, individuals verbalize explicit reminders to themselves and others about identity: "I'm the pitcher and I've got to get control of the situation here." "I'm the boss and I decide what the standards are." [11]

Identity announcements, whether they are made overtly to others or avowed inwardly to the self, are ways of directing one's own conduct and influencing that of others. A verbalized identity—"I'm the boss here!" —reinforces the motivation to act by sharply focusing the perception of objects and reducing the attention paid to extraneous events. Where circumstances make situated identity mildly or seriously problematic, a verbalized identity has the effect of re-establishing identity and thus re-invigorating its capacity to focus attention and direct behavioral energies.

Assertions of identity are thus motives that have motivational import in the situation. When people tell themselves who they are, they tell themselves what to do, not only by consciously indicating to themselves the lines of conduct that their identities require but also beneath the surface of consciousness by focusing their attentiveness. The familiar slogan of prag-matism (and of functionalist psychology) that attention is a function of interest applies directly here: an assertion of identity defines and sharpens the person's interest in a situation and thus more sharply focuses attention on those situated events that are relevant to that identity.

The motivational significance of identity is not, however, limited to the situation, nor can one grasp the full significance even of situated identity by attending only to its capacity to organize the interest and conduct of the person from one moment to the next. For identity does not only exist in the situation, but is also something that human beings bring to each of the situations they encounter and each of the roles with which they become engaged. "Identity" has a longer duration and a larger scope. It is considerably more than the appropriation of a role in a situation, even though it is on the appropriation of a role that it ultimately depends.

Identity is more than a situated phenomenon for several reasons, not least of which is the fact that human beings tend repeatedly to encounter the same situations and the same roles. One is, for example, a businessman, son, father, neighbor, husband, friend, colleague, enemy, leader, club president, and one is these roles over and over again in the course of day-to-day life. These roles occur in relatively familiar situations, which are in turn embedded in the routine currents of social life. Each day one moves from situation to situation and from role to role, making transitions that are very predictable. And even when we look at the person from a temporal perspective of longer duration, we see a life span that seems to embrace relatively predictable sequences of situations and social roles. One is first a child and later an adult; first a student learning an occupation and then a practitioner; first a young adult and then middle-aged; first a parent of young children and then of children who have themselves turned into adults. Moreover, situations and roles are themselves bundled within larger organizational and institutional contexts. One is a colleague, business associate, ally, enemy, or conspirator, in the world of the organization or the profession. One is a wife, mother, daughter, sister, husband, father, son, or brother within the boundaries of the nuclear or extended family. One is a student, friend, playmate, or peer within the world of the school or college. Situations and roles are organized within larger social structures that contain and organize the identities of their members.

The organized currents of social life thus seem to carry the person along and, in so doing, to provide for a more-than-situated identity. The flow of everyday situations provides a series of images of self—a succession of "Me's"—that, taken together, produce the illusion of a continuous and integrated self much as a strip of motion picture film yields an illusion of life and movement. If social life is well organized and can account for every part of the person's day and every bit of the person's energies, then there is really nothing except situated identities and the external social framework on which they are suspended and moved about. This is a view of the person that is often conveyed in the work of Erving Goffman, who tells us that the person is nothing apart from situated identities and the social framework on which they are hung.[12] Ideas that people may have about being something more or different from their roles are, from this point of view, merely illusions. The self is merely a product of the situation, not in any sense a cause of it.

Such a view of the person is fundamentally distorted, and fails to capture the human experience even for those whose lives are contained within organic community. There, one finds a relatively finite environment, a shared culture and a social structure of known and fixed borders that can sustain a round of situations and roles that might keep self-consciousness to a minimum. Even within such a world, however, individuals tend to construct their own frameworks, their own cognitive devices on which to arrange their various situated identities. The effort required to do so is probably not very great, for the round of everyday life is sufficiently predictable and routine that habit rules and self-consciousness is largely kept within the boundaries of particular identities. Nonetheless, even though the effort required to do so may be slight, the person constructs and maintains a consciousness of identity that transcends the immediate situation and its role.

The self in the modern world is even less able to depend on a social framework that carries the person from one situation to the next and thus from one identity to the next. For in a culture in which contradictory objects figure so prominently and in which the person is more likely to be confronted with dilemmas of choice than a smoothly organized and functioning set of organizations and institutions, there is no self-evidently legitimate flow of life into which individuals can allow themselves to be swept. Modernity makes for increasing self-consciousness: There is no easily sensed, coherent culture with which the person can identify; there are few self-evident community boundaries that contain this culture and provide a perspective from which to view the self comfortably; there is no steady and automatic succession of "Me's" to sustain the illusion of continuity.

The human experience thus makes for consciousness of identity on grounds that transcend situation and role, and not simply consciousness of the self that is experienced from one moment to the next. There is an impulse to perceive the self as a continuous and integrated entity—to anchor the experiences and activities of the moment not simply in a role as it is experienced in the situation but in a larger and longer sense of personhood. What is this sense of personhood, how is it created, and what are its forms and manifestations?

Two concepts are necessary if we are to grasp the experience and importance of identity, and particularly if we are to convey its significance in the modern world. The larger and longer sense of personhood that transcends particular situations, roles, and group memberships, for all human beings, is anchored in two fundamentally different forms of identity. On the one hand, *social identity* provides for continuity, integration, identification, and differentiation by linking the person to a community and its culture. On the other hand, *personal identity* provides for the same essentials of personhood through a more autonomous and independent construction of self in which the main focus is not on a community that provides a perspective from which the person has experience of self, but on the self as an autonomous entity that provides its own platform.

Social and personal identity are fundamentally different, and in some sense opposite, modes of personal organization. They are, I will argue, fostered by different forms of social structure, the former especially by the world of organic community, the latter by modernity. Both, however, are present in any society. Organic community fosters social identity at the expense of personal identity, but cannot fully command or obliterate the latter. Modern culture and society make it possible for human beings to experience personal identity to an extent not possible within organic community, but social identity retains significance. In the remainder of this chapter, I will first provide an account of social identity, then consider personal identity. Chapter VI will examine in more detail the results of their opposition for the construction of self in modern society.

Social Identity

Social identity may be defined as the individual's sense or feeling of integration, continuity, identification, and differentiation in relation to community and culture.[13] Like situated identity, social identity becomes something of which the individual is conscious only when it is somehow problematic. Its frame of reference is not the individual's role in a single situation, but rather a community, which is the source of a generalized sense of place or perspective, and a culture, which defines that community and provides purpose for the individual's life. Social identity rests upon a sense of cultural *meaning* and community *belonging*. It is developed over time on the basis of situated identities, but it transcends these identities in its capacity to organize and energize the individual's adoption of them.

We can understand the organization and functioning of social identity by comparing it with situated identity, for there are clear parallels between these two levels. Situated identity is tied to role and it liberates the individual's energies to act from the perspective of a role. Social identity is tied to a sense of membership in a community in which there are many roles and diverse situations, and it liberates the individual's capacity to adopt a situated role. In other words, where situated identity shapes responses *in* the situation, social identity shapes responses *to* situations. Just as situated identity is requisite to everyday conduct, social identity is requisite to the adoption of any situated identity. Viewed in this way, social identity thus derives a sense of integration from community membership. Fundamentally, to have a social identity is to have a sense of belonging that arranges and orders the various particular roles the individual is called upon to occupy.

Situated identity is also tied to the meanings and purposes inherent in any joint action, for to have situated identity is to make such purposes one's own and to base a sense of personal continuity and meaning upon them. Social identity is tied to the broader meanings and purposes of the community, which are themselves summarized by the term culture. The meanings and purposes of situations are self-contained, whereas those of culture are more encompassing and have as one of their functions the organization and legitimation of situated meanings. Social identity derives a sense of continuity from culture and its purposes. To have a social identity is thus to have a sense of meaning that arranges and orders the purposes adopted in specific situations.

Social identity thus consists of feelings of integration supplied by the community or communities to which the individual belongs and of continuity supplied by culture. It also entails feelings connected with and generated by the tension between identification and differentiation, and community and culture likewise supply the means for handling this tension. Culture provides a sense of likeness and is thus the basis of identification. The essence of identification is perceived likeness of impulsive response to situations and likeness of objective meanings. In other words, the condition upon which mutual identification depends is the perception that others' responses to a situation are the same as one's own. In the situation, identification rests upon a particular joint action carried on within the defined situation and its role structure. In the broader community, identification rests upon more general perceptions of similarity of response —emotions, abstract principles, values, norms, and other components of culture.

The essence of differentiation is the perception that others are in some ways different. The diverse roles provided by and contained within the life of a community provide for this sense of difference, for it is in occupying particular perspectives within the situation that the individual remains distinct from others and thus able to maintain self-control. In the broader community, individuals routinely engage some roles but not others: they are men or women, but not both, or they are children, adults, or elderly, but not all three simultaneously. Roles thus differentiate people beyond the immediate situation, providing a large part of the minimum sense of differentiation that is requisite to individual conduct.

A shared culture thus encourages identification with others, while roles encourage differentiation. These two forces also moderate one another, for the culture of a community exerts a countervailing force to that of differentiated role structure. What the distinctive perspectives of roles—as, for example, the roles of men versus those of women—try to pull apart, culture attempts to bring back together. That is, role differentiation tends to make people less likely to identify with one another and culture makes them more likely to identify. Looking at things the other way around, role differentiation tends to make people more conscious of the things that make them different, while culture tends to make them conscious of similarities.

Why does social identity come into existence? Why cannot we conceive of human beings simply as carried along by social inertia, transported from one situation to the next and, in each, wound up like so many toy soldiers and set down to do what their situated roles demand? Indeed, what is the evidence that things are not so arranged?

Social identity arises from the problematics of situated identity. Human beings are constantly exposed to doubt, conflicting demands, and transformations of situated identity. Hence, they are constantly made self-conscious and, more pointedly, identity-conscious by the ordinary events of everyday life. Social identity thus should be thought of as a practical response to such circumstances, a response that generates an organizing view of self that resolves the everyday problematics of identity. Such an organizing view is derived from an image of community and its culture. It should be conceived, in its simplest sense, as an effort made by ordinary people to make sense of themselves in relation to community and culture. Social identity thus amounts to a pragmatic "construction" of personal reality.

Perhaps the most general motivational assumption we can make about human beings is that they are naturally driven to make sense of experience. Living in a symbolic world, they are beset by consciousness of self and its alternative courses of action. They inhabit a world of time, one with a remembered past and one with alternative possible futures. Theirs is an abstract world, furnished not only with material things, but with ideas, hopes, principles, possibilities, values, and wishes. It is often an unpredictable world, for others do not act as wished or expected, hopes are dashed, and values are not realized.

The drive to render experience sensible is essentially practical: in order to act, human beings must know where they are, what others are doing, what others expect them to do, what others will do if they fail to act in the expected manner, what ills will befall them if they refuse to perform their appointed tasks. The world is rendered an orderly and therefore a safer place partly by the development of stable images of it. When men and women engage in what Peter Berger and Thomas Luckmann have called "the social construction of reality," they are trying to make the world a more predictable place, one in which they can anticipate what will befall them and how they might respond to it.

The self is a part of the world that must be made predictable. Human beings are inescapably a part of their own environment, for in adopting the perspectives of others in order to exert self-control they become a part of the environment with which they must contend. Individuals, every bit as much as the world that surrounds them, are potentially unpredictable. Unable to gain control over conduct until an impulse is half-released, they sometimes experience considerable anxiety in relation to self, for they are in some elemental sense unpredictable. Confronted with conflicting demands and sometimes errant impulses, people need a purchase on personal order every bit as much as they require a grasp of social reality.

Social identity is thus something people are driven to create. It is a cognitive response to potential or actual disorder within, just as images of culture and community are cognitive responses to disorder without. Social identity is a hypothesis, a tentative conviction about what this internal order is like, a hypothesis that permits the individual to act toward the external world, to take a place in the community with other human beings, to know a sense of place in relation to them.

Social identity is typically a concrete rather than a highly abstract creation. Its usual orientation is to the world of practical affairs and its problems rather than to the realm of abstract ideas. It can consist of a secure feeling that one does things other people value, that people can be counted upon for help and comfort tomorrow as yesterday, that one is the kind of person one should be, neither too different from others nor too much like them. And while the foregoing illustrations suggest a secure and positive social identity, that is clearly not always attained. When people worry about whether they are valued, or whether they can count on people, or whether they are what they should be, they are also having feelings that constitute social identity. Positive or negative, secure or not, social identity amounts to a hypothesis about the self and its relation to others and their purposes.

Social identity may be regarded as the product of individual effort—

a sense of continuity and integration constructed and reconstructed by the individual through time as a result of experience with diverse situations and social roles. But to view social identity in this way is not to regard it as something that is continuously salient for the individual as a self-consciously indicated object of attention and action. An approach to identity that regards it as something for which individuals "search" or "quest" weakens the concept and distorts the nature of human experience. How, then, is social identity a product of individual effort but not always (or perhaps even often) an objective in its own right?

Social identity is primarily a response to the problematics of situated identity. People occasionally experience discontinuity because the effect of social life is often to make the self an object whose various manifestations seem temporally unrelated to one another. They now and then feel themselves to be a disparate set of fragments because social life has disintegrating effects. They experience as well a tension between identification and differentiation, between their own impulses and the pull of a role or social group that would absorb them. These problematic experiences provide the occasion for self-reference, for reflection about the relationship between one situated identity and another. Out of this reflection arises an objectification of self—a name, an assertion of priorities, a definition of personal essence, a sense of the "real" self.

Social identity thus arises in acts of reflection in which the person resolves problems of continuity and integration. Typically, such acts of reflection result in a sense of defining essence experienced as a sense of membership in a community and couched in the language and culture of that community. It is a sense of how the various parts of the person fit together, of where he or she has been and will be. It arises as the person identifies with those who are perceived as similar and differentiates self from those who are not community members and who do not share its culture.

Social identity has community and culture as its guarantors, but it is invariably a product of particular situations. The spatial and temporal referents of social identity extend beyond the bounds of the immediate situation, but it is nonetheless produced and reproduced only in the concrete and particular experiences of everyday life. The circumstances under which it may arise are varied: A heart to heart talk between friends might provide an occasion on which each is able to formulate a social identity and have this self-placement certified by the other. But, of equal likelihood, a frustrating day at work might provide the occasion for reflections on the course of one's life and for sorting out what is important from what is not. When such reflections become public announcements—"I'm going to look for another job where the pressures aren't so great and I have more time for my family"—we have evidence of a reformulated social identity. Or, when a man announces that he is happiest when he is able to go fishing with his buddies, we likewise have an announcement of social identity.

Social identity thus appears to others in much the same manner as motives appear—that is, as an announcement of purpose or intention, often made in the face of questions, challenges, or some other problematic situation.[14] A woman who says that she puts her family ahead of her work asks that this self-objectification be taken into account in grasping the significance of her conduct. Like a motive, which arises in response to a question, social identity also usually arises in response to a real or implied question or challenge from others: Why does this woman not give more energy to her work? Why does she always leave work promptly at five? Why isn't she more committed to the company? And, also like a motive, the function of social identity is to explain to self and others why a person behaves in a particular way—why certain decisions are made, why role conflict is resolved in certain characteristic ways.

Like motives, social identities have motivational import. That is, once the individual announces a social identity and has this act confirmed by significant others, it becomes an internal state that affects the person's subsequent response to a variety of social situations. Announcements of social identity not only attempt to transform the attitudes and expectations of others, but they transform the persons who make them. When a social identity is asserted, it is factored into that complex array of internal sensitivities that unconsciously shape the individual's selection of stimuli and the impulses that are released in any given situation.

Paramount among the effects of any given social identity is its capacity to shape the degree of commitment and energy devoted to particular situated roles. Social identity, which often arises in response to the inevitable conflict among the many roles the individual must make, comes in its own turn to shape the person's responses to those situations and roles. To have a social identity is, in effect, to have a principle that orders and arranges various situations and roles, assigning some to a more central and salient place than others. Although this ordering may be articulated in various ways by the individual, its effect on the person is motivational—once formulated it sinks beneath the level of consciousness and shapes impulsive responses. That is to say, responses to situations—the adoption of roles within them and the investing of time and energy to their fulfillment—come under the control of the person's organized sensitivities to the social world, which are not themselves directly accessible to consciousness.

Yet, of course, social identity is always capable of being asserted, and when it is, what is formulated on the surface of consciousness reorganizes that which lies beneath it. Having socially placed himself or herself in a certain community and defined himself or herself in terms of its culture, the individual then carries on in the world, endeavoring to balance various roles and to perform appropriately in various situations. The announced family-centered individual nevertheless has to hold a job and devote time and energy to it, sometimes more than he or she had intended to devote. Social identity is thus an ongoing project, something that is never quite finished, for the simple reason that social life itself presents a series of challenges and problematic situations.

Social identity is thus a homely product of everyday situations that in turn affects those situations. It consists of feelings about self that are aroused when people experience social rebuffs or interpersonal warmth, when they reflect upon their lives or when they experience role conflict. These feelings, these objectifications of self, in turn shape the selection of situated roles, the degree to which energy is devoted to these roles, and the extent to which the individual identifies with others or feels estranged from them.

Evidence that social identity exists may be found in the trouble it sometimes makes for people and in the regularity and quiet ferocity with which it is defended. Social identity sometimes erupts into the midst of a situated role performance and catches the individual by surprise. Thoroughly caught up in a situation, acting energetically from within a situated identity, we can suddenly find ourselves highly conscious of ourselves in that identity. The salesperson in the midst of her pitch finds herself in the shoes of the customer, witnessing the performance of a dedicated actor, amazed to find that it is she standing there. In such experiences one is conscious of the sound of one's voice, of each contrived gesture or expression, every assumed posture, every effort to look and sound convincing. There one is, earnestly performing a role and yet simultaneously conscious of oneself being earnest.

Only a concept of social identity accounts for such experiences. Because human beings have an organized sense of themselves from the wider perspective of community and culture, they now and then find themselves inspecting a performance from that point of view, looking at how they are doing in a particular role. Such experiences are not evidence of personal pathology, nor of an essentially deceptive or theatrical quality of human life. Membership in a community and possession of its culture makes the development of social identity inevitable—which is to say that it makes it inevitable that people will view particular role performances in the larger context of themselves, their community, and their culture. These experiences do not ordinarily linger, for soon we are once again caught up in a situated role and no longer so self-conscious.

One can also witness social identity at work in every episode where an individual tries to put distance between self and role. Such episodes— Erving Goffman has called them *role distance* and given them an interpretation rather different from the present one—are marked by various efforts to signal that identity is not equivalent to a current role.[15] Baseball players talk about their wives and not just their sport; college professors and business people put pictures of their children on their desks; serious role players often make light of serious matters, seeming to deprecate themselves and their involvements. These social actors are partially in the grip of social identity when they respond to a situation by introducing aspects of themselves that do not seem appropriate to a current role. To signal in some way that one has other situated identities is to reveal the presence of social identity, a hypothesis about oneself that there are a variety of roles that somehow fit together.

And many of the minute occurrences of everyday life can be construed as defenses of identity, both of our situated identities and of the social identities that lie behind them. The excuses people offer for their mistakes, the disclaimers they put forward in advance of their offenses, and the justifications they offer for wrongful conduct all represent efforts to protect identity. The child who breaks a family rule and offers an apology is seeking not only to preserve a "good child" identity in the immediate situation but more essentially to preserve a social identity that is grounded in the family, in its community and its culture. Such mundane expressions are, in fact, one of the prime ways in which culture is experienced and reaffirmed in everyday life.[16]

Social identity is thus an objectification of self in relation to culture and community. In much of everyday life the person is an object to self only from the perspective of a single situation and the roles and concrete others it contains. But now and then the individual takes a broader, more encompassing point of view, looking at self as something that exists over a longer span of time, with purposes that exceed the immediate situation, in relation to others who are not immediately present. Social identity can erupt spontaneously in the midst of the most energetic role performances. It can emerge when one role performance is threatened by another, or when the individual moves from one situation to another, or when a situation becomes somehow problematic. Such experiences are the essence of social identity. When social identity comes to the fore, the individual forms a conscious view of self in relation to the broader culture and community of which he or she is a part. This view of self in turn affects subsequent behavior.

Personal Identity

Sociological accounts of identity often stop with the depiction of social identity (or its conceptual equivalent), on the grounds that the self is so thoroughly social that there is little need to posit any other form of personal organization. If identity is social placement, then the situation and its roles, together with the larger community and its culture, locate, energize, and direct the individual in both the short and long run. The practical impulse toward an orderly and predictive grasp of self is satisfied by a community that serves as a generalized other capable of assigning the individual a sense of place and purpose. Hence, there is no perceived need to go beyond the concept of social identity, which seems to embrace everything that the sociological social psychologist need know about the psyche.

There are at least two reasons to reject this view and to press toward a more complex view of identity. First, the pragmatist tradition portrays organisms in general, and human beings in particular, as less in thrall to their environments than do our standard forms of sociological and psychological determinism. Even the organic community and its culture do not provide the individual's only means of releasing impulses toward continuity, integration, identification, and differentiation. The human symbolic capacity creates personal as well as social projects, and inclines men and women to look within as well as without as they seek order and predictability in their lives. Second, although organic community is generally able to assert itself successfully over the inner voices of most members, the culture and social structure of modernity give individuals a stronger voice. As I argued in Chapter IV, modernity has encouraged the release of impulses toward freedom and autonomy that are every bit as much a part of human nature as are impulses toward authority and community. To grasp the modern experience, therefore, we must explore the theoretical bases of these contrary impulses and show how modern people manage their contradictory pulls.

Personal identity may be defined as a sense of continuity, integration, identification, and differentiation constructed by the person not in relation to a community and its culture but in relation to the self and its projects. Like social identity, personal identity is a matter of both individual announcement and social placement, but in its full expression in modern society, personal identity locates the individual on the larger and more abstract stage of society rather than the more enclosed and concrete stage of community. Personal identity often locates the person against or in contrast to specific communities, it gives more weight to differentiation than to identification, and it rests on a societal rather than on a communal mode of social participation.[17]

To portray the concept of personal identity in any depth we must reconsider the "I," one of two commonly known but much less commonly understood terms George H. Mead adopted in building his analysis of the self. The reality Mead sought to depict by using these terms—the "I" and the "Me"—is crucial to an understanding of the relationship between person and society, and thus to a full account of social and personal identity.[18]

The "Me" is generally and properly understood as the "social self"— that is, as the various objectifications of self the person creates through the process of role-taking. In contrast, Mead's "I" continues to perplex social psychologists, for even though it seems to point to a crucial element in human experience, the concept remains ambiguous. Without some way to grasp the creative and resistive elements of the person, symbolic interactionists are left with an "over-socialized" conception of humankind. Yet Mead himself left us in a state of confusion about the matter, and theorists since Mead have done little to extricate us from our predicament. The first problem, therefore, is to clarify the nature of Mead's "I."

The "I" is best understood by linking it to William James's conception of the self as "knower" versus the self as "known."[19] That is, on the one hand, we have an aware and acting creature (designated by the term "I") that looks around itself and responds to events and circumstances according to its own imperatives. The "attention" of this knowing self is, in a pragmatic sense, a function of its "interest"—that is, of its wants, needs, and sensitivities as they are organized at a particular moment. On the other hand, this creature also looks at and is aware of itself from the standpoint of others; it constitutes itself as a "Me." More precisely, it becomes aware of the direction (that is, the objects) of its own responses to external events and, having become aware, responds to the image of itself formed as it becomes aware. This image of self acting in a particular direction is the self as a known object.

The image of human conduct to which this formulation gives rise is a fascinating and powerful one, but it is not without its own limitations. Conduct is seen as the constant interplay of "I" and "Me." The person responds (I) to an event, becomes aware (Me) of that response by taking the role perspectives of others, responds (I) to that awareness (that is, to the Me) by forming a new image, to which it subsequently responds. The alternation of "I" and "Me" continues until the desired act is selected and released. In this constant shifting of consciousness from an external world of events to the self—from the world that stimulates a response to the response itself—lie the roots of both social control and individual autonomy. For it is by virtue of successive images of self that the person is able to adjust conduct to the expectations of others. In the standard Meadian and symbolic interactionist vision, those images can only be formed by imaginatively assuming the perspectives of others, for there is no other mirror. At the same time, the capacity to make and use symbols (upon which this self-designating depends) confers the ability to inhibit a response, to refuse to meet those expectations, and to choose otherwise. Human beings have the capacity not to act—not merely to inhibit an immediate response but in many instances to refuse to respond at all, whether to a pressing external world or to those very images of self that are formed as it tries to act in and upon its world. This capacity for refusal lies at the heart of the human capacity for autonomy.

The twin dangers in the Meadian formulation are an over-socialized conception of human conduct and excessive behaviorism. The former is a problem because it is tempting to make the social order the sole source of images of self on which the selection of acts depends. It can be stipulated that society is the major and original source of perspectives from which the self may be known. Individuals grasp the directions of their acts by taking the perspectives of others and seeing how their acts fit into a developing line of conduct. They grasp and attribute motives using a socially standardized vocabulary, and they act within a framework of typical joint actions that, so far as individuals are concerned, are a pre-existing part of reality. It is a small step from this stipulation to the notion that conduct is really nothing more than the selection of individual acts that fit the expectations of others as they are expressed in developing social acts located within defined situations.

But Mead's formulation of "I" and "Me" also lends itself to a behavioristic interpretation. If one posits that individuals try to adjust their responses so that they fit the developing expectations of others and thus meet with their approval, then it is easy to conclude that autonomy is an illusion and reinforcement is everything. For if the succession of responses (I) to self-images (Me) produced through role-taking merely revises conduct in a socially approved direction, then Mead's analysis merely says in a roundabout way what can be said more directly: Human beings learn to respond to themselves in ways that meet with social approval, that is, in ways that are rewarding because others praise them, or because they lead to successful interaction.

It thus does not seem sufficient to describe the "I" merely as the *response* of the individual to stimulation, whether that stimulation comes from the environment or from itself (in the form of a "Me"). Nor can we treat the "Me" as nothing more than a momentary image of self constructed solely and simply through role-taking. Instead, we must take seriously the notion that there is something more "in" the person, some process that makes human responses susceptible to more than external rewards. The "I" clearly involves what we could call "conditioned" responses to stimuli, so that in some degree the self as "knower" is a conditioned self whose awareness of the world is formed out of repeated experiences with it. And the "Me" clearly arises out of a process of role-taking in which individuals take the attitudes of others toward themselves. But there is more to the self, and to the relationship between "I" and "Me," than conditioning in a social context, for the "I" responds to others and to the "Me" with resistance as well as cooperation, and the "Me" seems in many ways to be more than the sum of its social parts. It is a major goal of an interactionist theory of identity to clarify what "more" there is, and to show the nature of this resistance.

Some help in this task is available from Donald Carveth's insightful essay on psychoanalysis and social theory. Writing about the Freudian view of biologically grounded instincts, which he thinks erroneous, Carveth addresses himself to sociological adherents of a "world-open" view of human nature, who would agree with his rejection of Freud's theory of instincts and argue that instincts have been fully replaced by culture, and that human nature is therefore simply and fully cultural.[20] There is, from such a perspective, little reason to posit a tense and conflicting relationship between the person and society. Carveth disagrees:

> Although there exist no instincts to oppose the socio-cultural pro-gramming, the latter does not simply take the place of the former— man's social nature does not simply replace his missing human nature. Rather, the rules, roles, and rituals of the established social order with which a person may consciously identify and seek to affirm are often opposed by his simultaneous, but unconscious, commitment to an alternative vision of reality and identity.[21]

This "alternative vision" is not provided by biology, nor can it be reduced to the social experience of the person, even though it is social experience that provides its source.

Carveth seems to suggest that alongside a social "reality" that is con-structed in interaction with others, there is a personal "reality" that is built up by the individual. Moreover, in addition to the conscious control of conduct—which may involve the posing of personal and social visions of reality against one another, often in the form of conflicts between the interests of the collectivity and the desires of the individual—there are unconscious processes as well. The Meadian "I," in this vision, is no well-socialized responder to role-taking, for the person acquires a perspective of his or her own that may or may not encourage the same behavioral choices as the perspective afforded by one's own role or the roles of others.

Social identity emerges as a more-than-situated self that provides for continuity, integration, identification, and differentiation. But this emer-gent social identity has another consequence not yet sufficiently appreci-ated. It lays the foundation for personal identity—for a sense of continuity anchored in personal biography rather than the flow of social life, feelings of integration that are the person's own property and not only an artifact of social placement, identification with self and not only community, and differentiation from others and not just identification with them.

The experience of a continuous self is guaranteed first by a commu-nity, which provides, through its culture and through its organized flow of joint actions, a sense of purpose and direction for the individual. Social identity, by attaching the person to the community, makes the person's sequence of actions as well as the events that befall him or her meaningful, which is to say, directed and purposeful. But this sense of direction and purpose, which is derived from the community, becomes the *property* of the individual. It is something taken on from community and culture, but once acquired it begins to have a life of its own.

To put this another way, human beings are creatures of *biography*. They have memories of themselves and their experiences as well as imagined futures. The former are subject not simply to recall but to formulation and reformulation, for the past is not only an objective reality that occurred once and cannot be repeated but a series of events that can take on new meanings as life progresses. The latter are formulated and reformulated again and again as plans, daydreams, fantasies, hopes, and aspirations, some of them to be realized in one way or another, others to be abandoned, and others to exist always just out of reach.

A biography is the property of the individual, although it is clearly dependent upon social experiences, couched in familiar cultural terms, and constructed with the collaboration of others and not only by the person acting or thinking alone. Others help us interpret the meaning of our past and plan for the future, reminiscence is an important social occasion, and the meanings of past and future selves are obviously dependent upon the language we use. Still, it is our biography and not someone else's, and much of the conversation in which we construct and reconstruct it occurs within ourselves and not in interaction with others. Others may try to convince us that we have been successes, or that we are bound to fail, but in the last analysis we individually are the ones who decide which view is the correct one.

In more familiar interactionist language, a biography can be thought of —much like a role—as a *perspective* from which to act. Formed out of social experience and stock social materials, the individual's biography nevertheless comes to have a reality as a perspective from which the individual acts, a perspective that is sometimes as important and perhaps even more important than other perspectives. For, just as human beings take the attitude of others toward themselves as incumbents of roles or members of communities, they can also take the attitudes of others toward themselves as themselves. Once there is a self—that is, once the person is socially located by a social identity—the person begins to develop a perspective that is in some degree the person's own property, independent of the other perspectives to be taken into account.

Human beings always act from perspectives. They know the world, not in its entirety, not fully or completely, but from one or another perspective. It has become conventional for symbolic interactionists to assert that human beings act from the perspective of roles, and that they are able to do so by taking the roles of others toward themselves, grasping their own acts as manifestations of their roles by imaginatively inserting themselves into the roles of others. I am proposing here not a radical departure from this vision, but an extension of it. We act from our own concrete and biographically singular perspectives as much as from the perspectives afforded by roles, and we do so through the familiar mechanism of role-taking. We cannot, in other words, grasp our own, unique, individual perspective directly, but must do so by imagining the possible responses of others to us or by interpreting their real responses. Nonetheless, the perspective we come to grasp is not simply that of a role, nor of a situation, nor even of ourselves as socially identifying creatures. It is, as well, our very own, personal, individual perspective, the perspective we associate with a particular individual.

One way in which we grasp and formulate this perspective is in terms of some idea of biography—of a life that is separate, different, perhaps in some ways unique, but in any case a life that is the individual's and no one else's. This life has a beginning and an end, an imagined course, an interpreted meaning—in short, a reality that is the property of this particular, concrete individual. This experience of biography rests on at least three foundations: First, human beings have bodies as well as selves; second, they have personal names as well as social names; and third, typifications play an important part in the way human beings grasp reality.

The fact that human beings are not disembodied selves but embodied actors is sometimes hard to discern in what sociologists say about them and their conduct. We write as if we believed our own rhetoric that it is the role and not the person that is significant, not only for the limited purposes of sociological analysis but in the conduct of life itself. Yet the body is important, not because it has biologically rooted impulses that shape its conduct, though it surely does, but because it is a particular living form that is born, lives, and dies that has the experiences on which the self is hung. However important the social framework, the biological skeleton is also crucial, for it is a particular creature—a concrete, living, breathing, sentient being—that identifies with others and develops a self.

Moreover, this real being has a name, not only a name that links the person to society and its roles but also a personal name that identifies this individual. John Smith is, to be sure, a "Smith" and not a "Brown," and he is the "husband" of Susan Smith and the "father" of Mary Smith, and is thus linked by these names to other people and identified as the incumbent of various social roles. But naming does not identify merely by linking the person to others, for it also establishes a label that differentiates the person from others. John Smith is not any other human being but John Smith. True, there may be several John Smiths, and this fact may occasionally cause confusion or consternation, but each John Smith ordinarily has no difficulty recognizing that he is not the same as all other John Smiths, and is, in fact, keen to stress this fact.

Finally, human beings grasp reality through typifications, which affect the perception of the self as much as of any other aspect of experience.[22] We do not perceive reality in all its blooming, buzzing confusion, but through typifications that simplify and organize the welter of sense data. We can grasp and make sense of the activities of a physician because we have a typification of a physician's role that lets us interpret his or her actions as typical of the role. In much the same way, human beings develop typifications of *self*. These typifications of self—images, pictures, and ordered portrayals of the person—make it possible for us to recognize ourselves in the complex, varied, often discontinuous "data" of our own actions and sensations. They are our constant guides in a varying and inconstant world, and while they are built up through social experience and use social materials, they are nevertheless our own typifications of our own selves. We regard them as our property and use them as ways of interpreting our own experience.

The self, then, is potentially its own perspective. The person owns a biography that comes to be typified in certain relatively continuous ways, that is attached to and associated with a particular body and personal name. Biography provides for a sense of continuity, which is to say that when people speak or think about themselves in a biographical way, they lend a sense of continuity to personal experience. This sense of biography—and therefore of an emergent self that is constant even while it is transformed—is linked to social identity. The daily, weekly, and yearly round of life in the social units of which the individual is a member and with which he or she identifies provides a context for this emergent sense of self. One has a biography—a life—in interaction with others. But the emergent sense of self we call biography is never fully encompassed by society or community. It is, finally, the person's own meaning and the person's own perspective, even in the world of organic community where this life is fully and constantly surrounded by an ongoing stream of community life that provides it with direction and purpose. Even there, I would argue, this emergent object, the self, is able, if only in a small way, to become its own perspective and to grasp itself as a discrete object moving through time. In the contemporary world of American culture, the temptation and to some extent the capacity for the self to locate itself autonomously in society as a unique, unfolding entity is particularly strong.

Biography is not the only important feature of personal identity, for the self is not only an *emergent* object to itself but one the individual sometimes seeks to grasp in its entirety, as a whole that exists and has qualities and attributes that make it distinct and in some ways unique. And the very same facts of the human experience—corporeal existence, the possession of a name, and typifications—that shape biography shape the apprehension of the self as a whole, integral entity.

In the course of their everyday lives human beings must occasionally pause for self-objectification. Such pauses, which occur when something interrupts routine conduct, literally refresh the meaning of the self, for they are the occasion on which the person is able to assemble its discrete bits and pieces into some kind of coherent whole. Social identity is one of the means for such refreshment, for the person can render the self whole by seeing it from the vantage point of a community with which the person identifies. Identification with a community and adoption of its perspective provides one of the means through which human beings can achieve integration and thus think of themselves as having a reality that endures beyond the immediate situation. Thus, their bodies provide the anchor points for names that link them to a community of others as well as to the stock typifications of its culture.

But there is no reason why the community should provide the only perspective from which the self can be made whole. Human beings experience themselves indirectly, from the imagined perspectives of specific other people, social roles, situations, and communities. Any perspective whatsoever can serve as a perspective from which the self may be perceived and interpreted and thus made whole. Thus, to the extent that the individual can imagine the perspectives of a role, of the situations in which interaction with role partners takes place, or of the community as a whole, these perspectives become available for the purposes of self-definition. What we must understand, in addition, is that because human beings have memories of self-objectifications from a variety of perspectives, and because they assemble these memories into social and personal biographies, they become more or less durable objects to themselves. They form more or less stable typifications of themselves that they attach to a named body.

The important extension of Mead's analysis is thus that the person's emergent typification of self becomes a *perspective* from which the self may be grasped. We have the capacity, at any point, to imagine ourselves not only as incumbents of a role, participants in a situation, or members of a community, and thus to act from those perspectives, but also as ourselves and thus to act from our own perspective—that is, from the perspective of the typification we have created in collaboration with others. We can, in essence, make the emergent object self that is continually created in social interaction with others a perspective from which it may act.

Social experience thus creates a situated self that is defined by its location in the immediate flow of social interaction and is able to be an object to itself from the imagined vantage point of specific others, their roles, and the situation as a whole. Moreover, it creates a social self—what I have called social identity—that is defined by the person's location in one or more communities and is able to be an object to itself from the imagined vantage point of community and its culture. And, crucially, it creates an emergent object—a self here designated as personal identity—that is defined by a far more abstract and open process of social location and is able to (and must) be an object to itself, to a great extent, by imagining its own perspective.

This view is, I believe, not only consistent with Mead's analysis, but a necessary extension of it. Although it is customary to speak of the self as formed in a process of role-taking in which the person imagines the responses of others to an impending act and adjusts conduct accordingly, Mead's social psychology lays the basis for a much more general and powerful analysis. As the person responds to stimulation, the emergent response becomes available for interpretation, so that the person is able to grasp the meaning of an incipient act. Role-taking is a crucial aspect of this process of interpretation, for we do not directly interpret the meaning of our incipient actions, but rather grasp their meaning by imagining them from another perspective, quite often the perspective of a specific other person or of that person's social role. In more general terms, what we do when we respond to ourselves is to take the perspective of another in order to grasp our own emergent act as itself the manifestation of our own perspective. That "other" perspective can be that of a role; it can be that of a specific, concrete person whom we typify in ways that reflect a history of social interaction and not simply a role; it can be the perspective of a situation as a whole; it can be the perspective of a whole social unit.

Since the self becomes an *object* with social location, not only in the immediate situation but beyond, it too becomes available, much as any other object, as a perspective from which the person can act. To have a body, a name, and a self-typification is to have a perspective that, while surely formed and shaped by social experience, is nonetheless somewhat apart from it. Everyday social interaction calls upon us to act as role incumbents or community members, but it also enables us to act as ourselves. We can only grasp that we are being ourselves indirectly, from the standpoint of others, for we have no direct apprehension of the way our acts do or do not fit our self-typification.

This raises a crucial question for analysis, a question we can appreciate by examining the way the person has self-consciousness as the incumbent of a role or as a member of a community. When the person acts from the perspective of a role, he or she adopts (in acts of imagination) the perspective of role partners in order to judge the degree of fit between the role being enacted and the line of conduct being formed. In social interaction "in role," people cognitively structure a situation into roles and then inspect their own conduct from the imagined perspectives (roles) of others. When the person acts as a member of a community, he or she adopts the perspective of the community as a whole in order to conceive of self as a community member and of his or her acts as meeting community expectations. As members of communities, we inspect ourselves from the standpoint of the community with which we identify.

The question, then, is how we cognitively structure the situation when we seek to act from the perspective of ourselves and not of our roles. If we have more or less stable typifications of ourselves, how do we imagine the perspectives of others in order to know whether what we are doing fits with those typifications? The answer to this question is that we cognitively structure the social world in a way that differs from our structuring of situation or community. Both the concrete situation and the larger community tend to attract our identification. Although we do not necessarily adopt the perspectives of specific others, we identify with them as participants in the situation. Similarly, although we do not always do the bidding of community, we identify as members of the community. But to act from the perspective of ourselves we must to some extent set ourselves against others and against the community. We must, in other words, cognitively structure not a situation with interlocking roles, nor a community of mutually identifying members, but a social world of independent and different selves.

To put this in another way, personal identity inclines the person toward a conception of self in opposition—to others, to situations and their requirements, to social roles, to communities. To one acting from the perspective of personal identity, "the other" is thus imagined as one with a perspective that leads him or her to oppose, resist, deny, limit, or constrain. The perspective of personal identity is that of a biographically and existentially separate and perhaps even unique human being. This perspective is grasped and sustained, I would argue, by developing a sense of opposition and resistance, by imagining others who want to limit or restrict one's actions. "The other" thus becomes, in a sense, the incumbent of a role or the member of a community who is imagined to identify fully with community or role and to want to "reduce" one fully to a role and a member.

By conceiving of the self in this way, we make the "I" more than a mere product of social conditioning. That which responds, the knowing self, is moved not only by a history of being socially rewarded in particular ways for its activities, but also by its own inner logic, by its own sense of integrity and continuity, its own demand for meaning and sense in its own terms. This responding, knowing subject has the capacity to say no, to deny not only the responses it has been socially conditioned to make, but in some instances also its own developing imperatives. It can begin to respond in a way that has previously met with approval, and then know that this response, while it meets with the expectations of others, constitutes a denial of its own program of activity. It can decide to remain celibate or to commit suicide or to refrain from eating. By these lights, then, the "I" is not merely a product of conditioning nor a matter of biology, but it is rather a manifestation of an "existential" self, a knowing, animated, self-producing, and self-reproducing creature that, having been given a name and an existence by virtue of its birth into the society of its fellows, then claims for itself an existence and a reality that is separate and independent of this society.[23]

It is crucial to emphasize that this self-in-opposition—this personal identity that locates the person in opposition to community rather than by identification with it—is a social phenomenon and not a biological one. The social process, by giving the person perspectives from which to act and communities to which to belong, creates a being with a perspective of its own, a being that can resist society. Human beings apprehend personal identity much as they apprehend social identity, by imagining the way they appear to others. Social identity leads us to see a self identified with its role and with others and made continuous and whole to the extent that its actions are appropriate expressions of its role and memberships. Personal identity leads us to see a self that is differentiated from others and therefore ultimately one that identifies only with itself, and so a self that is made continuous and whole to the extent that its actions are appropriate expressions of its own essence. Personal identity is thus social in the way it is experienced.

It is also social in its origins, for this is no raw biological creature with fixed instincts that run counter to social and cultural demands. It is a social creature with self-interests that it can interpret as counter to social demands, and that it can even interpret as counter to biological needs and urges. Personal identity is a social force, not a biological one, and it impels the person not by dint of hormones, but by virtue of the way the person imagines both his or her own being as a project and the way others are perceived to support or oppose this project.

The "I" is thus crucial to social theory because, without it, we have an over-socialized and overly behavioristic conception of human beings and their conduct. Stripped of this element of the self, the individual is no more than an actor fully programmed by society. And that kind of actor is better explained by some form of psychological or sociological reductionism. For, if there is nothing in the person except what is supplied by society and culture, then only two kinds of explanations of human conduct are possible. At the aggregate level, culture should enable us to predict conduct perfectly; and at the level of the individual, we need not look any further than what culture and society have pumped into the person and under what circumstances and schedules. But if the social process yields a creature it cannot hold leashed, then there is no adequate explanation of that social process or its outcomes without attending to this creature.

Next . . .

This account of situated, social, and personal identity undergirds the analysis of the experience and prospects of the person in American society. Faced with cultural polarities, tempted by societal as well as communal modes of social participation, and offered a variety of forms of community, how does the person respond? In Chapter VI, I will attempt to depict the main strategies of self-construction available in contemporary American society.

CHAPTER VI

Strategies of Self-Construction

Social identity and personal identity are major contending forces in contemporary self-construction. Each is a potential solution to the problematics of situated identity in everyday life—a way of producing continuity and integration while also managing the tension between identification and differentiation. Each links situations and their roles into meaningful sequences and creates a sense of wholeness that combats the fragmentation of everyday life. Each provides a way of handling the inevitable conflict between the individual's need (and the community's demand) for identification and the individual's quest for (and the community's resistance to) differentiation.

Although social and personal identity both construct a self that outlives the self of the immediate situation, they do so in opposite ways. Social identity provides for the continuity and integration of the self primarily through identification with community, and thus attenuates the significance and scope of individuation. It organizes situated identities temporally and in relation to one another by reproducing the life of the community within the person, so that the structure of the self mirrors social structure. Personal identity guarantees continuity and integration through the formation and elaboration of a personal project, and thus rejects identification with others in favor of differentiation from them. It organizes situated roles temporally and in relation to one another through deliberate and self-conscious acts, so that the self's structure is self-created.

Both personal and social identity are engendered by modern life, which in its American version provides opposing but equally attractive objects: freedom and security, autonomy and intimacy, past and future. Americans are thus drawn toward two contending visions of society and individual: One is of a world, often depicted as having been lost at some point in the past, in which social identities were secure and people lived in warm community. The other is a vision of a world in which personal identities may be made at will and the individual is a free agent of his or her own destiny.

These visions stand both mutually opposed and mutually dependent, for each finds its own meaning in part by negating the other. The community-centered, tradition-oriented, security-conscious pole of American culture favors the development and indeed dominance of social identity. To emphasize social identity is to choose conformity over rebellion, staying over leaving, and dependence rather than independence. The autonomy-seeking, future-oriented, freedom-loving pole of the culture favors the development of personal identity. It incites rebellion, urges departure, and favors going it alone in the construction of a special and individual self. But the selection of one course of action over another seldom obliterates the opposite choice from view or removes it from consideration.

American culture thus exacerbates the tension between these two forms of identity. It is essential to realize that it does so in the same individuals, that each American is in some degree pulled toward both visions of self and society and hence also toward the construction of both social and personal identity. Although Americans become differentiated from one another on the basis of which of the two poles of the culture they espouse and which of the two forms of identity predominates, the dynamics of American identity turn upon their continuing opposition.

To explore these patterns of cultural polarization and individual ambivalence further it will be helpful to theorize about the strategies of self-construction available in contemporary life. The three strategies I will examine are ideal types that seek to capture the problematics of identity in contemporary America and to explore the ways people cope with them. At one extreme lies the strategy of *exclusivity,* which emphasizes social identity at the expense of personal identity through an overpowering identification with a single community. At the opposite extreme lies the strategy of *autonomy,* which cultivates personal identity at the expense of social identity through a pronounced emphasis on the differentiation of the person from others. These extreme strategies are inherently difficult to sustain, even though many contemporary Americans devote considerable behavioral and discursive efforts to the task. Although some succeed at one or the other, most seek a middle way, a *pragmatic* strategy of self-construction, in which social and personal identity are maintained in varying degrees of harmony and tension.[1]

Exclusivity

The strategy of exclusivity, which promotes social identity at the expense of personal identity, seeks to construct the self through membership in and identification with a single community that can provide the organized standpoint from which its members' acts and experiences can be meaningfully interpreted. Those who follow the strategy of exclusivity view their community as an enclave, often portraying it as opposed to the society at large or to other communities. Its culture is frequently seen as requiring some defense against the inroads of other communities. Its members are apt to feel that their community is in sole possession of the truth, and occasionally they will claim moral ownership of society. They typically feel superior to other communities and their cultures, even when they wish only to be left alone and have no desire to impose their culture on the rest of the society.

Continuity entails a sense of an emergent, meaningful self, of links between past and future, whether measured in minutes, years, or stages in the life cycle. Exclusive identifiers attempt to sew together the disparate events and acts of everyday life by confining themselves within a community of like others, thus seeking organic community within modern society. Transitions from one role or situation to another are made the basis for a continuous experience of self by interpreting them within the framework of a morally required, normal round of everyday life associated with membership in such a community. Exclusivity thus renders acts, roles, and situations relevant to a continuous sense of self by accepting the rhythms of communal life as the key reference points of experience. In the face of the discontinuities of everyday life, one makes sense of what one does and one legitimates it by referring it to communally shared ways and sequences of thinking, acting, and feeling.

Although exclusive identifiers "wish" to see no further than the boundaries of the community of identification, such restricted vision is in fact impossible in modern life. In organic communities, problematic situations that threatened the continuity of the self arose within the enclosed life of the community and were solved by reference to its culture. Exclusive identifiers want to make the community the sole reference point for the self, but in the modern world the sources of discontinuity often lie outside the community, and its culture can often be defined only by contrasting it with the culture of other communities. Society and its other communities always stand as a visible and in some respects threatening presence.

Those who identify strongly with their religious communities illustrate these points. Christians who seek to identify exclusively with a Christian community—many Evangelicals or Pentecostals, for example—are in effect trying to construct a day-to-day existence that is ordered by the ethical, moral, and theological precepts of a Christian culture.[2] The same is true of Jews who make membership in their community the main basis of identity. Ideally, the culture of a religious community would consist solely of objects that invite desirable forms of conduct and provide a complete basis for interpreting personal experience. It would, in other words, define a morally self-sufficient community.

Modernity, however, whether in its American or any other version, makes moral self-sufficiency difficult, if not impossible. The everyday life of any strongly religious person in a secular society is regularly interrupted and its continuity threatened by the larger society. The Christian fundamentalist, for example, rubs shoulders in jobs and in the marketplace with those who do not share the same views of life, and a sense of personal continuity established on the basis of Christian precepts is thus constantly threatened by alternatives. Other people seem to face fewer restrictions on their conduct, or the daily rhythm of their lives is different, or at week's end they look forward to spending their Sunday on the golf course rather than at church. Moreover, few religious communities possess an organic culture that can provide a full round of everyday activities and a fully taken-for-granted set of objects. Instead, the culture and community of most contemporary religious groups must be significantly defined in oppositional terms. Their cultural unity and community integrity seem to be provided for in large part by resisting the influence of the modern world. There is a strong wish to look no further than the culture of the religious community to decide what to do next or to make sense of life as it has been lived so far. But this culture can be grasped and maintained only through a perception of community boundaries and their cognition as barriers between "us" and "them." The exclusive religious identifier thus seeks refuge from a world whose very existence is crucial to the definition and maintenance of his or her own culture, community, and identity.

This fact, as much as theology, may account for the preoccupation with and incessant discourse about sin among many Christian denominations. Preachers warn their audiences of the dangers of backsliding, vividly portray the many available ways of sinning, and seem to view the secular world as determined to tempt unsuspecting Christians into sin. Discourse about sin functions as a way of enhancing community solidarity through discourse about the moral boundaries of the community. Although solidarity is surely enhanced, so is the perception of the secular world—in other words, "society"—as a tempting place. Talk of sin also seems to afford vicarious participation in a forbidden social world that is forever visible and important to those who choose to reject it. Such discourse helps maintain a sense of boundaries between the secular world and the religious community, and supplies part of the tension needed to reinforce its solidarity.

A sharp sense of boundaries characterizes virtually all exclusive identifiers in modern society. Evangelical Christians seem in many respects motivated in the same way as Orthodox Jews, who strive toward an organic community in which day-to-day life has a guaranteed continuity of personal and social meaning from which alternatives are excluded. The Orthodox ideal is a community life structured by the dictates of Jewish law, a community where the details of everyday life are regulated by tradition and are guaranteed by ritual. They seek a taken-for-granted round of everyday life that sweeps the person along in its flow and thus keeps discontinuity to a minimum and, when it does occur, deals with it in terms of the community and its meaning system. But alternatives are always available—indeed, since the Enlightenment the larger society has tempted Jews —and boundaries between the Jewish community and the larger world assume a tremendous psychological and sociological significance.[3]

An acute sense of those boundaries—of what Jewish law requires versus what the others do, of how Jewish tradition interprets the person and his or her experience versus how non-Jews view life—thus becomes an important basis of personal continuity. One knows what to do next and what one's life means by linking it to Jewish law and by seeing its contrast with actions that do not accord with Jewish law. One does not have a taken-for-granted identity, but a social identity that must be repeatedly invoked. The underlying motivation for continuity provokes the reaffirmation and reinvigoration of identity through motive talk that focuses on social identity. Children are told that "we do this because we are Jews"; adults remind themselves of the specifically Jewish rationales for their acts and attitudes.

Talk about social identity also strengthens the resolve of the community and the clarity of its boundaries. Because the cultural differences between the religious community and the outside world are often perceived by at least some members to be smaller than they are alleged to be, a fact that makes the outside world more appealing and the community less capable of holding its members, something must be done both to retain identification and to emphasize differences. Exaggerated talk of the larger society and its other communities and cultures, and of how different and problematic they are, thus becomes a necessary device through which the culture and boundaries of the community are constructed. And discourse that explicitly links everyday acts to the community's culture and differentiates them from the acts of outsiders is especially useful in preserving social identity and the boundaries on which it depends.

But the need to be self-conscious of community and of the social identity it sustains perpetuates the very discontinuities a social identity seeks to repair, as well as a sharp sense of contrast between communal and societal modes of life. Exclusive identification with the quasi-organic ethnic, religious, or other enclave provides the rationale for decisions that affect the life course as a whole (whom to marry, for example) as well as less consequential matters (whether to go to a baseball game or to church). One does things, and one tells oneself and others that one does things, because of who one is. But the very existence of choice—and the nature of that choice, which is between confinement and freedom—is the source of discontinuities in the self. To decide that one's social identity requires a course of action is to remind oneself that other avenues of thought, feeling, and action are open. In particular, it is to remind oneself that a societal mode of social participation, which imposes far fewer restraints and seems to require a less explicit rationale for every act, is open to choice.

Exclusivity seeks integration of the self by adopting the perspective of a *generalized other*—that is, the imagined, shared perspectives of a quasi-organic community. So long as the person can sustain a sense of personal continuity in relation to this community, he or she can hold in mind an image of the community as a whole, and thus have a perspective from which to view the self as a whole. Particular roles become expressions of more general community purposes, and instead of fragmenting the person they contribute to a sense of place and purpose within the community. Each role becomes a facet of a self whose value is recognized by a community; each situation becomes a means of realizing that self and the community purposes it represents.

The quasi-organic community is not real organic community, however, and just as continuity remains problematic for those who choose exclusivity, so does integration. The quasi-organic community is not a spontaneous, natural world unto itself, but has a "constructed" character that makes integration a more self-conscious and less automatic achievement.

Moreover, the sense of opposition between the quasi-organic community and the society is as problematic for integration as it is for continuity.

It is tempting to view the organic community of the past as one in which there was a true generalized other—that is, a truly shared set of common perspectives that the members of the community could take toward themselves. To some extent that is an illusion we have about organic communities, for even there, the shared perspectives and common responses that George H. Mead had in mind when he wrote about the generalized other must be seen as products of the imagination as much as realities of conduct. It may well be that in the organic community those reciprocal imaginations are widely shared, but it remains the case that significant symbols do not fully guarantee intersubjectivity and that responses to common situations are varied as well as uniform. Even in the organic community of the past, then, both the boundaries of the community and the content of its culture are artifacts of perception or imagination and not simple and objective realities. When people in such communities achieved personal integration by adopting the perspective of the generalized other toward themselves, they *imagined* this generalized other, and its perspective was more uniform and integrated in their imaginations than their individual perspectives were uniform and integrated in actuality.

What was true of the "genuine" organic community is even truer of the quasi-organic communities constructed within modern society. Because communities are not simply or even mainly territorial entities where people live in constant association with one another and where imaginations are constantly measured against reality, but are more likely to be abstract and dispersed, all modern communities are to a great extent products of the imaginations of their individual members. The generalized other that each person uses as a means of assessing and integrating the self requires both more prodigious feats of imagination and more explicit confirmation than in the organic community.

Many Christian denominations, for example, emphasize a simple theology based on the role of Jesus in the individual's salvation. Such a theology may be essential for the personal imagination and social construction of a generalized other by people who are geographically dispersed, constantly surrounded by competing visions, and seem to lack a more spontaneous and less self-conscious basis for the imagination of a generalized other. The answer to the question of why Jesus is so crucial a figure and why a "personal relationship to Jesus" figures so prominently in the vocabularies of motive of many Christians cannot be found solely in the theology of Christianity, which assigns a specific historical and religious meaning and function to Jesus. An important part of the answer lies in the fact that Jesus becomes the embodiment or personification of the generalized other. Here is a community composed of people of diverse racial, ethnic, and social class origins who share little in the way of a common culture, it would seem, except their belief in being "born again in Jesus." This constant stress on the person of Jesus signifies that a particular individual has come to represent the responses of this community as a whole, to be the person who must be imagined not only as a way of guaranteeing the wholeness of the person but also the integrity of the community. Jesus thus becomes *the* generalized other who stands for and certifies the reality of the community as a whole.[4]

Where people more widely and reliably share actual responses to a variety of situations, particular figures are far less likely to personify the generalized other. Orthodox Jews, for example, have several centuries of experience as organic communities; they do, in fact, share a culture that is not defined by abstract theological principles but by a long-established and codified set of rules. Even among the Orthodox, however, there is a preoccupation with those rules, with the culture, with the exact prescriptions of the law. For Orthodox Jews in the modern world Torah has a function similar to that of Jesus for Christians. That is, the law becomes a representation of the generalized other, a constant point of reference that defines the shared responses of the community. If the Christian makes himself or herself whole by establishing a personal relationship with Jesus, the Orthodox Jew attains and maintains an integrated self by constant study of and reference to the law. The Christian takes the perspective of Jesus toward himself or herself and asks what Jesus wants him or her to do; the Orthodox Jew takes the perspective of the law and asks what it requires. In either case, under the trying conditions of community in modern life, the generalized other is constructed in a more explicit and self-conscious way than would be necessary in a genuine organic community.

The explicit construction of a generalized other is also spurred by the sense of opposition that exclusive identifiers feel with modernity. All quasi-organic communities are to one degree or another efforts to deal with, come to terms with, oppose, avoid, or repeal modernity. So, too, exclusivity always has modernity in its mind as something to be dealt with. If the Christian feels whole because he or she takes the perspective of Jesus toward himself or herself, he or she also feels whole because so much of what Jesus tells him or her to do has to do with modernity and how the individual ought to relate to it—reject it because the temptations of society are sinful, accommodate to it, seek to change it, or even accept some of its gifts and luxuries because there is no conflict between them and a belief in Jesus. The Orthodox Jew finds in Torah all of the objects and interpretations necessary for the construction of a whole self, and also derives a sense of integration from the belief that Torah puts the rest of the world in its place.

Much of the foregoing analysis also pertains to identification and differentiation. Exclusive identifiers regard their community as the repository of a full culture—a place where even innermost impulses are shared by significant others and lead members to feel, think, and act similarly. The similarity may be more or less real from the standpoint of an outsider, but it is tangible and crucial from the perspective of the identifier. Exclusivity implies that only those in this community are like one, and that those who are not in this community are not like one. Thus, identification—a sense of likeness and oneness with others—rests in part on a contrast with the world beyond the community of identification. Others—those who haven't been saved, the Goyim, the unwashed, the pagans, the secular humanists—are important not only because their negation of the community's culture helps to define it, but also because they help establish one's sense of differentiation from others.

This last point is crucial. In the organic community, the main basis of differentiation is role, for it is the distinctive role set of the individual that permits a sense of global difference from others and establishes a place for the person within the community. In modern society, however, the circumstances of identification and of differentiation are quite different. For those who choose the exclusive strategy it is a sense of attachment to one community and one community only that provides both for identification and for differentiation. One is like and thus allied with and can make common cause with those who are similar to one because they are members of the same community; one is different from those who are not members of the community. As a result, an individual sense of differentiation is achieved by exclusive identifiers in relation to society as a whole: there is this large, heterogeneous society, and I am different from others by virtue of my membership in this community and the fact that most members of the society are not members. Exclusivity thus tends to give the person a sense of separateness from others in a very different way than people attain in real organic communities. In the real organic community, the person is both like and unlike others on the basis of discrete combinations of social roles. In the quasi-organic community, there is a tendency for an exaggerated sense of oneness with community members and an exaggerated sense of difference from those who are not members.

Although I have developed a theoretical image of exclusivity by using ethnic and religious identification as a main source of examples, the strategy is far more widely practiced. Exclusivists can be found anywhere—in voluntary organizations, corporations, universities, social movements, urban neighborhoods, and small towns. Nevertheless, some kinds of social units are more likely than others to serve as the basis of exclusive identification. Ethnicity, religion, social class, small towns, neighborhoods, and some social movements seem the most likely candidates, and for two main reasons. First, the exclusivist is looking for a close approximation of organic community, and propinquity thus plays a major role in the construction of community. Exclusivists need others who can confirm a sense of community and shared culture through their own conduct as well as through overt approval. Second, these forms of community provide for a sense of opposition to or, at least, isolation from the broader social stream. Other possible bases of community are either too dispersed, too integrated, or too ephemeral to attract exclusive identification.

Exclusivity thus fosters a definite pattern of choices and attitudes as the person faces the behavioral dilemmas posed by American culture. First, it encourages conformity to community standards, often an aggressive conformity that suggests the presence of undertones of rebellion or the fear of rebellion. In the face of the temptation to rebel against the expectations of a tightly integrated community the exclusivist chooses determinedly to conform and to subdue doubt with a firm and often vocal sense of conviction. In the face of its awareness of the potential for rebellion, the community tightens its scrutiny and turns up the volume of its own demands.

Second, exclusivity fosters a resolute commitment to stay in and remain attached to the community, but with the option of leaving always available in principle and often both feared and desired. "Staying" is a highly self-conscious act for many exclusivists, a choice made in the knowledge that one might instead leave. It is therefore a choice made, sometimes repeatedly, by people who are tempted to leave and who fear their own temptation, or who fear others will leave. Precisely because there are so many opportunities to fall away from the community and because these opportunities are tempting, exclusivists stress not only conformity to the community's traditions but the need for members to demonstrate their loyalty by remaining as members.

Third, exclusivity promotes a sense of attachment to and dependence upon others, but always with the knowledge that independence is possible and perhaps rewarding. Exclusivity fosters a belief that common purposes take precedence, that "life is with people," that true joy is to be found in subduing the wish to be alone and free and replacing it with the comforts of dependence upon others. But the strength of such beliefs and the urgency with which they are asserted show the power of the opposite inclination to put one's own needs first, to go it alone, to be independent.

Exclusivity is thus an effort to face the dilemmas of choice fostered by American culture through the construction and maintenance of a social identity and the strict subversion of personal identity to it. It constructs an economy of the self in which the costs of subverting personal autonomy are viewed as more than compensated by the rewards of social participation, security, and certainty provided by membership in and identification with a community. And as much as it is a way of perceiving the self, exclusivity is also a way of perceiving community and society. It fosters the cognition of community as a warm, safe, and supportive place and of society as a hostile, threatening, and foreign place.

Autonomy

Autonomy is the opposite of exclusivity, for where exclusive identifiers flee from society and embrace community, the autonomous seek the freedom of society and eschew community. Exclusivists feel continuity to the extent they can fit their daily, weekly, and yearly rounds of activities to the rhythms and cycles of the community. The autonomous construct a sense of continuity by regarding their acts as contributing to the attainment of individual goals, purposes, or projects. Autonomy thus requires a life plan, a constantly reiterated design or blueprint against which every act can be measured. Conduct is legitimated by its contribution to the design, and the person derives a sense of continuity by surmounting obstacles to the attainment of goals.

Autonomy entails a sense of the person as independent, as a creature of individual will who can set personal goals and then seek to attain them. One variety of autonomy fosters an intense devotion to and preoccupation with the achievement of wealth, status, power, or other valued objects. Americans often measure achievement by the attainment of "success," an object sufficiently abstract to encompass a variety of financial, political, and intellectual accomplishments. Although there is ample evidence that Americans are often willing to settle for the outward signs of success, the genuine article—real, self-made success—is still held out as the ideal.

Just as "success" is a measure of autonomy, the "successful" provide models for the would-be autonomous person to emulate. Both particular individuals and idealized character types provide such models. The entrepreneur, for example, is a recognizable historical character type in America, and there are contemporary entrepreneurs who can serve as models worthy of emulation. Steven Jobs, for example, one of the co-founders of Apple Computer, is the subject of magazine articles about modern entrepreneurs, and his well-publicized departure from the company he helped found and his creation of a new computer enterprise (Next, Inc.) dramatizes the possibilities of contemporary entrepreneurship. In both myth and reality, entrepreneurs are the topic of discourse, not only about what it takes to be a successful creator of business or other enterprise but also about the possibilities of autonomy.

Although the entrepreneur had been seen as a vanishing social type, there has recently been a revival of interest in entrepreneurship through the publication of books and magazines that portray entrepreneurs, hold them up as worthy of emulation, and sometimes purport to show how to duplicate their success. It is instructive that the revival of entrepreneurship as a model of character comes partly in response to its widely portrayed and much-lamented demise. Just when the "organization man" and the "manager" had been supposed to have supplanted the nineteenth-century "entrepreneur," the latter character makes a comeback. This should come as no surprise, for these character types personify the antipodes of American culture. The entrepreneur is beholden to no organization, but makes an autonomous way in life, creating a self as well as a successful business rather than simply fitting the self to the enterprises of others. The entrepreneur thus provides an important concrete model of autonomy, showing those who choose the strategy of autonomy how to construct themselves in this mode. And the entrepreneur also models one pole of the culture.

There are other contemporary models of achievement for the autonomous to emulate. The sports hero, for example, becomes a "somebody" —a person to be reckoned with, to be taken into account, to be heeded— through exceptional athletic performance. Likewise, hard-driving political leaders (Jesse Jackson), rock stars (Tina Turner), scientists or scientific popularizers (Carl Sagan), even corporate executives (Lee Iacocca) embody part of the meaning of autonomy in contemporary life.

One of the key aspects of autonomy is its connection with fame and celebrity. To be truly autonomous is to have a name others instantly recognize, to be somebody, to need no introduction. The reason for this connection is obvious: the strategy of autonomy requires the person to abandon the small and enclosing world of community for the larger, more open, more competitive stage of society. Autonomy thus requires applause, name recognition, even adulation as evidence that autonomy has been achieved. Most people rely on occupational, ethnic, familial, and other roles and group memberships to establish their identities when they interact with others. The ultimate quest of autonomy is for one's name alone to be a sufficient identifier, so that wherever one goes in society, the mention of one's name is sufficient to establish an identity. The autonomous seek to interact not as incumbents of roles but as themselves.

Entrepreneurs and other successful individuals are thus significant because they both reveal some of the means individuals might use to become successful and display success as a measure of personal identity. Not only is success possible, such tales seem to say, but so is the autonomous self. The Steve Jobses, Jesse Jacksons, and Lee Iacoccas of the world seem to be testimony to the possibility of a thoroughly personal identity. They appear to have carved a place for themselves in the social world not only because of what they have accomplished but because of who they have become. Their place in the social order is not defined by their roles, but by their selves. Sociologically, we might say, they are not merely incumbents of positions but are themselves fixtures of social structure.

In the orthodox sociological view of social structure, of course, the distinction between the position and the person is firm. Social roles and organizations are sharply distinct from the persons who hold temporary incumbency or membership. In the real world, however, the distinction is frequently blurred. It is not simply that incumbents to some degree shape every role as they see fit, but more fundamentally that some roles become in essence equivalent to the selves of those who create or hold them. One could easily argue, for example, that (at least in the public eye) the presidency of the United States readily accepts the personal imprint of the incumbent. Ronald Reagan was President of the United States, but he was as much, and perhaps more, Ronald Reagan, a seemingly autonomous individual who defined his job as much as it defined him.

The autonomous thus need no introduction in the same sense that the role of a physician needs no explanation. We know who a physician is and what a physician does because we know the role, which is an element of our basic conception of the occupational structure. In the same way, Ronald Reagan, Lee Iacocca, and other models of autonomy are known to us not primarily through their roles, but through our conceptions of them as individuals. They, too, are elements in our conceptions of the social world; incumbents of roles, they nonetheless stamp those roles with themselves. And in the same way that roles outlive their incumbents, some of the autonomous outlive their bodies by becoming heroes and remaining so even after their deaths.

The desire for autonomy is easily transformed into a quest for mere celebrity, and admiration of the genuinely successful readily degenerates into fascination with the merely famous. Autonomy requires the person to carve out a distinctive place in society, a task at which only a few are destined to succeed. It is relatively easier, however, to cultivate the appearance of autonomy, to parlay modest accomplishments into the trappings of great success and thereby to acquire an instantly recognizable name. (And, with bows to Robert Merton, it may also be easier for some to secure illicit success and thus gain a place through infamy.[5]) Likewise, it is easy to be deceived—to watch and applaud the famous without any effort to assess the accomplishments on which their fame (or infamy) is based.

A quest for achievement—to make a million or to do one's "personal best"—is not the only form autonomy takes. Some of those who seek to "fulfill" or "actualize" or "discover" themselves, or to experiment with various "lifestyles" that will foster "growth" may also be pursuing autonomy. The cultivation of a self, the quest for uniqueness or distinctiveness, the search for the "real self," and similar preoccupations can provide the goals or purposes on which autonomy is founded just as much as can success, and such a route to autonomy may be more widely accessible than economic, political, or scientific achievement.

At the root of contemporary humanistic psychology as well as the popular psychologies it has spawned lies a belief that under the proper conditions the self will flourish and grow and develop its own distinctive character. Therapies that share a general philosophy of self-realization, differing largely in details from one another, have proliferated in the last quarter century. Transactional Analysis, Therapeutic Sounding, Heartworks, Client-Centered Therapy, Rebirthing, Body/Mind Centering, and numerous other psychological and bodily therapies of greater or lesser repute promise to teach the person methods to discover the true self, find peace of mind, and restore harmony with one's fellow human beings (or with the universe).

Not all of these therapeutic movements are vehicles for the pursuit of autonomy, nor are all who participate in them seeking autonomy, but the movements and their leaders are important to some who would construct an autonomous self. Such popular therapies provide a language for describing and talking about an autonomous self, a community of discourse that can provide legitimacy to the quest for a truly personal identity, and most of all an alternative to success as the basis for autonomy. Therapeutic seekers have not necessarily abandoned a quest for material success (their gurus, in fact, often do well financially), but they seem, by and large, to be expressive rather than utilitarian individualists. Their project is to discover who they are, not by stamping themselves upon the world, but by discovering and nourishing the self within. Nonetheless, it is autonomy many of them seek, since it is the differentiation of self and its unique characteristics from others, rather than comforting identification with others, that is their object.

These therapeutic movements are generally the creations of individuals who put a highly personal stamp on their version of the truth. Not only does the therapeutic movement itself emphasize the autonomy of the person, but its leaders express this quest in their own autonomous efforts to create distinctive modalities of treatment and to secure fame and fortune by doing so. The creation and promotion of therapeutic methods seems to be an activity in which the successful therapeutic entrepreneur achieves autonomy through fame and fortune, while urging a more expressive form of autonomy upon followers. Doubtless some therapeutic leaders do this with great cynicism, while others believe in their own methods even while securing autonomy through the more conventional route of achievement and celebrity.

The analysis of such therapeutic movements (as well as of achievement) as avenues for the pursuit of autonomy always risks portraying greater uniformity of meaning and purpose than actually exists. The preoccupation with self encouraged by such therapies, for example, has led critics to see them as both encouraging and feeding a more deeply rooted narcissism in American culture. In the same way, the "myth of the self-made man" and of "rugged individualism" has for generations been the object of the hostility of social critics. Such critical discourse can easily lead one to imagine that therapeutic seekers or Yuppie entrepreneurs are single-minded pursuers of their particular brands of autonomy. But, in fact, the lines between expressive and utilitarian individualism are readily blurred. "Self-actualization," as the phrase is interpreted by ordinary people, can seem very close to "winning" the battle to beat the other guy to the top. Moreover, therapeutic seekers may be especially prone to transform a therapeutic movement into a community by virtue of their strong identification with it.

Here as elsewhere in social life there is no one-to-one correspondence between the central public meanings of an activity or an ideology and the motives of individual participants. Strategies of self-construction do not necessarily correspond closely with the concrete goals people form and the activities in which they regularly participate. Achievement is an important route toward autonomy, for example, but we cannot assume that all those who seek or achieve success, in whatever field, are therefore also seeking autonomy. The cultivation of a special and unique sense of self is another way of seeking autonomy, but we must not assume that all those who speak in the vocabulary of self-actualization really do so because they have chosen a strategy of autonomy.

There is no simple correspondence between the outward forms and social characteristics of conduct and the inner forces that motivate it. Autonomy seekers find meaning in everyday acts by linking them to individual goals that lie in the future; that is the real test of autonomy. Many people seek or attain success, but continuity and integration in their personal meaning systems do not lie in their achievements, but elsewhere. Thus, for example, an Orthodox Jew may place a high value on success in business, but it may not be the goal of success that guarantees personal continuity, but rather his participation in a religious community. Similarly, some of those who seek self-actualization genuinely seek autonomy, in the sense that they measure their acts against some standard of self-actualization. But there are others who find in the vocabulary of self-actualization the basis for identification with a community, and whose sense of continuity is much more guaranteed by a sense of membership in it than by any specific progress they make toward self-actualization.

The strategy of autonomy thus seeks continuity by locating the meaning of discrete acts in their contribution to a personal project. The project may entail a specific form of achievement, the cultivation of fame or celebrity, the development of a unique and special sense of self, or merely the display of eccentricity. Whatever the project, it assigns meaning to specific acts by treating them as manifestations of the plan at work, setbacks on the road to success, means whereby the project may be accomplished. Thus, the self-actualizer can interpret an outburst of temper as a sign that the true self is breaking through its repressive institutional crust; the entrepreneur can treat a business failure as a valuable lesson that will aid future success; and the budding celebrity author can define grueling promotional trips as part of the dues that must be paid for success. Everything can be and in a sense must be interpreted in relation to the quest for a fully autonomous personal identity.

Like exclusivity, autonomy requires self-consciousness, calculation, and rationality. But where exclusivity demands that the individual interpret the details of his or her life in relation to the community, autonomy requires careful attention to the construction and maintenance of a distinctive and unique life story. Where the exclusive identifier is provided with a script to which the details of a life must be adjusted, the autonomous person must write a script, defining the plot as the action progresses and writing an appropriate part and lines.

How do the autonomous find integration? If human beings require some kind of community in which there are widely shared perspectives, such that the person can reflect on a variety of activities and involvements and see himself or herself whole, where does the autonomous person find this community? What generalized other do the autonomous find?

The strategy of autonomy achieves an integrated self by cultivating a very abstract generalized other—an abstract community—whose scope is as wide as society itself. All generalized others and communities—even organic communities—are abstract, of course, for the very notion of a "community perspective" is itself an abstraction. But autonomy cultivates an especially abstract sense of community. It fosters fewer concrete precepts for behavior and a larger number of abstract rules and premises, which are not tied to particular situations and offer less specific behavioral guidance.

In the organic community, people judge their behavior according to whether it accords with traditional expectations. People have a reasonably exact idea of what they must do in any situation and a fairly clear sense of when they have fallen short of the mark. This is not to say that people in such communities are merely automatons programmed to enact a minute set of behavioral requirements—that gives too little credit to the inventiveness of human beings and to their propensity for autonomy even under conditions where conduct is exactly prescribed and closely supervised. It is to say that people have well-focused ideas about the responses they share as members of a community. But in modern life, and especially among those who seek autonomy, there is less concrete and specific guidance for behavior and more general and "philosophical" guidelines. Ethics are apt to be "situational" rather than "specific." The generalized other enunciates principles rather than rules, abstract standards for conduct rather than specific directions.

Several phenomena of modern life lend themselves to interpretation in such terms. The Calvinist belief in a calling and the salvation of the elect, for example, is an instance of the tendency to construct abstract guidelines in modern life. One is not told exactly what to do, only what one's actions and experiences might possibly mean in terms of the theology. In much the same way, the contemporary belief in "self-actualization" does not direct the individual along a specific behavioral path, but rather toward a way of finding meaning in acts and experiences. And contemporary social science also shares in this proclivity for the abstract precept: Lawrence Kohlberg's hierarchy of types of morality, for example, is an expression of the same tendency toward abstractness. It is a manifestation of higher moral development, in this scientific ethics, to do something because one perceives the rightness of it according to a general principle of behavior than to do it because one is told to do so or because one is following a rule.[6]

The propensity for abstraction is not difficult to understand. Any modern society, but especially one as large and as ethnically and religiously diverse as American society, contains varied and conflicting normative precepts and cultural objects. Indeed, as I have argued, it is in the nature of a modern society to generate a great many communities, each with its more or less distinctive generalized other. It is therefore impossible to constitute the whole society as the generalized other, except by developing a sufficiently abstract way of conceiving it. Mead, in fact, thought that one of the ways social conflict would be overcome is through the developing conception of a more inclusive human community (internationally as well as within nation states) defined by more abstract and general ideas about what people held in common.[7] Whether or not Mead was correct in his prediction about the direction of human evolution, his microscopic thinking seems sound: one way of achieving the integration of people who are economically and morally in conflict is by acts of imagination in which they perceive the common ground that makes them alike rather than the matters on which they disagree. The quest for a societal generalized other by the autonomous is a quest for common, and necessarily more abstract, cultural ground on which those who would otherwise be at odds can agree.

In its pure form, then, autonomy fosters the evaluation of personal goals and purposes by the standards of a very abstract generalized other. The individual achieves integration not by fitting into and behaving appropriately in a concrete community with explicit rules, but by viewing self from the perspective of a generalized other manifest in abstract principles. This abstract generalized other defines the community; that is, it is a set of principles that provides the perspective from which the self is constituted and made whole. This generalized other provides the most abstract kind of community one can imagine, for it is not embodied or personified, except perhaps by those who are exemplars of autonomy. The generalized other is simply and only an abstraction. It is none other than society itself, made into a community of all.

The nature and dynamics of autonomy must be understood, in the same way as exclusivity, by examining its problematics and pathologies. Two features of autonomy make it problematic. First, it is extraordinarily difficult to hold an abstract community in mind as a perspective from which to view self and achieve integration, so that the autonomous person is almost constantly tempted to retreat into a more concrete and specific conception of community. There is in modern society an available "pool" of existing communities, as well as singular principles on which new communities can be constructed, that tempt the autonomous person. Specific religious or psychological ideologies carried within the bosom of existing communities, for example, remove some of the protean burden of creating a generalized other and community from the shoulders of the autonomous. Because it is difficult to give birth to oneself, it is tempting to find and use ready-made templates.

Second, the would-be autonomous person does not eat abstract food, is not raised in an abstract family, does not have sexual relations with abstractions, and is not only a member of an abstract community. This individual is raised with others, eats and sleeps with them, forms alliances and interpersonal relationships, and is a member of groups and organizations. These experiences generate feelings of obligation, lead to a need for the satisfactions of social intercourse, and impose requirements. In short, the real experiences of real people tend to pull them away from pure autonomy and to embed them in less abstract organizations and communities.

Yet the would-be autonomous person is apt to feel considerable ambivalence toward such concrete ideological, interpersonal, organizational, and community attachments. Concreteness is comforting because it eases the constant burdens of self-definition. But the desire to construct oneself as one sees fit, which is so powerfully urged by American culture, makes it hard to yield to the temptation toward community and attachment. Community is appealing, but also frightening, for it threatens to subvert the person's capacity to construct a future of his or her own choosing and to replace it with a future dictated by others.

One response to this ambivalence is a tendency to construct the self in opposition to others and to the social restrictions they are perceived to impose. Wariness of the potential for confinement that lies in every attachment to others readily promotes a sense of the social world as filled with "rules" and "regulations." Ralph Turner's "impulsives," for example, exhibit this response when they conceive of the social world as a set of restrictive norms that threaten at every turn to submerge or overwhelm the "real self." Instead of a sense of attachment to a defining community and its *values*, there is an effort to remain free of restricting social *norms*.

Another response to ambivalence is narcissism. Resisting the appeal of others who offer something more concrete than an abstract quest for the future but who also threaten to control the individual, some who choose the strategy of autonomy have a proclivity to project the self onto the generalized other, and thus to be conscious of nothing more than the self. Where Turner's impulsives create a sense of opposition between self and society, narcissists find no perspective save their own from which to view self. Where exclusive identifiers find a well-developed, explicit community perspective to which they can fit themselves, narcissists see only their own perspective when they consult the social mirror.

Narcissism entails the imagination of a generalized other that resembles one's own tastes, wants, and ideals. It involves projecting the personal project upon the world, defining personal truth as community truth, and visualizing a community made up of others who are exactly like oneself. The result of narcissism is unhappiness, for to the extent that the individual seeks to imagine society only in his or her own image, that image tends to dissolve. There is nothing to confirm it, nothing to certify its accuracy or legitimacy, nothing to validate its satisfactions. Indeed, there can scarcely be a self under these conditions. Continuity and integration are undermined, for in the absence of external validation, every act is equally meaningful and therefore equally meaningless. There can be no basis for deciding what to do next when any possible act can be interpreted as contributing to one's personal project. And instead of an energizing tension between identification with a community and differentiation from others, there is only the self with which to identify and from which to differentiate.[8]

Short of opposition or narcissism, the would-be autonomous person seeks a whole self by identifying with an abstract community, feeling a sense of likeness with all human beings who share a similar commitment to autonomy. In the pathological case of narcissism, the would-be autonomous individual identifies only with self, feels a sense of likeness only with self, and has a culture that does not go beyond the boundaries of the self. Some make the social world, particularly the institutional world, a negative community, a generalized other whose praise is to be avoided and whose condemnation is evidence of success. But those who to one degree or another succeed at autonomy—and in the main they are able to do so because of their willingness to yield some degree of autonomy—are apt to feel themselves differentiated from the great mass of people who, in their eyes, have not achieved their state of grace. From the perspective of the autonomous person, most other people are slavish conformers, parochial, lacking in drive or purpose, or otherwise unsuccessful. The important point, of course, is that the successful maintenance of autonomy depends upon a contrast with those who have failed to be autonomous. If exclusives compare their sense of security and certainty with the loneliness, lack of direction, and idolatry of those who are not members, the autonomous compare their independent sense of self-worth and mastery with the conformity and dependence of others.

There is a crucial theoretical point here. Each American not only selects a particular type or mode of personal identity, but maintains it in part by imagining the other choices he or she might have made and rejecting them or rationalizing their rejection. People do not always develop their strategies in a highly self-conscious way, but they do seem to maintain them by self-conscious reference to contrasting modes. Religious fundamentalists need secular humanists as demons whose threatening presence strengthens their resolve. The inner-directed have conformists as their opposites, and they need them in order to maintain their conceptions of themselves. Impulsives have institutionals as a contrasting category of person to whom they can favorably compare themselves. This tendency to use opposite identity types as a support for one's own choice is probably more noticeable at the extremes than in the vast middle, but even among those who fall somewhere between the extreme strategies of exclusivity and autonomy there is a tendency to look at other identity types and be thankful that one has made a different choice (even while in many cases continuing to be tempted by another choice).

Autonomy thus fosters its own patterns of choice and attitudes as individuals confront the behavioral dilemmas posed by American culture. First, it is apt to view rebellion positively as a main symbol of autonomy, and conformity to any social demands as a symbol of its loss. In the face of the inescapable temptation to yield to identification with some community, and thus to conform to its dictates, the autonomous are frequently drawn either toward some form of rebellion (however symbolic) as a main technique of self-construction or toward the avoidance of any generalized other save for one projected by the needs and wishes of the self. And because such communities as the autonomous may construct in the search for a generalized other are either completely imaginary or dependent upon the mass media of communication as the principal social structure of community, there is little to hold the person to such communities for very long.

Second, autonomy fosters wariness of any roots, even though the autonomous have a variety of experiences that incline them to put down roots. To "leave"—whether by quitting a job, separating from a spouse, abandoning one personal project for another—comes to symbolize autonomy. "Leaving" is thus as self-conscious a choice for the autonomous as is "staying" for the exclusives. Because it is tempting to remain in place and to begin to compromise one's personal project by acceding to the wishes of others, "leaving" comes to be seen as a choice necessary to the integrity of the self.

Third, autonomy promotes a sense of independence from others, but always accompanied by covert inclinations or wishes to become involved and perhaps even dependent. Autonomy views the person as entitled to put his or her own needs ahead of the interests of others and asserts that one must, in order to remain true to oneself, sometimes make the painful choice of refusing to acknowledge the dependence of others upon one or even one's need to depend upon them. And the persistence of a belief that one must go it alone and the strength with which this belief is sometimes asserted masks an opposing inclination to throw in one's lot with others and make their purposes one's own.

Autonomy is thus an effort to face the dilemmas of choice fostered by American culture through the construction and maintenance of a personal identity and the strict subversion of social identity to it. It constructs an economy of the self in which the costs of isolation, uncertainty, and a sense of opposition to or alienation from social life are perceived as offset by the rewards of freedom, self-mastery, and independence. And as much as it is a way of perceiving the self, autonomy is also a way of perceiving community and society. It fosters the cognition of society as a stage on which the autonomous person may operate, in the company of other autonomous people, to construct a free and independent self. And it promotes a view of community as a place of real dangers to personal freedom and integrity and of uncertain rewards of approval and interpersonal contact.

The Pragmatic Strategy

Successful exclusivity and autonomy require dedicated efforts to suppress the opposing impulses to which American culture gives rise. To maintain a social identity rooted in a community and define personal identity as subsidiary to it requires an extreme commitment to that community. To construct a personal identity to which any social identity remains subsidiary one must seek autonomy with a vengeance, refusing commitments and involvements that might reduce this autonomy. Both exclusivity and autonomy require the construction and rigorous maintenance of a meaning system; to yield to the temptation of an opposite meaning system is to feel alienated from the chosen community or from the self under construction.

Most people find exclusivity and autonomy either beyond their reach or undesirable. Religious and ethnic exclusivists are prone to the temptations of the outside world, and many of them succumb. Social movements run their course—their leaders die, their goals are reached or superseded, other movements gain public favor—and leave their most devoted adherents stranded. Small towns and urban neighborhoods cannot command the loyalties of residents, who see and sense the freedoms that lie outside these domains even as they are comforted by the easy familiarity and certainty they foster. Achievement or celebrity elude the autonomous, or else taste less sweet than they were imagined. Self-actualization, partly because it is so ambiguous a goal, can always seem just out of reach. For a variety of reasons, people employing these strategies fall short of their mark, abandon or drift away from them, and seek less confining or demanding modes of self construction.

The exclusive identifier, for example, wants to remain within the boundaries of a quasi-organic community but finds society tempting and cannot remain entirely within the community of identification. Where does the person turn when a personal meaning system based entirely within a quasi-organic community begins to unravel, or when the person offends that community and is thus excluded from it?

Exclusively identifying Jews and Christians who stray from their respective religious and ethnic communities illustrate the possibilities. Beyond the boundaries of their exclusive communities lie more permissive and less demanding communities of Jews and Christians whose members are not isolated from the modern world and who, in a variety of ways, embrace it. The "traditional" Orthodox Jew who begins to stray, for example, can identify with the "modern" Orthodox movement and affiliate with a less traditional synagogue, with one of the other institutional varieties of Judaism (Conservative, Reconstructionist, or Reform), with the Jewish people as a whole, or with Israel. These are alternatives that permit compromise with the future-oriented, choice-laden, autonomous aspects of modern life even while preserving some of the security and certainty of the past, its traditions, and the security to be found within an enclosing community. The same may be said of fundamentalists, who have a variety of alternative versions of Christianity to which they can turn and in relation to which they can manage the ambivalence associated with modern life in ways that are less strenuous and confining than those involved in an exclusive identification.

In much the same way the person who has constructed a self by an exclusive attachment to a social movement can find ways of retreating into a less confining and demanding way of life. The revolutionary may change his or her mind about liberal reform, the radical environmentalist may join the Environmental Protection Agency, the student activist may enter politics. In such cases, the individual drifts away from an exclusive identification with a group, organization, cause, or community, and develops a moderate, less single-minded, and relatively more balanced orientation.

Movement away from exclusivity and toward a more balanced mode of identification is by no means the only possible response to the problematics of exclusivity. One alternative is a radical shift from one community of exclusive identification to another—migration, as it were, from one exclusive identity to another. The person who abandons the truth of religion, for example, may seek the truth of revolution. Others may seek to construct a self through rejection of the former exclusive identity. Many American ex-communists of the 1940s and 1950s provided a striking illustration of how to build a career and an identity on the rejection of a former identity. In essence, those who abandoned their earlier embrace of communism for a later vehement rejection of this movement migrated from one exclusive identity to its opposite.[9]

More typically, perhaps, those who once followed a strategy of exclusivity begin to attenuate their identification with the former community and to change their frame of reference, to imagine a community that is more inclusive, less demanding, less confining, and more able to satisfy those impulses that steer them toward choice and autonomy. Such individuals begin to feel a sense of attachment to a community that, while clearly important and central in the construction of a new personal meaning system, is less dominant than the former community and has more the character of a base from which the individual operates *in* society than of a shelter or refuge *from* society. To explore this strategy further it will be helpful first to consider those who abandon autonomy.

Where does the seeker of autonomy turn when it becomes too difficult to remain a solitary actor seeking success or "self-actualization" in a societal mode of membership and participation? The range of choices is wide; the person can turn to a circle of friends, a social movement, a long-neglected religious or ethnic tradition, a family, or some other social unit that can function as a community and provide a generalized other. The individual selects some group, organization, or commitment as a primary and ordering one, making it into a context for experiencing life in the communal mode. By doing so, the person shifts into a different mode of managing ambivalence, from attempting to suppress social identity altogether to admitting it into the personal system of meanings.

Thus, for example, the hard-driving entrepreneur who has sought only success and who has had contempt for anyone who would allow family, friends, and other social impediments to stand in the way begins to "soften," to make more time for family, for example, and make spouse and children more central in the construction of self. For such an individual the family may well become the context for experiencing life in the communal mode. Another person may begin to invest effort in neighborhood or city, making one of these social entities a community. Another may rediscover ethnic roots, relearning an identity that was consciously (or unconsciously) shed in childhood, or perhaps even one discarded by a previous generation.

In instances like these, a personal project becomes attached to a community, whether the very small and concrete community provided by the nuclear family, the more abstract community provided by neighborhood, or the very abstract community afforded by a social cause. To say that the personal project becomes attached to a community is to say that it becomes redefined, that the person finds a way of linking something that was formerly a project of the self to a community and its collective purposes. The successful business executive or entrepreneur, for example, begins to speak of "repaying a debt" to the community. In doing so, this person begins to link personal success to the welfare of others, redefining the personal project and thus simultaneously legitimating a past self and linking it to a new self.

So far I have looked at pragmatic identification as a refuge from the vicissitudes of exclusivity and autonomy. The task now is to approach the pragmatic strategy more directly as a form of identification that, regardless of how people get to it, has its own characteristics, its own problematics, its own ways of providing for continuity, integration, identification, and differentiation, and its own approach to the inherent ambivalence of modern life.

Pragmatic identification builds a personal meaning system in which the individual experiences self *both* in a community, which provides the principal supports but not the exclusive container of social identity, *and* in the larger society, which provides the main basis of personal identity. The community may be a quasi-organic community with which the person identifies less than exclusively (even though many of its members are exclusive identifiers); it may be some other social unit (a family, a social movement, a neighborhood, a work organization) with which the person identifies and that he or she treats as a context for life in the communal mode. Whatever the community, its hold over the person is partial and not total, and the social identity it affords must compete with a personal identity that is anchored in "society." For the distinctive mark of pragmatic identification is that the person repeatedly moves from one context to another—from community to society, from social identity to personal identity—and back again.

Pragmatic identification constructs the person as an individual in a community, rather than only as a member of a community or only as an individual. This strategy of self-construction thus requires the development and cultivation of a more or less coherent idea of self—that one is, for example, a "religious person," a "family man," a "liberal," "dedicated to the community," or "first and foremost a physician." The person is not any of these things exclusively, but rather the person is so "mainly," "primarily," "first," or "above all else." This idea, or "theory" of the self, links the activities of yesterday to those of today and tomorrow, makes the person whole, and provides for identification and differentiation.[10]

The pragmatic construction of self is achieved by taking the perspective of two generalized others. First, there is generally a community of principal identification, which provides the values, ideals, and standards of conduct in terms of which social identity is built. And second, there is the imagined perspective of the larger society, a much more abstract generalized other whose chief functions are to certify the legitimacy and validity of the person's pragmatic identification and to support personal identity. Continuity, integration, identification, and differentiation are achieved by managing a complex and often tenuous balance between a communal and societal mode of social participation.

Continuity in the self depends upon the way people connect their experiences, actions, and purposes from day to day, from year to year, and throughout their lives. Exclusives attempt to make connections by relating every act and experience to the purposes of a defining community; the autonomous attempt to connect everything to a personal project. Pragmatic identifiers have a more difficult task, for they are most alive to the inherent contradictions of modern life and wish to balance and compromise rather than exclude whole areas of experience or modes of action from consideration. The open reaches of a society in which one can become what one wishes are tempting, but so are the comforts of family, neighborhood, ethnic group, and other forms of community. Every act and experience, in its essence, seems linked to one or the other of these spheres: hard work advances one in society but may alienate the person from family; participation in familiar ethnic rituals is reassuring and warming, but may make one seem parochial to others and may be perceived as restricting opportunities for employment or mobility. The pragmatic identifier attempts to make a primary choice, but does so in a way that is not intended to preclude other involvements.

The problematics of continuity for pragmatic identifiers stem primarily from the conflicting claims that a variety of groups, organizations, and collectivities make on the person's time and energy, and from the wish to honor many of these claims. Where the exclusive can subvert everything to a community and its ideology and the autonomous can view every experience or act in relation to an over-riding purpose, the pragmatic identifier has to juggle not only investments of time and energy but investments of self, of identification. Where the exclusive knows what to do next and realizes what it will mean if he or she does not do it, because there is a real or imagined community that supplies solid guidance, the pragmatic identifier has a variety of things to do "next," and can find a rationale for doing each. Where the autonomous individual evaluates what he or she has done in relation to its contribution to a defining purpose, the pragmatist is often in the position of second-guessing, wondering whether a different course would have produced a better result. The underlying theme is one of ambivalence, of being pulled in competing directions, not only by the familiar contradictory cultural objects but by the concrete individuals, groups, organizations, and collectivities that embody and assert them.

Although this formulation perhaps over-emphasizes the conscious aspects of pragmatic identification, we can say that the pragmatic identifier, in selecting a particular community and making it the center but not the sovereign of the self, is looking for a way of resolving ambivalence so that day-to-day decisions can be made and rationalized. To define the self primarily in terms of work, for example, and to feel a sense of community predominantly with one's fellow workers, is to attempt to order the various situated identities that one assumes and sheds over time, to establish some principle that will settle questions of how much time one spends at work, whether one will honor its claims on one's energy, and how much it should be allowed to shape other areas of life, such as family. Identification with a work community also is an effort to fix the meaning of work, a meaning that is typically revealed in those encounters where the person must refuse to honor claims in other spheres. The professional whose identification is with the profession is able to spend less time with family because the professional community provides an ideology that explains and justifies professional demands. The busy lawyer or physician uses this ideology as a resource for motive talk, explaining to spouse and children why a vacation is out of the question or a family celebration will have to be missed.

It is possible, of course, for pragmatic identification to verge on autonomy, on the one side, and exclusivity, on the other. That is, the pragmatic strategy must be conceived as a rather broad one in which, at either of its extremes, pragmatic identifiers begin to resemble either exclusive or autonomous identifiers. Some professionals, for example, identify so thoroughly with their professions that, for all practical purposes, the profession becomes an exclusive focus, a quasi-organic community. Everything in life is seen through the eyes of the profession and the professional, and the professional meaning system is sufficient to explain and justify everything. Others find in their profession not a community of identification but merely a vehicle for the pursuit of autonomy; they seem to identify with the profession, but in fact have far more in common with the autonomous individual. Although pragmatic identification thus has a rather broad range, my focus here is on the ideal-typical "middle-of-the-road" pragmatic identifier.

The pragmatic identifier is frequently faced with dilemmas of choice and filled with ambivalence about what to do. But this ambivalence should not be viewed necessarily as debilitating, as a "problem," or as something that absorbs so much personal energy that it allows no time for other involvements. It may well be as much a source of creative tension as of anxiety. For the pragmatic identifier, the community of principal identification provides the sense of *purpose* on which the experience of continuity rests, but it is a sense of purpose that reaches beyond the community. Thus, for the individual who makes being Jewish the mainstay of identity, Jewish values provide not an end in themselves, but rather a framework into which a variety of other purposes and activities may be assimilated. There is some degree of tension between particularistic ethnic commitments and broader, more universal and "societal" commitments; and there may well be tension between the natural comfort one feels in being with other Jews and a desire to operate in a pluralistic society. But these tensions may be energizing-as well as debilitating. They may provide the impetus for imaginative solutions and creative intellect as well as for paralyzing indecision.

Pragmatic identification makes it possible to put the purposes of one sphere of life first and to make other purposes subsidiary to them, but it does not require the abandonment of other purposes. The pragmatic identifier can have "the best of both worlds," therefore, in the sense that some sense of community and of concrete attachment to others can be sustained at the same time as the person operates within the broader reaches of society. The pragmatic professional identifier finds a way (or tries to find a way) to integrate not only the "demands" but also the positive rewards of work and family, enlisting family members as a part of a support system that makes continued dedication to the profession possible, but also contributing to their individual and collective needs.

This last formulation points squarely at a major problem of pragmatic identification. From one standpoint, we see a rosy picture: the individual puts one sphere of life first, but does not try to deny the relevance or importance of other spheres; there is a stable social world—a work organization, for example—in which important activities take place and in which the self is confirmed as an actor on a societal stage; and there are other social worlds, such as the family and the local community, that are also important, to which a share of energies is devoted, and that provide for life in the communal mode. The problem, of course, is that others may not define the situation in the same way as the pragmatic identifier. The families of professionals notoriously feel deprived of the time, energy, presence, affection, and attention of the professional. And if the professional identifies chiefly with family, this may be a cause for concern among fellow professionals, who sense less professional commitment than they would like.

The crucial point is that pragmatic identifiers are always subject to pressures to identify more with some contexts and less with others. Whatever the pragmatic identifier's own feelings about the matter, others may well resist his or her choice of identification. Implicit in pragmatic identification is the idea that the individual has multiple identifications and multiple communities. Because many of these communities—whatever their structural nature, whether as organizations, primary groups, collectivities, quasi-organic communities, or whatever—are not merely artifacts of individual perception but have a collective life, they act *upon* the individual and do not always readily accept the degree of importance they are assigned by the individual.

It is the experience of cross-pressures from a variety of potential and actual communities that gives the life of pragmatic identifiers a quality of tension between the person and others. The exclusive identifier resolves tension by settling all issues of self and other through a commanding social identity rooted in the community of identification. The autonomous resolve tension by making "the other" so much an artifact of the imagination that there can scarcely be any tension. But the pragmatic identifier, who identifies partially with a variety of groups and organizations, even though mainly with one, is often not let alone by others. Families, communities, professions, ethnic groups, friends, and others demand more of the individual—more time and energy, more loyalty, more identification.

One of the characteristic ways in which this aspect of pragmatic identification is reflected in contemporary life is in discourse about "assertiveness" and "individuality." It is tempting to dismiss this discourse as a reflection of the narcissism and selfishness of contemporary Yuppies. Such a dismissal is a poor analysis, for a concern with assertiveness—worries about whether one is too easily swayed by others and about how one can possibly learn to assert oneself more effectively—is inherent in the pragmatic mode of identification. To the extent that the individual is open to a variety of communities and their purposes, he or she is subject to cross-pressures and so more or less constantly has to deal with them and to find some solid ground from which to do so.

Where is that solid ground? To some extent it comes from the mainstay community itself, which provides at least part of the wherewithal to resist some demands while acceding to others. But the very essence of pragmatic identification is to withhold absolute privilege from any single community of identification, even though the person does select one as more central than others. As a result, the pragmatic identifier must find solid ground not only in the mainstay community but also in some more independent and unique sense of self or personhood. This sense of individuality is qualitatively different from that of the exclusives and of the autonomous. The exclusives are individuals only within the context of a community and the social roles it provides; they are "unique" in their combination of roles. The autonomous feel so absolutely unique that individuality is not really in question. To be a fully autonomous member of society is to project oneself into the world so effectively that one is the only other with which one must be concerned. Pragmatic identifiers are concerned with their individuality, with their separateness from others and their capacity to make their own decisions, because they are the people who expose themselves to cross-pressures from the variety of communities with which they identify and from the societal pole as well. They talk about "assertiveness" because it is an integral part of their experience to feel the need to assert themselves.

The key words for pragmatic identifiers are thus "individuality" and "individualism," words that convey a sense of self as an individual who is in reasonable and legitimate ways unique, a separate being worthy of respect and decent treatment regardless of group membership or individual accomplishment. Against the oppressive demands of warm community and the frightening temptations of life in the societal mode, "individuality" is a position of compromise and "the individual" is the embodiment of the idea that the person can be both allied with others and apart from them, a loyal community member and an actor on a larger stage, both similar to others and in valued ways different from them.

"Individualism" is thus not a pathology of modern life but a necessary adaptation to it, and the contemporary critique of individualism is thus far wide of the mark in its condemnation of the excessive individualism of

American society. Individualism is an unavoidable and functional product of modern culture. Ideas about "individuality" and "individualism" provide a means of compromise between the interests of the individual and those of the community. "Individuality" based on a mainstay community is a way of finding community with others while also securing a degree of autonomy from them. "Individualism" as an ideology provides some insulation of the individual from social demands while avoiding the narcissism and solipsism of autonomy.

It is also "individuality" that assigns to discourse its crucial role in self-construction among pragmatic identifiers. What is the nature of this discourse and why is it so important?

The discourse of pragmatic identifiers can be understood in part by contrasting it with that of exclusive identifiers and the autonomous. Those who seek identity exclusively within a community engage in considerable discourse focused either on the relationship between individual conduct and the community's culture or on the differences between community members and outsiders. When individual acts become problematic, they are likely to be so because they violate community standards. Thus, in accounting for their actions, identifiers must show likeness with other community members and difference from outsiders in order to construct interpretations of their conduct that will prove acceptable to other community members. To the extent that such interpretations can be constructed, the individual's claim to be a community member in good standing will be upheld and his or her identity will thus be certified.

The autonomous also engage in discourse, but it is more likely to be self-stimulated than requested by others. Autonomy requires a personal project that becomes the standard by which the individual evaluates his or her actions. But since the project is personal and individual, the person alone has standing to evaluate how particular actions either contribute to or detract from the project. The autonomous will seek the approval of what audiences they can find or imagine, but in the last analysis applause provides only temporary comfort and no lasting certainty about the self. Thus, it seems likely that the autonomous are likely to carry on an internalized discourse and to act as prosecutor, defense, judge, and jury.

Pragmatic identifiers are in a peculiar position, for although they attach priority to one community, they are likely to be receptive to the demands of several communities to account for their actions in relation to community standards. And since they pursue individuality, although not the commanding project of the autonomous, they will also prosecute and judge themselves. They will seek signs of their individuality and be alert for the danger signs of excessive conformity to community pressures.

One result is that pragmatic identifiers are a ready market for discourse about the self. Exclusive identifiers have little need for externally created ideas about the self and its relation to society, for the relatively restricted world in which they seek to live has established its own view of the person and will devote its ideological apparatus to elaborating and promulgating it. And the autonomous likewise can dispense with the formulae of social scientists, psychologists, and social critics. Autonomy is its own answer to such questions. But the pragmatic identifier, who is exposed to cultural cross-pressures and thus has both personal and social identity mobilized, seeks solace in talk, and so is a good market for the scholarly and popular categories on which talk depends. Scholars' discourse about other-direction and identity, as well as journalists' discourse about Yuppies or the declining work ethic, is thus useful to the pragmatic identifier.

The practical value of such discourse lies first in its capacity for concrete representation of opposing cultural objects. The pragmatic identifier who feels in danger of being over-shadowed by a community of identification can take refuge in concern about other-direction or conformity. The pragmatic identifier who feels adrift because it is difficult to respond to several communities as well as to the larger society and maintain any coherent sense of self can take comfort in talk about identity and its vicissitudes or in the expression of concern about narcissism.

There is a sense in which such discourse about the self and its relation to society creates its own structure of communities, ephemeral and barely visible, to be sure, but nonetheless significant. Those who read and then talk to one another at cocktail parties or in church discussion groups about *Habits of the Heart*, for example, constitute a temporary community of those who recognize the dangers of excessive individualism and who thus steer themselves back toward a somewhat stronger commitment to community. This book, like others of its genre, will make few practicing converts to its theology of communitarianism, but it will tend to reinforce such communitarian sentiments as already exist in its readers. Perhaps more significantly, the analytical categories of such books concretize the fears of pragmatic identifiers and, in thus attaching specific labels to diffuse anxieties, may help to discharge them.

Popular discourse about "Yuppies" conducted under the auspices of *Time* and *Newsweek* has a similar effect. It seems unlikely that sermons in the pages of a news magazine will strongly shape the conduct of its flock, but it is not implausible to suggest that such discourse is a mild instrument of social control. If the pragmatic identifier fears too much autonomy as well as too little—and too much or too little community— talk about Yuppies provides a context in which limits may be set. The selfish, stylishly clad, BMW-obsessed Yuppie is a useful stereotype that helps define the limits of what is good and proper.

By the same token, the discourse of one or two generations ago, which focused on conformity and identity rather than upon selfishness and narcissism, also helped to define limits. The other-directed, organization-controlled "man in the grey flannel suit" of the 1950s embodied an opposite set of dangers to which the exclusives and autonomous could remain oblivious, but to which pragmatic identifiers had to remain attentive. Then it was in some ways the communitarian pole of American culture that seemed the greater danger and individualism the lesser, to the lay users if not the professional authors of the principal terms of discourse, and so talk focused on the former problem rather than the latter.

In many respects, the most important form of discourse is everyday motive talk, a genre well studied over the past several decades. Beginning with C. Wright Mills's early analysis of *vocabularies of motive,* those universes of discourse in which people talk about questioned and untoward conduct in an effort to restore social interaction to its intended course, social psychologists have explored a number of forms of motive talk. Disclaimers and accounts, for example, are prospective and retrospective methods for responding to real or potential challenges from others and thus fending off disruption in the first instance or smoothing it over in the second. Each offers an acceptable motive and claims legitimacy for an intended or completed act, and thus seeks to have the potential or actual challenger accept the act and leave the actor unchallenged. In accounts, for example, *excuses* seek to attribute questioned acts to causes outside the actor's control ("I was late to work because my child suddenly became ill"), and *justifications* challenge the challenger, in effect claiming acceptable motives for a reasonable act ("I know I've been spending a lot of time at the office lately, but there's no crime in doing one's best for one's family, is there?"). Disclaimers try to establish good motives for impending acts and thus avoid subsequent challenges. The *sin license,* for example, acknowledges the potential for legitimate challenge, but seeks to defuse it with a claim of other commitments or needs ("I know I have obligations as a mother, but I'm an individual too, and that's why I want a few days away from you and the children").[11]

Such modes of discourse invariably refer as much to the identities of those who use them as they do to the moral status of their acts or their relationship to challengers. In the most general terms, as social psychologists have conceived it, motive talk is an effort to preserve socially desirable identities. When social actors succeed in claiming legitimate or understandable motives for their acts, they also succeed in maintaining and reinforcing their identities. That is, they persuade others to see them, and they are enabled to see themselves, as individuals acting in socially desirable and approved ways, and thus to be identified with others and with shared conceptions of the good.

A distinction between social and personal identity—and the recognition of tension between the two, particularly in American society—calls for some modification of those conceptions of motive talk. First, we must recognize that motive talk frequently speaks not only to a gross distinction between desirable identities and undesired negative retypifications but to distinctions between one social identity and another or between personal and social identity. Each social context in which the pragmatic identifier interacts with others is a potential source of challenges to acts, not on the basis that they are wrong in some absolute sense but on the grounds that they are not the acts called for in that context. The worker is subject to censure for not coming in early enough, and alleges the prior claim of another context, the family, as an excuse. The professional cites the pressures of work and the desire to succeed on the family's behalf as the reason for absence from hearth and home. In such responses to challenge, individuals at least temporarily establish the priority of one social context and its associated identity over another context and its identity. Similarly, the husband or wife who claims the right to time away from the family on grounds of individuality is asserting, at least for the time being, the priority of personal over social identity.

Second, it is equally essential to understand that motive talk provides a temporary way to restore balance in the tightwire act of pragmatic identification. Exclusive identifiers and the autonomous seek the security of a solid platform from which to perform, but pragmatic identifiers live on the wire. An account or disclaimer functions as a balance pole to shift the person's center of gravity temporarily in one direction or the other, warding off the inclination to fall toward either social or personal identity. Thus, an assertion of individuality provides enough energy to sustain personal identity against the appeal of social identity or the assertion of its priority by another.

The social psychology of pragmatic identification thus seems to require an adroit use of motive talk. To say this is not, however, to argue that a high degree of self-consciousness underlies its use. Social and personal identities operate in large part at a motivational level; they shape sensitivities beneath the level of consciousness and are not necessarily formulated by the person in so many words. The motive talk we can observe is the surface manifestation of more complex and tumultuous underlying motivational states. We cannot directly observe the ambivalence that seems to characterize pragmatic identifiers, only the motive talk that continually arises as these individuals strive to respond to their own impulses and to the actual and imagined responses of others to them.[12]

It is in part the variability of motive talk—its tendency to tip the balance toward assertions of social identity at one moment and personal identity at another—that perhaps underlies the view that the late twentieth century has produced a new form of self, which Louis Zurcher has termed the *mutable self*. The portrait of a self that is always prepared to change its emphasis and orientation, to become what circumstances dictate that it must become, is an appealing theoretical construction. More than Riesman's conception of other-direction or Turner's conception of the impulsive self, both of which focus rather narrowly on a single criterion of differentiation, Zurcher's formulation is somewhat broader and recognizes the necessity of frequent, if not constant adaptation, to the vicissitudes of modern life. The mutable self is one way of depicting what I have called the pragmatic strategy of self-construction.[13]

Pragmatic identifiers thus hold themselves together by combining and balancing two views of themselves. On the one hand, day-to-day life is organized and directed by keeping one community paramount in mind as the community of reference and the source of the generalized other. One looks at oneself primarily from the vantage point of the family, for example, and sees oneself as a member of society whose selection of the family as a primary community is legitimate. On the other hand, because one is always subject to competing demands, there is a tendency to develop an image of oneself as an individual, as someone who lives in the company of others and who shares their goals, but also as one who is separate, deserving of consideration as an individual, in some ways unique, an object that has never before existed in the world. One's individuality, then, becomes as important a mark of place in the world as one's loyalty to a mainstay community; indeed, it is the attachment to the mainstay community that makes the individuality both necessary and possible. One sees oneself, from the vantage point of mainstay community and larger society alike, as an individual, as one who is like others and yet different from them.

The pragmatic identifier is thus rendered whole by acts of imagination that involve both membership and individuality, by the use of both a mainstay community and a larger society as generalized others who will confirm both a sense of belonging and a sense of separateness and uniqueness. Instead of an integral self that is held together by massive identification with a community or single-minded identification with an individual goal, there is an integral self that is more a piecemeal assembly, an ongoing project, an object that is constantly being edited and reworked, and that needs the reassurance of discourse about the self and its prospects. Wholeness is established by taking the perspectives of a variety of others: the imagined perspective of a mainstay community; the imagined perspective of other communities to which the person feels attached; the imagined perspective of the larger society. And the person feels whole not simply as a member of any particular community, but as a unique and separate individual.

Identification is thus a relatively complex matter for pragmatic identifiers. Such individuals feel "at home" in the community with which they mainly identify, but also in the variety of other contexts in which they participate and with which they feel some sense of identification. The person feels "like" a great many others rather than only a single category of others, capable of moving in several circles rather than one. As Joseph Gusfield points out, modern individuals—pragmatic identifiers in my terms—can to some extent pick and choose, now emphasizing the societal component of their identities and then selecting a more particular community.[14] Sometimes this selection is quite intentional, and at other times it is more a response to a particular situation than a self-conscious decision. Pragmatic identifiers now feel identified with their families, now with their occupations, now with a social movement. They feel most identified with and most at home in their mainstay community, and yet it is this sense of having a major purpose and a main community that makes it possible to work toward other purposes and to identify with others.

From whom does the pragmatic identifier feel different? In one sense, pragmatic identification encourages a sense of individuality in which the person feels different from all other human beings. Individuality, a sense of defining and unique essence or being, means that the person is like no other person. The sense of individuality toward which pragmatic identifiers tend operates in every social context to provide a counter-point (and a counter-weight) to the tendency of that context to draw the person toward identification.

Yet differentiation is also a complex matter. Within any given social context, the individual whose principal identification lies elsewhere feels differentiated not only by individuality but also by a difference of identification. The "family man" at work feels some sense of discomfort because others work harder and show more commitment, for example, but he can also feel some superiority over them because of his family commitment. Indeed, he may have to think of himself as a superior human being in order to counter their disapproval. The social movement participant who makes the movement a mainstay community can feel a sense of difference from others in the society, rooted to some extent in the feeling that he or she has a better vision of what the society should be or how life should be conducted. The contemporary peace activist, for example, feels not only a sense of community with other peace activists, but also a sense of difference from those who are, regrettably in the activist's view, oblivious to the truths the activist holds so dear.

Pragmatic identification thus fosters a difficult pattern of choices and attitudes as the person faces the dilemmas of conduct fostered by American culture, for this strategy takes the sometimes hazardous middle way. First, the impulse to conform is satisfied (and the fear of conformity somewhat attenuated) by the voluntary obligations to community the individual takes on. So long as the security of a community can be defined as chosen and its control seen as only partial and temporary, the person is able to identify strongly enough to sustain a sense of belonging and to define the self in terms of the community and its purposes. Under these circumstances, rebellion is apt to be sporadic and often symbolic, with individuals only threatening to leave, or leaving temporarily and then returning. The assertion of individuality—of a personal identity—is not a constant and defining project, but an occasional activity that seeks to restore a balance threatened by the claims of others.

Second, the pragmatic strategy provides for both staying and leaving because it encourages movement between communal and societal modes of social participation and thus between social and personal identity. By occasionally shifting and rearranging the hierarchy of identification with various communities, the pragmatic identifier has an experience of personal change that is the symbolic equivalent of leaving. By alternating between communal and societal modes of participation, the impulse to find greener pastures elsewhere is likewise permitted at least partial release. Yet the distance traveled is never very great, for the pragmatic identifier does not abandon one community, but only gives it lesser prominence, selecting another as the community of principal identification. Thus, pragmatic identifiers leave, but they also stay; they find greater rewards or fewer challenges elsewhere, yet elsewhere is not so far removed as to prevent a return.

Third, pragmatic identification cultivates a balance between independence and dependence. In the societal mode of participation, the person can construct a personal identity and thus maintain a sense of self as an independent actor on a large and open stage. In the communal mode of participation, the person can satisfy those apparently natural and inevitable impulses toward dependence upon others that are our common human legacy. Each mode of participation is available as a retreat from the other when the going gets rough: community offers haven to those injured during a sojourn in society, while the latter offers an escape route to those who feel confined by community.

Pragmatic identification is thus an effort to find a middle path between the opposing objects of American culture and to avoid the absolute behavioral choices it fosters. It constructs an economy of the self in which ambivalence—sometimes explicitly recognized and perhaps more often lurking in the motivational background—figures prominently. It fosters a view of the person as an individual in community, choosing to feel obliged to others but also free to shift loyalties and to act as an autonomous self and not only as an agent of community purposes. And it constructs the social world as a dual reality of community and society—as an assembly of supportive yet also confining others, of a free yet often frightening open social space.

Next . . .

The exclusive, autonomous, and pragmatic strategies of self-construction are theoretically derived ideal types. My goal in formulating them has not been to catalog exhaustively the range of personal experiences in contemporary American life, but to portray in broad theoretical strokes the alternatives open to people who live in this society. Such a view of self-construction must ultimately be subject to empirical test and revision, a task beyond the capacity of this book but nonetheless an important one that I hope this analysis will help stimulate.

The time has come for a summing up, for a review of the principal images and conclusions of my analysis and of their implications for the further study of the self and of American culture and society. This is the task of Chapter VII.

CHAPTER VII

In the Last Analysis

My goal in this book has been to reconstruct our view of the self and its relationship to American society. Major critical constructions of the American self have faltered in two key ways. By assuming that their major task is to account for changes in the self, many analysts have failed to recognize the divided nature of the culture, and so have merely expressed its main axes of variation rather than analyzing them. By making individualism their chief target, some critics have overlooked an important communitarian dimension of American culture. Moreover, the critics have relied on theoretical tools inadequate to their purposes. From Riesman's analysis of modes of conformity to Lasch's depiction of narcissism, the theoretical perspectives brought to bear on the analysis of the self have been either too limited in scope or ill fitted to the American experience. And the analysis that has most recently received wide attention, *Habits of the Heart*, seems to abandon theoretical rigor in favor of the sermon.

Social psychologists working in the symbolic interactionist tradition have developed a useful theory of the self, but they have done so with too little regard for the cultural foundations and implications of their work. They have wisely put the concept of identity at the center of their analysis of the self and given this concept a properly sociological emphasis. But in making role the major theoretical underpinning of identity, they have insufficiently stressed that the individual imaginations and collective constructions of the social order on which the self depends typically extend well beyond the situation and its roles and encompass images of both community and society. As a result, they have emphasized situated identity to the neglect of the biographical self, and so have failed to grasp the central problems of identity fostered by a culture divided along an individualistic-communitarian axis.

My goal has been to combine the major strengths of these largely separate traditions of analysis, and thereby also to avoid their weaknesses.

Although the critical tradition has often failed to move sufficiently far from participation in cultural discourse to portray the culture of which it is a part, it has at least called our attention to the problematics of self-construction. Its formulation of character types has typically relied on an excessively narrow conception of the concerns of ordinary people, and its frequent insistence on seeing these types in the context of social change has blinded it to the real dilemmas of choice people face as they construct themselves and their lives. But it has at least provided glimpses of the cultural objects that attract and repel. And, although social psychologists have only occasionally turned their attention to the cultural circumstances in which people construct identities, they have created the conceptual foundations on which we can build a more encompassing analysis of self-construction. In these final pages I want to review and amplify the basic ideas I have employed in my effort to reconstruct self theory.

Culture as the Human Environment

At the heart of my analysis is a dual effort to recapture the concept of culture for social psychology and to construct a useful analysis of American culture. Social psychologists of the self have typically approached their topic seemingly oblivious to culture, investigating the antecedents of self-esteem or the presentation of self under the assumption they would discover universal processes at a distinctive social psychological level of analysis. In my view, culture must be brought into the analysis if we are to discover and fully understand such processes.

To bring culture into the social psychology of the self requires a conception of culture, but finding a useful one is no small task. A view of culture as *meaning*—in whatever particular terms it is conceived—is appealing to the symbolic interactionist, as is an emphasis on the ubiquity and necessity of the *interpretation* of meaning as a key human activity. The problem with most interpretive approaches to culture, however, is that they treat meaning and interpretation extensively and imaginatively, but neglect the relationship between culture and conduct. And structuralist approaches to culture either ignore conduct completely or make the person a cultural robot. It is one thing to describe the meaningful world in which humans reside—to convey a rich sense of how they interpret events in this world or to show how constraining culture is. It is quite another matter, and for the social psychologist a very important one, to explain what people actually do.

Although both the interpretive and the symbolic interactionist traditions emphasize the centrality of meaning in human conduct, it is the latter that has been willing to risk attempting to explain what people do and to construct theories of human conduct that at least in principle make it possible to link meanings to actions. Hence, early in my consideration of culture as meaning I found it necessary to shift from an interpretive to an explanatory stance. To do so, I essayed a brief interactionist treatment of culture.

From the perspective of Mead's pragmatism, human beings live in a world of objects. They are not simply creatures with fixed sensitivities and capacities that cause them to respond to the stimuli that emanate from a fixed external world, but naturally active organisms whose capacity to invent and use symbols requires them consciously to designate that toward which they are acting. They do not attend merely to discrete and raw stimuli given in "nature," but to symbolically designated objects of conduct.

An object, as Mead intended the term, is a paradoxical thing. On the one hand, it is a resultant of human attention and activity, for whether we consider such tangible objects as a "meal" or more abstract objects like "freedom," the object requires an acting subject. Its meaning lies in the way people at any given moment are prepared to or actually do respond to it. Whether a meal is a hasty stoking of biological fires, an occasion for leisurely conversation, or the price of sexual favors depends on how it is regarded by those who eat it. Whether freedom is a cherished political fact or an illusion likewise depends on the stance human beings take toward their world. Objects are constituted by acts.

On the other hand, because objects are named and represent a variety of actions that may be undertaken toward them, they also "contain" meaning. They both invite conduct and constrain it, for when objects are sighted and named, they constitute an environment that subsequently affects what people can do or wish to do. The sight of a meal calls forth an impulse to eat, and in much the same way talk of freedom evokes a wish to enhance freedom and makes one conscious of constraint. The impulse to eat, which seems merely biological, is in fact much less biological than it seems, for the meal holds a great many meanings that have nothing to do with nutrition. The impulse to seek freedom, which appears not at all biological, is in fact much more so than it seems, for the hunger for this object may be experienced as keenly and as viscerally as that for food.

Objects thus exist because human beings individually and jointly act toward them; and, because they are named, they exist independently of any single individual and both evoke and constrain individual and joint acts. This relationship between human beings and their objects is thus one of mutual determinism, and it is so precisely in the sense that Mead and other pragmatists intended their more general image of mutual determination of organism and environment. That is, on the one hand it is the response capacities of the organism that determine its world, for only that to which the organism can in some way respond is a part of its effective environment. On the other hand, the environment has had a hand in shaping the sensitivities of the organism as they have evolved over time, and it is the source of events that evoke responses from the organism. The human world differs from that of other organisms because human beings have the capacity for complex symbolic responses. Thus, our responses constitute a different kind of world—a world of named objects—and not merely a world of stimuli. Nonetheless, in all cases the responses of the organism constitute the environment in which it lives; and the constituted environment in turn shapes the organism's responses to it.

It thus seems reasonable to conceive of *culture* as the environment—that is, the world of objects—in which human beings live, for, by doing so, we are better able to link *meaning* and *action*. Human beings live in a world of objects whose meanings they must designate before they can act. Because the events that befall human beings typically invite a variety of actions, they must designate objects before they can act, and sometimes they must choose between one object and another. In other words, a process of *interpretation* is inherent in human conduct, for to know what we want and how to act so as to get it, we must interpret the circumstances in which we find ourselves. But interpretation is not all there is to life; human beings do not simply search for meaning and interpret their world, but they act in and on it. They are drawn toward some objects, repelled by others, and in general engaged in individual and social projects.

To develop a pragmatist concept of culture as environment is also to recover a concept of *motivation*, of the underlying springs and motors that give direction and force to human conduct. Motivation is a concept symbolic interactionists have generally eschewed, and for good reason. Social psychologists have been too willing to posit such putatively universal motivations as "self-esteem" or "self-consistency," and in doing so to neglect the fact that these very terms are a part of culture. Recognizing that it is relatively easy to postulate invisible but underlying motivations to account for conduct in any way one wishes, interactionists have concentrated instead on the analysis of *motives*. That is, they have focused on what people say about themselves and their conduct—on the reasons, explanations, and interpretations they claim underlie their acts—and avoided coming to grips with underlying motivations. But although there are pitfalls in dealing with motivation, it is unavoidable that we do so.

The concept of culture as environing objects is an effort to incorporate motivation in a way that avoids the problems of the concept while acknowledging its importance. Conceived as a world of objects, culture is deeply implicated in human motivation. Although its objects are created and sustained only because human beings attend to and act toward them, they also constitute an external and constraining world that attracts attention and effort at the same time as it both facilitates and interferes with human acts. The human environment—culture—both mirrors and shapes people's sensitivities as they act in relation to it.

To make proper use of a concept of culture one must be alert to its complexities and built-in contradictions. Culture does not landscape the human world smoothly or harmoniously, but presents broken surfaces. Its objects, as often as not, invite opposite forms of conduct, both facilitating and interfering with any particular course the person might chart. Although particular cultures may appear as uniform worlds of objects and thus motivationally consistent, there are always opposing objects and hidden streams of conduct.

This is true of any culture, but it is especially true of American culture, which confronts its inhabitants with sharply and visibly opposed objects. Although the underside of a culture is often kept out of sight, breaking through mainly in times of crisis or in rituals of release from its constraints, the opposing objects of American culture are starkly visible. "Freedom," for example, attracts diverse efforts to become and be "free." But "authority" is an opposing object that is seldom far from view, even when attention is resolutely focused on freedom. To be "free" often means to overthrow or subvert authority; to exercise "authority" often means to subdue those who seek to extend their freedoms.

The result is that American culture fosters a considerable fund of ambivalence—cognitive, conative, and affective—that underlies and shapes the construction of self. It fosters a perception of many goals as mutually inconsistent, encourages opposing inclinations, and causes many objects to evoke contradictory sentiments and emotions. "Community," for example, is an object of desire, for it generates warm feelings of attachment to one's fellow human beings and of sharing a way of life and a world-view with them. But it is also an object of fear, since it often seems to exact conformity as the price of support. And it seems difficult for Americans to see "community" and "individuality" as mutually consistent goals. Instead, they are apt to feel torn between staying in a community and accepting its interpersonal supports or leaving it in order to find freedom and individuality. They are likewise apt to sense they must make difficult but necessary choices between conformity and rebellion and between dependence and independence.

This view of culture as the complex and divided human environment, and of American culture as fostering ambivalence, is the first necessary element in a reconstruction of our ideas about self and society. The failure to recognize the divided nature of the culture has led social theorists and critics into rather simplistic assertions of change in character, identity, and other foundations and experiences of self. The failure of social psychologists seriously to consider culture, and of symbolic interactionists to give motivation its proper due, has led to incomplete analyses of the forces that attract and repel human activity. The view of culture sketched in these pages affords a more useful way of characterizing the problematic linkage between person and society in the contemporary world.

Social Structure and the Self

The concept of culture draws our attention to the *ends* toward which human life is directed, but the reconstruction of our understanding of self and society requires an additional step. To portray the relationship between self and society requires a grasp of social structure as well as culture —of the way social life is organized as well as the ends toward which it is drawn. Here, again, two correctives must be applied. First, the conventional wisdom of sociology has interpreted modernity as a transition from community to society, and has therefore made its understanding of the modern self contingent on an analysis of social structure in which community has declined and society has become the dominant force. This interpretation needs revision. Second, although symbolic interactionists have well understood that the self's structure is shaped and constrained by social structure, their concept of social structure has been far too limiting, not only because it has seldom gone beyond the concept of role but also because it has failed to recognize the inherently opposing tendencies of modern life.

At the very heart of modernity lies an inherent conflict between communal and societal modes of social participation and self-construction. Modernity has widened the conceptual boundaries of social order beyond the local community to a more abstract unit, "society." In doing so, however, it has not merely substituted *Gesellschaft* for *Gemeinschaft*, but has instead made the contrast between the two a fundamental aspect of modern experience. Modern life offers the freedom of a larger, less confining stage where the person can perform with greater autonomy and a lessened sense of the weight of others. It encourages people to put behind them the communities of their birth and to build lives of their own design. But this larger stage, from which the past is banned and on which the future is everything, is also frightening and coercive. Moreover, it requires the abandonment of much that human beings seem inherently to value, including habitual forms of conduct that require only "tradition" to legitimate them as well as established ties to familiar and reliable others who value the whole person and not merely the role. The result is that "community," with its security *and* its constraints, remains an appealing construction of social order, even in the face of the opportunities and freedom of society.

A tension between communal and societal modes of social participation, inherent in the modern experience, is amplified by the axes of variation that characterize American culture. The preoccupation with "freedom," for example, encourages the pursuit of life in the societal mode, for it is a society of autonomous people that seems to offer the best route to the attainment of freedom. Yet whichever form of autonomy the person seeks and at whatever stage of the life cycle he or she does so, the communal mode of social life and its objects are not far from view. To seek the "freedom" of society is both to abandon the "security" and to escape the "constraints" of community. As a result, modernity in the American context is typically marked by a sense of life as confronting the person with difficult and painful dilemmas—whether to stay in a community or to leave it, whether to conform to its expectations or to rebel against them, whether to build an autonomous and independent self or to construct a self dependent upon (and depended upon by) others.

A view of social structure that emphasizes the ongoing tension between community and society as opposing ways of imagining the social order also enables us to escape some of the limitations of the symbolic interactionist approach to the self. By and large, symbolic interactionists who have theorized about and empirically studied the self have recognized the importance of social structure. Both in theory and research, symbolic interactionists and those sympathetic to this perspective have understood that the self is always implicated in a social world that provides the materials and the perspectives out of which the self is constructed.

Unfortunately, the conception of social structure on which social psychologists have relied has been severely limited. This is partly because the concept of role has occupied theoretical center stage. When social psychologists approach the study of identity, for example, they tend to do so with the concept of role uppermost in their minds. To think of an identity is to think of the role on which it is based. This is not surprising, given the greater interest of symbolic interactionists in situated identity than in the nature of identity beyond the immediate situation. Situated identities are largely based on roles, which provide the secure perspectives from which the self may be perceived by others and experienced by the person.

Of equal and perhaps even greater importance, social psychologists have been reluctant to theorize about social structure, and even more recent symbolic interactionist approaches to social structure have not been terribly helpful. Symbolic interactionist students of the self often adopt a relatively orthodox sociological reading of social structure, utilizing such common concepts as group, organization, bureaucracy, social class, and community in its depiction of social structure. Although Ralph Turner's analysis of institutional and impulsive forms of self-anchorage hints at a recognition of how problematic these conventional categories may be, other social psychologists have made little effort to revise the way we think of social structure.

Although symbolic interactionists over the past fifteen years have increasingly turned their attention to issues of social structure, their work has borne little fruit for social psychology. This is in part due to their tendency to regard social structure as the resultant of processes of social coordination and negotiation and to neglect the ways people construct social structure through acts of objectification and identification. The "negotiated order" perspective, for example, has been useful and fruitful for symbolic interactionism as a whole, but not especially for the analysis of the self. It captures the crucial fact that social order is not an objective given but an ongoing and constraining outcome of various processes and contexts of negotiation. It captures less well, however, the fact that the construction of self depends not only on the negotiation of role performances but also upon the naming of and identification with social units. Some of the latter provide the immediate contexts in which roles are made and situated identities are constructed, but others are larger, more abstract units whose social psychological implications have to do with social and personal identity.

In this book I have sought to apply a pragmatist approach to the conceptualization of social structure, emphasizing the practical significance of the way people construct social order and see themselves in relation to it. The construction of self, whether in the immediate situation or beyond, necessarily relies on the postulation of a social order, which provides the conceptual platform from which the self is named and perceived. Likewise, a social order is no thing standing autonomously by itself, but is named and perceived by human beings acting individually and jointly. In the immediate situation, a definition of the situation as a whole, with its resultant structure of named and familiar roles, provides the basis for the construction of order and of self. Beyond the immediate situation we must look at the way people construct social order in a larger context and over the longer term if we are to understand how they construct themselves.

My approach to this more encompassing construction of social order and self has emphasized the contrast between community and society. In accounting for the self beyond the immediate situation we must not look only to the conventional categories of social structure on which sociologists have relied, but also (and more importantly) to the conceptual distinctions people make as they survey themselves and their social worlds. The inherent conflict between communal and societal modes of social participation and identification underlies one of their key distinctions.

The most important implication of such a broadened view of social structure is that we must reformulate the conventional view that the structure of the self mirrors the structure of society. In modern society, at least in its American version, what the self mirrors is an ambivalent construction of social order. Instead of an orderly conceptual grasp of community *or* society as containing and defining social entities that provide the generalized other in relation to which the self may be constructed, Americans seem to construct a social order in which these entities are in conflict. The result is that the structure of the self—viewed in terms of identity, for example—cannot be described simply in terms of a hierarchy of roles or of group memberships. Although at any given moment there probably is some such hierarchy, it exists not because of an essentially static social structure to which the person has adapted, but as a temporary outcome of and solution to ambivalence.

The Nature of Identity

Finally, a better understanding of the fate of the contemporary self and the continued development of self theory both require revisions in the concept of identity. In a divided culture that fosters both communal and societal modes of social participation, much of our conceptualization of the self seems inadequate to the task of depicting the experience and prospects of the person.

One of the key contributions of symbolic interactionism to social psychology, as to sociology more broadly, has been its emphasis on the "situated" character of human conduct. In a discipline frequently inclined to "explain" conduct by citing the determining influence of an array of "variables," symbolic interactionists have steadily voiced their pragmatist conviction that conduct is assembled in real situations as people confront and attempt to solve problems. The social psychological dimension of their approach has stressed the situated character of the self. Against psychologists' accounts of stable needs and traits of the person that shape conduct, symbolic interactionists have posed an account of a self that takes its shape and color not only from its society but also, and crucially, from the particular situation in which it finds itself. The "self" of symbolic interactionism is one that acquires identity by adopting the perspective of a situated role, and by moving adeptly from one situation to another.

Although much is gained by emphasizing the situated nature of identity, something is also lost unless we apply two correctives. First, we must see identity not only as the product of a situation and its roles, but also as a resource the person brings to the situation. This more durable and transportable form of identity must be conceived as dual—as personal identity as well as the more familiar social identity. And it must be seen as a force that shapes social reality just as social reality has shaped it. Second, we must examine more carefully the problematic situations under which all forms of identity arise, and doing so requires us to theorize about both the specific dimensions of continuity, integration, identification, and differentiation, as well as about the social circumstances that make them problematic.

To conceive of identity as a resource is to emphasize the pragmatist vision of the organism as insurgent. Although we are surely products of our environment and of the history of our relations with it—and in this sense we "take" or "receive" identity from our social surroundings—we are also shapers of the environment. Our capacities to respond to and act upon the world help us to shape what the environment is or will become. In this sense, the personal and social identities that the person brings to each situation are environment-determining, and are not merely environmentally (that is, socially) determined. Social experience shapes and transforms social and personal identity, but the latter themselves shape and transform social experience.

Let me put this less abstractly. It is true that in each situation the person is confronted with objects and roles that shape both conduct and identity. When I walk into my office, many things—students, telephones, my colleagues, a stack of unread papers—clamor for my attention, and I am apt quickly to become engrossed in my professor role. In this sense, my social surroundings seem to determine who I am and what I do. They lead me to see myself as a professor and to find continuity in a series of professorial acts. For a time I *become* a professor.

But matters are not so simple. Although the simple mechanical fact of my stepping into an office does induce me to become what that office demands, only what I bring to that office equips me with the skill and energy to become it. It is not only that I have brought with me a host of memories and trained capacities that permit me to appear and act as a professor is supposed to act, although these are clearly essential. More fundamentally, it is because *I* have some conception of where this professor role fits in *my* overall scheme of things that I am able to engage in it and become it. Whatever energy, commitment, or fervor I bring on this particular occasion, I bring because of a larger and more durable sense of self. The larger communities with which I identify and the personal projects I have undertaken are what enable me to engage the professor role and identity.

Moreover, my personal and social identities do not only permit engrossment in a situated role, but shape the way I perform it, and thus indirectly shape the situations and social entities in which this role is located. If I identify strongly with the university and its purposes, my acts will have an energy and commitment that will not only validate my situated identity as a professor (and reinforce my social identity) but also shape the university itself. My actions will give life to the institution, and I will likely serve as a role model for others, not only representing to them how to be a professor but also personifying the university's values. If my loyalties lie elsewhere—if I seek fame in the profession and not the local context of the university—I will select those aspects of the professor role that advance my goals and give as little attention as I can get away with to those that do not. In making such a choice I will likewise shape the quality of the organization, and if enough of my fellow professors identify and act as I do, we will make the university lifeless.

To conceive of identity as a resource that influences the person's responses to situations and roles is thus to give more emphasis to the active, insurgent potential of human beings, to regard them as individual as well as social creatures, who seek identity in personal projects as well as community attachments. And to do this is to regard them as the creators of their world and not merely as its products. Neither image by itself is adequate, for neither an unrealistic vision of human beings as able to do and be whatever they choose nor a fatalistic account of persons as in thrall to society captures our essential human nature.

The necessity of a second corrective arises out of two common but fundamentally erroneous views of the modern world and its relationship to the past. In one of these views, modern people are portrayed as engaged in a self-conscious, incessant "quest" for identity. This perspective makes identity a key object of everyday conduct, which is to say, it makes the pursuit of identity not only an underlying motivational state but also a frequently verbalized motive. But such a view is erroneous, for identity is secured even when it is not sought, and the use of "identity" as an interpretive device to make sense of conduct for self and others is not a sure signal of the underlying motivation for the conduct.

In the other view, identity is portrayed as a problem unique to the modern world. In the organic communities of the past, according to this view, identities were taken for granted, perpetually secure, and fully social. Although such a romantic image holds a strong appeal for some of those interested in pursuing a communitarian agenda, it is strongly distorted. It is hard to think of an example of an organic community so free of conflict, so stable in its relationship to its environment, or so unchanging that it could provide a secure place for everyone, make every social identity appealing, and make every bit of human conduct an appropriate enactment of an identity. And even if one could conceive of a community in which every problem had been anticipated and solved, there is good reason to think that personal projects would still arise to supplement and sometimes challenge community needs and expectations. In creating a self, society creates self-interest and thus lays the basis for personal as well as social identity.

A conception of identity as a practical accomplishment helps us to escape these false visions of humankind. Like all human knowledge, identity arises out of human efforts to adjust to unexpected or problematic cir-cumstances. It need not be conceived either as a fundamental motivation or as a particular object of conduct. Instead, identity is at bottom a way of conceiving of something, a way of knowing a part of the world in order to be able to surmount the problems with which humans are regularly confronted.

A pragmatic conception of identity views it as a form of knowledge that facilitates adjustment to the world. Like all knowledge, identity can take a variety of forms, although the common focus of all is on the person's relation to the social world. For some individuals, identity is a tentative hypothesis, regularly adjusted to meet the test of facts. For others, it is a more systematic and rigorously maintained theory, changed or aban-doned only under great pressure. For others, perhaps, it is a matter of faith or dogma to which the person adheres even in the face of a reality that strongly contradicts it.

Whatever form it takes, and regardless of whether the focus is on social identity, personal identity, or some mixture of the two, the test of iden-tity lies in its use. Assertions about self and about the self's relationship to others arise out of difficulties of adjustment. To say that one's destiny lies with a religious or ethnic community, or that one must be true to oneself, or that one is going to spend less time in the rat race and more time with one's family is to assert a proposition about identity that can possibly be of use in facilitating adjustment. (It need scarcely be said that "adjustment" in this context does not mean a peaceful surrender to social constraints, tractability, tranquility, or the complete resolution of tension between the person and the social world. "Adjustment" fundamentally means the restoration of the person's capacity to act, to find and pursue purposes, to meet needs, to live, by overcoming those obstacles the envi-ronment continually throws in the path of conduct.) Such assertions are "true" to the extent that they work.

Pragmatically conceived, identity arises out of at least two different types of effort to meet problematic situations. On the one hand, there are the problematics of the human situation as a whole. The social organiza-tion of conduct (by situation, role, group, organization, etc.) is itself an important source of the problematic in everyday life. Roles provide for continuity in personal meaning, but transitions from one role to another disrupt that continuity. A role makes the person whole, but new roles re-quire new and different constructions of personal order. Moreover, while the social organization and control of conduct requires identification with others, it also requires some measure of differentiation. Social and personal identity are the practical results of human efforts to make sense of disrupted or challenged personal meaning—to link situations and their roles in some sensible way by identifying with a community or by conceiving of one's acts as the expression of personal projects, or both.

On the other hand, there are problematics that arise out of particular cultures and the social organizations that contain and perpetuate them. In the modern world people experience a strong contrast between an imagined or remembered world of organic community and the promised freedoms and rewards of life on a societal stage. Both community and society are inviting, and each provides in its own way for continuity, integration, identification, and differentiation. In American culture, this sense of contrast is heightened, and so is individual ambivalence. Here, a natural and inevitable tension between social and personal identity is emphasized, for there are strong temptations either to identify completely with a community or to eschew identification with any community.

As a practical accomplishment, identity is constructed by using strategies adapted to and occasioned by the particular circumstances in which the person finds himself or herself. Given the strong polarity of community and society fostered by American culture, and a corresponding sense of opposition between social and personal identity, three strategies are most salient in America. Exclusive identifiers construct the social world entirely on the model of organic community and find a predominantly social identity within its reassuring limits. The autonomous construct the social world entirely on the model of society, building a chiefly personal identity on its open stage. Pragmatists, recognizing the appeals of both community and society, seek a mode of adjustment in which both personal and social identity can more or less coexist.

Last . . .

In many small ways and a few large ways the ideas expressed in this book differ from what has come to be the conventional wisdom of social criticism and social psychology. As a pragmatist, I believe that the test of ideas lies in their use. Hence, it seems fitting to end this book not by insisting that my ideas are true, but rather by encouraging their use. Those concerned with the fate of the person in American society have, I hope, been led to question whether the standard critiques of individualism enable us to grasp this fate as well as they had thought and to consider the alternative vision sketched here. I hope that social psychologists have found useful theoretical stimulation and guidance for their continued study of the self and its relationship to society. And since the construction of self is too important a task to be left to professional social critics and social scientists, I hope that students and those outside the scholarly world who have labored through these pages have been stimulated to think about the self and its prospects in new ways.

NOTES

Chapter I

1. Representative among the "pessimistic" analyses of recent decades are the following: Robert N. Bellah, Richard Madsen, William M. Sullivan, Ann Swidler, and Steven M. Tipton, *Habits of the Heart: Individualism and Commitment in American Life* (Berkeley: University of California Press, 1985); Orrin E. Klapp, *The Collective Search for Identity* (New York: Holt, Rinehart, Winston, 1969); Thomas Kreilkamp, *The Corrosion of the Self* (New York: New York University Press, 1976); Christopher Lasch, *The Culture of Narcissism* (New York: Basic Books, 1978); Christopher Lasch, *The Minimal Self: Psychic Survival in Troubled Times* (New York: Norton, 1984); Philip Rieff, *The Triumph of the Therapeutic* (New York: Harper and Row, 1966); David Riesman, with Nathan Glazer and Ruel Denney, *The Lonely Crowd: A Study of the Changing American Character* (New Haven, Ct.: Yale University Press, 1950); Richard Sennett, *The Fall of Public Man* (New York: Knopf, 1977); Warren I. Susman, "Personality and the Making of Twentieth-Century Culture," pp. 271–290 in his *Culture as History* (New York: Pantheon, 1984); Lionel Trilling, *Sincerity and Authenticity* (Cambridge, Mass.: Harvard University Press, 1972); Ralph H. Turner, "The Real Self: From Institution to Impulse," *American Journal of Sociology* 81 (March 1976): 989–1016; Allen Wheelis, *The Quest for Identity* (New York: Norton, 1958); William H. Whyte, *The Organization Man* (New York: Simon and Schuster, 1956).

2. Whyte, *Organization Man*.

3. Riesman *et al.*, *Lonely Crowd*.

4. Wheelis, *Quest for Identity*; Klapp, *Collective Search for Identity*.

5. Turner, "Real Self."

6. Trilling, *Sincerity and Authenticity*; Susman, "Personality and the Making"; Sennett, *Fall of Public Man*; Lasch, *Culture of Narcissism* and *Minimal Self*; Rieff, *Triumph of the Therapeutic*.

7. See Donald Meyer, *The Positive Thinkers: Religion as Pop Psychology from Mary Baker Eddy to Oral Roberts* (New York: Pantheon, 1980); Charles A. Reich, *The Greening of America* (New York: Random House, 1970); Carl Rogers, *Client-Centered Therapy* (Boston: Houghton Mifflin, 1951); Carl Rogers, *A Way of Being* (Boston: Houghton Mifflin, 1980).

8. Bellah *et al.*, *Habits of the Heart*, pp. 32–35.

9. See, for example, Richard Hamilton and James D. Wright, *The State of the Masses* (New York: Aldine, 1986); R. D. Rosen, *Psychobabble: Fast Talk and Quick Cure in the Era of Feeling* (New York: Atheneum, 1977); Edwin

Schur, *The Awareness Trap: Self-Absorption Instead of Social Change* (New York: Quadrangle-New York Times, 1976); Philip Slater, *The Pursuit of Loneliness* (Boston: Beacon, 1974); Ralph H. Turner, "Is There a Quest for Identity?" *Sociological Quarterly* 16 (Spring 1975): 148–161; Joseph Veroff, Elizabeth Douvan, and Richard Kulka, *The Inner American: A Self-Portrait from 1957 to 1976* (New York: Basic Books, 1981).

10. See Irving Howe, *The American Newness* (Cambridge, Mass.: Harvard University Press, 1986) for an analysis of American culture in the era of Emerson and Hawthorne.

11. See Meyer, *Positive Thinkers.*

12. Emile Durkheim, *The Division of Labor in Society*, trans. George Simpson (Glencoe, Ill.: Free Press, 1964).

13. George Herbert Mead, *The Philosophy of the Act* (Chicago: University of Chicago Press, 1938).

14. Lewis O. Saum, *The Popular Mood of Pre-Civil War America* (Westport, Ct.: Greenwood, 1980).

15. For an excellent sociological discussion of the frontier, see Lee J. Cuba, *Identity and Community on the Alaskan Frontier* (Philadelphia: Temple University Press, 1987), chap. 1.

16. Kai T. Erikson, *Everything in Its Path* (New York: Simon and Schuster, 1976), pp. 79–84. I will, however, modify Erikson's conception by moving it toward a more explicitly pragmatist conception of culture.

17. The analysis of American culture developed here, and especially in Chapter III, has been influenced by numerous authors. In addition to those cited elsewhere, the following have been especially influential: Sacvan Bercovitch, *The American Jeremiad* (Madison: University of Wisconsin Press, 1978) and *The Puritan Origins of the American Self* (New Haven, Ct.: Yale University Press, 1975); Rowland Berthoff, *An Unsettled People: Social Order and Disorder in American History* (New York: Harper and Row, 1971); Rex Burns, *Success in America: The Yeoman Dream and the Industrial Revolution* (Amherst: University of Massachusetts Press, 1976); John Cawelti, *Apostles of the Self-Made Man* (Chicago: University of Chicago Press, 1965); Joseph Featherstone, "John Dewey and David Riesman: From the Lost Individual to the Lonely Crowd," pp. 3–39 in Herbert Gans, Nathan Glazer, Joseph R. Gusfield, and Christopher Jencks, eds., *On the Making of Americans: Essays in Honor of David Riesman* (Philadelphia: University of Pennsylvania Press, 1979); Conal Furay, *The Grassroots Mind in America: The American Sense of Absolutes* (New York: New Viewpoints, 1977); Philip Greven, *The Protestant Temperament: Patterns of Child-Rearing, Religious Experience, and the Self in Early America* (New York: Knopf, 1977); R. W. B. Lewis, *The American Adam: Innocence, Tragedy, and Tradition in the Nineteenth Century* (Chicago: University of Chicago Press, 1955); Harriet Martineau, *Society in America* (New York: Saunders and Otlay, 1837); John J. McDermott, *Streams of Experience: Reflections on the History and Philosophy of American Culture*

(Amherst: University of Massachusetts Press, 1986); David M. Potter, *People of Plenty: Economic Abundance and the American Character* (Chicago: University of Chicago Press, 1954); Rieff, *Triumph of the Therapeutic*; Alexis de Tocqueville, *Democracy in America*, ed. Phillips Bradley (New York: Vintage, 1945); and, not least, the novels of Sinclair Lewis.

Chapter II

1. Clifford Geertz, *The Interpretation of Cultures* (New York: Basic Books, 1973), p. 5.

2. This formulation relies upon but also to some degree broadens Mead's conception of the "problematic situation," since it suggests that discourse—which entails both self-consciousness and explicit awareness of social objects—occurs not only when a line of conduct is unexpectedly blocked or impeded but also when it is unexpectedly facilitated.

3. See Helmut R. Wagner, ed., *Alfred Schutz: On Phenomenology and Social Relations* (Chicago: University of Chicago Press, 1970), pp. 79–122.

4. The works I have chosen for examination have in one way or another reached a general audience, either as best-selling books or through college instruction, and thus are works that have had maximum cultural resonance.

5. Ralph H. Turner, "The Real Self: From Institution to Impulse," *American Journal of Sociology* 81 (March 1976): 989–1016.

6. *Ibid.*, p. 991.

7. *Ibid.*, pp. 991–992.

8. Quotations in this and the next paragraph are from *ibid.*, pp. 992–993.

9. Lionel Trilling, *Sincerity and Authenticity* (Cambridge, Mass.: Harvard University Press, 1972).

10. Warren I. Susman, "Personality and the Making of Twentieth-Century Culture," pp. 271–290 in his *Culture as History* (New York: Pantheon, 1984).

11. David Riesman, with Nathan Glazer and Ruel Denney, *The Lonely Crowd: A Study of the Changing American Character* (New Haven, Ct.: Yale University Press, 1950). Citations in the discussion that follows are to the paperback abridged edition, with new preface (New Haven, Ct.: Yale University Press, 1961).

12. Riesman *et al.*, *Lonely Crowd*, p. 4.

13. *Ibid.*, p. 11.

14. *Ibid.*, p. 15, italics in original omitted.

15. *Ibid.*, p. 16.

16. *Ibid.*, p. 21.

17. *Ibid.*, pp. 241–260.

18. See, for example, Carl N. Degler, "The Sociologist as Historian: Riesman's *The Lonely Crowd,*" *American Quarterly* 15 (Winter 1963): 483–497, and Seymour Martin Lipset, *The First New Nation* (New York: Basic Books, 1963).

19. Allen Wheelis, *The Quest for Identity* (New York: Norton, 1958), p. 17.

20. *Ibid.*, p. 18.

21. *Ibid.*, p. 19.

22. *Ibid.*, p. 128.

23. *Ibid.*, p. 129.

24. *Ibid.*, p. 85.

25. Richard Sennett, *The Fall of Public Man* (New York: Knopf, 1977); Christopher Lasch, *The Culture of Narcissism* (New York: Basic Books, 1978). See also Peter Marin, "The New Narcissism," *Harper's Magazine*, October 1975, pp. 45–50.

26. Lasch, *Culture of Narcissism*, p. 5.

27. *Ibid.*, pp. 9–10.

28. *Ibid.*, p. 10.

29. *Ibid.*, p. 12.

30. *Ibid.*, p. 37.

31. In this sense the claim of the authors of *Habits of the Heart* that there is scarcely any language available to Americans save that of individualism is simply wrong.

32. For an elaboration of the latter point see John P. Hewitt, "Review Essay on *Five Bodies: The Human Shape of Modern Society* by John O'Neill," *Symbolic Interaction* 9 (Fall 1986): 276–280.

33. Mead's views are presented in George Herbert Mead, *Mind, Self, and Society* (Chicago: University of Chicago Press, 1934). For a contemporary exposition see John P. Hewitt, *Self and Society: A Symbolic Interactionist Social Psychology* (4th ed.; Boston: Allyn and Bacon, 1988).

34. Anselm L. Strauss, ed., *George H. Mead: On Social Psychology* (Chicago: University of Chicago Press, 1964), intro.

35. Joseph R. Gusfield, "On the Sociological Reality of America," in Herbert Gans, Nathan Glazer, Joseph R. Gusfield, and Christopher Jencks, eds., *On the Making of Americans: Essays in Honor of David Riesman* (Philadelphia: University of Pennsylvania Press, 1979), p. 48.

36. *Ibid.*, p. 51.

37. Erving Goffman, *The Presentation of Self in Everyday Life* (New York: Doubleday, 1959).

38. *Ibid.*, pp. 252–253.

39. For a discussion of early twentieth-century discourse in this vein see Susman, "Personality and the Making," pp. 276–284.

40. Carl Rogers, *Client-Centered Therapy* (Boston: Houghton Mifflin, 1951).

41. Carl Rogers, *Carl Rogers on Personal Power* (New York: Delacorte, 1977), p. 7.

42. *Ibid.*, p. 240.

43. *Ibid.*, p. 244.

44. *Ibid.*, p. 246.

45. *Ibid.*, p. 248, italics in original.

46. *Ibid.*, pp. 266–267.

47. *Ibid.*, p. 272.

Chapter III

1. The analysis of culture proposed here is in part an effort to emphasize the importance of the human agent—of what some would call "the subject"—in human affairs. Unlike structuralist and poststructuralist views of culture, which seek to rule out any notions of individual agency, a pragmatist analysis necessarily incorporates a view of the conscious, acting, resisting subject as well as of the world of obdurate objects that constrains human beings. For an excellent analysis of how pragmatism differs from various forms of structuralism, see Eugene Rochberg-Halton, *Meaning and Modernity: Social Theory in the Pragmatic Attitude* (Chicago: University of Chicago Press, 1986), chap. 3.

2. Mead's analysis of these concepts is found in several places, but especially important are his *Mind, Self, and Society* (Chicago: University of Chicago Press, 1934) and *The Philosophy of the Act* (Chicago: University of Chicago Press, 1938).

3. This view of culture was initially developed in Randall G. Stokes and John P. Hewitt, "Aligning Actions," *American Sociological Review* 41 (October 1976): 838–849.

4. The mutual determination of organism and environment is a main premise of pragmatism. An organism's environment is, effectively, that to which it pays attention and to which it can respond, and so the environment is in some sense "determined" by the organism. But the attention and interest of the organism are the product of an evolutionary (or learning) history, and so the organism is also "determined" by the environment.

5. Kai T. Erikson, *Everything in Its Path* (New York: Simon and Schuster, 1976), p. 81.

6. *Ibid.*, p. 82.

7. See Kristin Luker, *Abortion and the Politics of Motherhood* (Berkeley: University of California Press, 1984).

8. Erikson, *Everything in Its Path*, p. 83.

9. A highly visible effort to interpret American culture—*Habits of the Heart* by Robert N. Bellah, Richard Madsen, William M. Sullivan, Ann Swidler, and Steven M. Tipton (Berkeley: University of California Press, 1985)—well illustrates this point. The authors are so wedded to the assumption that this is a culture of individualism that they remain blind to evidence from their own interviews that American individualism is countered by powerful ideas of responsibility and community. Indeed, like many other sociological critiques of American culture, theirs is better viewed as an illustration of American culture than as an analysis of it. For various appraisals of this book see Charles H. Reynolds and Ralph V. Norman, eds., *Community in America: The Challenge of Habits of the Heart* (Berkeley: University of California Press, 1988). In this volume, Jeffrey Stout's cri-

tique ("Liberal Society and the Languages of Morals," pp. 127–146) is particularly cogent. Herve Varenne's *Americans Together: Structured Diversity in a Midwestern Town* (New York: Teachers College Press, 1977), which Bellah and associates approvingly cite, although they seem not to have learned from it, more realistically depicts the cultural meanings that guide American life, and my work has profited considerably from it.

10. Like other portrayals of American culture, including those examined in the previous chapter, mine may seem excessively shaped by a middle-class and perhaps also male perspective. Two arguments may be mounted in defense of the approach I have taken. First, although social class, as well as ethnicity, religion, and other variables, surely affects the way people respond to culture, I believe there is an American culture shared across these social divisions, and it is this shared culture I seek to describe. Second, axes of cultural variation often correspond to social divisions of class or gender. Hence, what may in one sense appear as the very different cultures of different social classes or of men and women may, in fact, stem from the axes of variation characteristic of American culture as a whole.

11. The social construction of American adolescence is well revealed in books of advice to parents. See, for example, Haim Ginott, *Between Parent and Teenager* (New York: Macmillan, 1969).

12. On middle age and its vicissitudes see Daniel J. Levinson, *The Seasons of a Man's Life* (New York: Knopf, 1978).

13. David H. Fischer, *Growing Old in America* (New York: Oxford University Press, 1977).

14. Richard D. Brown, "Modernization and the Modern Personality in Early America, 1600–1865: A Sketch of a Synthesis," *Journal of Interdisciplinary History* 2 (1972): 207–209.

15. Lewis O. Saum, *The Popular Mood of Pre-Civil War America* (Westport, Ct.: Greenwood, 1980).

16. Erik H. Erikson, *Childhood and Society* (2nd ed.; New York: Norton, 1958), p. 293.

17. *Ibid.*

18. *Making It* by Norman Podhoretz (New York: Random House, 1967) is one of the more vivid portrayals of movement from an ethnic to a wider social world.

19. The classic sociological work on this form of status politics is Joseph R. Gusfield's *Symbolic Crusade* (Urbana: University of Illinois Press, 1963).

20. See, for example, Philip Slater, *The Pursuit of Loneliness* (Boston: Beacon, 1974).

Chapter IV

1. Although sociologists have begun to refer to a "post-modern" era (perhaps to some extent in reaction to literary and artistic "post-modernism"), this term

seems to me usually ambiguous, often pretentious, generally premature, and probably a better indicator of the nature of modern culture than a tool for analyzing "post-modern" culture. Michael R. Wood and Louis A. Zurcher, among others, have even written of a "postmodern self" in their book, *The Development of a Postmodern Self: A Computer-Assisted Analysis of Personal Documents* (Westport, Ct.: Greenwood, 1988). Here, too, the ambiguity of conceptualization leads one to regard their analysis more as a document of the modern experience than as an analysis of it. Hence I have stayed with the term "modern" in this book. My use of the word "modern," of course, refers to *sociological* modernity and not to "modernism" as a cultural movement.

2. My analysis of community has profited especially from three sources: Lee J. Cuba, *Identity and Community on the Alaskan Frontier* (Philadelphia: Temple University Press, 1987), chap. 6; Joseph R. Gusfield, *Community* (New York: Harper and Row, 1975); and Dennis Wrong, "The Idea of 'Community': A Critique," pp. 254–263 in Irving Howe, ed., *Twenty-Five Years of Dissent: An American Tradition* (New York: Methuen, 1979).

3. My goal here is to construct a pragmatist, symbolic interactionist approach to social structure. Without denying the external and constraining nature of groups, organizations, social classes, institutions, and the society they form, the position I take here is that social order is a construction of reality as well as an external and objective fact. This should not be taken to mean that the social order is whatever members think it to be. Nor should it be taken to imply that human beings are driven by the prospect of anomie to construct any reassuring sense of order. Instead, a sense of social order arises out of a pragmatic effort to make sense of one's surroundings in the service of both individual and collective purposes. For a partial review of symbolic interactionist treatments of social structure and an elaboration of social order as a construction of reality, see John P. Hewitt, *Self and Society: A Symbolic Interactionist Social Psychology* (4th ed.; Boston: Allyn and Bacon, 1988).

4. The phrase "organic community," which is widely used in the literature of community, is used here to designate an ideal type. Few contemporary communities and not many historical ones closely resemble the ideal.

5. Raymond Williams, *Keywords: A Vocabulary of Culture and Society* (New York: Oxford University Press, 1976), p. 66.

6. *Ibid.*

7. Charles H. Cooley, *Human Nature and the Social Order* (New York: Scribners, 1902).

8. After writing the following discussion of social roles, I became aware of an excellent discussion along similar lines. See George Arditi, "Role as a Cultural Concept," *Theory and Society* 16 (July 1987): 565–591.

9. A critical theorist might argue that this conception of role is, in fact, one of the ways sociologists unwittingly reinforce the invasion and control of the indi-

vidual by the corporation and the state. That is, by making individuals into bundles of disconnected roles and acting as if this were the natural state of human affairs, sociologists make into "human nature" what is the specific and distorted nature of humankind under capitalism. This argument has some merit, for sociological ideas do at once reflect and reinforce prevailing ideas about the world. But it is an incomplete and therefore unconvincing analysis, for it fails to consider that there is more than one tradition of social thought, including critical theory itself, that resists this interpretation of person and role. Modern culture seems to spawn radical theories of individualism and critical sociological theorizing as much as it does the more orthodox sociological theorizing about role that I have been discussing. If the latter reflects and reinforces culture, so do the former.

10. See Charles H. Page, "Bureaucracy's Other Face," *Social Forces* 25 (1946): 88–95, and Peter M. Blau and W. Richard Scott, *Formal Organizations* (San Francisco: Chandler, 1962).

11. See, for example, Ralph H. Turner, "Role-Taking: Process versus Conformity," in Arnold M. Rose, ed., *Human Behavior and Social Process* (Boston: Houghton Mifflin, 1962), pp. 20–40.

12. Tamotsu Shibutani, *Society and Personality* (Englewood Cliffs, N.J.: Prentice-Hall, 1961), pp. 324–331.

13. William J. Goode, "A Theory of Role Strain," chap. 4 in his *Explorations in Social Theory* (New York: Oxford University Press, 1973), and Robert K. Merton, "Sociological Ambivalence," in his *Sociological Ambivalence and Other Essays* (New York: Free Press, 1976).

14. See Marion J. Levy, *The Structure of Society* (Princeton, N.J.: Princeton University Press, 1951).

15. See, for example, John O'Neill, *Five Bodies: The Human Shape of Modern Society* (Ithaca, N.Y.: Cornell University Press, 1985), pp. 82–90.

16. Ralph Waldo Emerson, "The American Scholar," pp. 52–70 in *The Collected Works of Ralph Waldo Emerson*, ed. Robert E. Spiller and Alfred R. Ferguson, vol. 1 (Cambridge, Mass.: Harvard University Press, 1971).

17. *Ibid.*, p. 52.

18. *Ibid.*, p. 53.

19. *Ibid.*, p. 56.

20. *Ibid.*

21. *Ibid.*, pp. 56–57.

22. *Ibid.*, pp. 69–70.

23. The American longing for the past is starkly evident in the widely popular social criticism that focused on dying, death, and the funeral industry in contemporary America. Elisabeth Kubler-Ross's *On Death and Dying* (New York: Macmillan, 1969) is a good example, for although its main focus is on a psychoanalytical account of the contemporary stages of dying, it rests in part on an idealized portrayal of dying in the past. "The best America is yet to come" was the slogan of the 1988 Democratic presidential candidate, Michael Dukakis.

24. Two brief qualifiers are in order here. First, complex and difficult issues are raised whenever we speak of people "wishing" or "desiring" certain feelings of "security" or "certainty." To speak of modern people as seeking the communal mode of social participation and its accompanying feelings is to speak elliptically —that is, to gloss over important issues of motive and motivation. These matters will be considered in detail in the following chapter. Second, although the organic community is often expressed or visualized as a moral ideal, there is no reason to assume that it has ever existed in the form in which sociologists have described it. Just as sociologists have lamented the decline or transformation of the self, so they also have lamented the decline of organic community. But this form of community is as much a moral ideal of sociologists as of anyone else; there is no reason to assume that it is grounded in the reality of the past. It is, instead, grounded in a moral interpretation of that reality.

25. Robert N. Bellah, Richard Madsen, William M. Sullivan, Ann Swidler, and Steven M. Tipton, *Habits of the Heart: Individualism and Commitment in American Life* (Berkeley: University of California Press, 1985), p. 72.

26. *Ibid.*

27. Arlie R. Hochschild, *The Unexpected Community* (Englewood Cliffs, N.J.: Prentice-Hall, 1973).

28. The sociological study of the emotions and their relation to organized social life has developed considerably in recent years. A broad review of the literature may be found in Steven Gordon, "The Sociology of Sentiments and Emotion," pp. 562–592 in Morris Rosenberg and Ralph H. Turner, eds, *Social Psychology: Sociological Perspectives* (New York: Basic Books, 1982). The concept of "emotion work" comes from Arlie R. Hochschild, "Emotion Work, Feeling Rules, and Social Structure," *American Journal of Sociology* 85 (November 1979): 551–575.

29. See Tamotsu Shibutani, "Reference Groups as Perspectives," *American Journal of Sociology* 60 (1955): 562–569, and Ralph H. Turner, "Role-Taking, Role-Standpoint, and Reference Group Behavior," *American Journal of Sociology* 61 (1956): 316–328.

30. Ralph H. Turner and Lewis M. Killian, *Collective Behavior* (3rd ed.; Englewood Cliffs, N.J.: Prentice-Hall, 1987), p. 4.

31. *Ibid.*

32. See John P. Hewitt, "Symbolic Interactionism and the Study of Communication," pp. 1–37 in Thelma McCormack, ed., *Culture, Code, and Content Analysis: Studies in Communication*, vol. 2 (Greenwich, Ct.: JAI Press, 1982).

Chapter V

1. See Donald L. Carveth, "Psychoanalysis and Social Theory: The Hobbesian Problem Revisited," *Psychoanalysis and Contemporary Thought* 7 (1984): 43–98 for a view of Freudian theory more sympathetic to a symbolic interactionist perspective.

2. The literature on identity is vast. For an excellent account of the introduction and transformation of this concept in sociology, see Andrew J. Weigert, "Identity: Its Emergence Within Sociological Psychology," *Symbolic Interaction* 6 (Fall 1983): 183–206. Major symbolic interactionist (and closely linked) analyses of identity include the following: Peter J. Burke and Judy Tully, "The Measurement of Role/Identity," *Social Forces* 55 (1977): 881–897; Peter J. Burke, "The Self: Measurement Requirements from an Interactionist Perspective," *Social Psychology Quarterly* 43 (1980): 18–29; Peter J. Burke, "The Link Between Identity and Role Performance," *Social Psychology Quarterly* 44 (1981): 83–92; Nelson Foote, "Identification as the Basis for a Theory of Motivation," *American Sociological Review* 26 (1951): 14–21; Erving Goffman, *Stigma: Notes on the Management of Spoiled Identity* (Englewood Cliffs, N.J.: Prentice-Hall, 1963); George J. McCall and J. L. Simmons, *Identities and Interactions* (rev. ed.; New York: Free Press, 1978); Gregory P. Stone, "Appearance and the Self: A Slightly Revised Version," pp. 187–202 in Gregory P. Stone and Harvey A. Farberman, eds., *Social Psychology Through Symbolic Interaction* (2nd ed.; New York: Wiley, 1981); Anselm L. Strauss, *Mirrors and Masks: The Search for Identity* (Glencoe, Ill.: Free Press, 1959); and Sheldon Stryker, *Symbolic Interactionism: A Social Structural Version* (Menlo Park, Calif.: Benjamin/Cummings, 1980). Recent efforts to examine identity in its social and historical context include Roy F. Baumeister, *Identity: Cultural Change and the Struggle for Self* (New York: Oxford University Press, 1986); Joseph A. Kotarba and Andrea Fontana, eds., *The Existential Self in Society* (Chicago: University of Chicago Press, 1984); Roland Robertson and Burkart Holzner, eds., *Identity and Authority* (London: Basil Blackwell, 1979); Andrew J. Weigert, J. Smith Teitge, and Dennis W. Teitge, *Society and Identity: Toward a Sociological Psychology* (New York: Cambridge University Press, 1986); and Louis A. Zurcher, *The Mutable Self: A Self-Concept for Social Change* (Beverly Hills, Calif.: Sage, 1977).

3. Stone, "Appearance and the Self," p. 188.

4. Social psychologists of the self who have focused on self-esteem and self-image *have* been more attentive to this dimension. See, for example, the work of Morris Rosenberg: *Society and the Adolescent Self-Image* (Princeton, N.J.: Princeton University Press, 1965); Morris Rosenberg, *Conceiving the Self* (New York: Basic Books, 1979); and Gregory C. Elliot, "Self-Esteem and Self-Consistency: A Theoretical and Empirical Link Between Two Primary Motivations," *Social Psychology Quarterly* 49 (1986): 207–218.

5. See Stryker, *Symbolic Interactionism*, chap. 3. For another statement of Stryker's structural version of symbolic interactionism and its relation to other approaches to role theory see Sheldon Stryker and Anne Statham, "Symbolic Interactionism and Role Theory," pp. 311–378 in Gardner Lindzey and Elliot Aronson, eds., *Handbook of Social Psychology* (New York: Random House, 1985).

6. Erving Goffman, *Encounters* (Indianapolis: Bobbs-Merrill, 1961), p. 6.

7. See John P. Hewitt, *Self and Society: A Symbolic Interactionist Social Psychology* (4th ed.; Boston: Allyn and Bacon, 1988), pp. 79–85.

8. For the classic analysis of role conflict and strain see William J. Goode, "A Theory of Role Strain," *American Sociological Review* 25 (1960): 483–496, which also appears as chap. 4 of his *Explorations in Social Theory* (New York: Oxford University Press, 1973).

9. Tamotsu Shibutani, *Society and Personality* (Englewood Cliffs, N.J.: Prentice-Hall, 1961), pp. 324–331.

10. The distinction between *conventional* and *interpersonal* roles clearly has particular utility in modern society, where, on one hand, individuals are free to associate with one another outside of the boundaries of conventional roles and, on the other hand, there is a circulation of individuals through particular roles, so that one does not necessarily interact repeatedly with the same individual in the performance of any particular role. There is, in other words, a heightened awareness of the distinction between the person and the role. We attribute behavior to *both* person *and* role, and we are aware of relationships as being influenced by both formal role requirements and those expectations and obligations built up between people as a result of their interaction. In this sense, the distinction between conventional and interpersonal roles merely ratifies an experience that, while not exclusive to modern life, is more characteristic than in the world of organic community.

11. The conceptual distinction between *motive* and *motivation*, although confusing because of the similarity of the terms, is nonetheless important. It stems especially from a classic essay by C. Wright Mills: "Situated Actions and Vocabularies of Motive," *American Sociological Review* 5 (October 1940): 905–913. A discussion can be found in Hewitt, *Self and Society*, pp. 116–118.

12. Erving Goffman, *The Presentation of Self in Everyday Life* (New York: Doubleday, 1959).

13. In the discussion of identity from this point on I give most attention to the person's social and personal identity in his or her own eyes. It is nonetheless the case that either form of identity is as much a matter of placement (or acceptance) by others as it is of the person's own claims.

14. See Mills, "Situated Actions and Vocabularies of Motive."

15. See Erving Goffman, "Role Distance," pp. 85–152 in his *Encounters*.

16. See John P. Hewitt and Randall G. Stokes, "Disclaimers," *American Sociological Review* 40 (February 1975): 1–11; Marvin Scott and Stanford Lyman, "Accounts," *American Sociological Review* 33 (December 1968): 46–62; and Randall G. Stokes and John P. Hewitt, "Aligning Actions," *American Sociological Review* 41 (October 1976): 838–849.

17. There is little agreement among symbolic interactionists as to what the term "personal identity" means; my approach draws from the tradition, but also departs from it in some respects. For other uses, see Goffman, *Stigma*; McCall and

Simmons, *Identities and Interactions*; and David A. Snow and Leon Anderson, "Identity Work Among the Homeless," *American Journal of Sociology* 92 (May 1987): 1336–1371.

18. George Herbert Mead, *Mind, Self, and Society* (Chicago: University of Chicago Press, 1934), pp. 173–178, 192–200, 209–213, 273–281.

19. See William James, *The Principles of Psychology* (New York: Henry Holt, 1890), chap. 10: "The Consciousness of Self." James's analysis of self and identity holds up remarkably well a century after its creation.

20. The phrase "world-open" is that of Peter L. Berger and Thomas Luckmann in *The Social Construction of Reality* (New York: Doubleday Anchor, 1967), and it is their view Carveth criticizes.

21. Carveth, "Psychoanalysis and Social Theory," p. 82.

22. See Helmut R. Wagner, ed., *Alfred Schutz: On Phenomenology and Social Relations* (Chicago: University of Chicago Press, 1970), pp. 116–122.

23. For several studies of "the existential self" see Kotarba and Fontana, eds., *Existential Self in Society*.

Chapter VI

1. This discussion is intended as a way of depicting the main *strategies* of self-construction in contemporary life, and not as a literal description of character or personality "types." It is interesting, however, that even in this work, in which I have taken pains to show the cultural resonance of various typologies of self, the construction of yet another typology proves impossible to resist. To depict a culture at odds with itself, it seems, one must portray those who personify its opposing moments. My use of "pragmatic" to designate one of the three strategies may seem strange for a "pragmatist." All three strategies are "pragmatic" in the sense that all human acts are efforts to adjust to or modify the environment. Here I use the term in its ordinary sense of "practical"—not practical in the sense of "unprincipled," but in the sense of seeking to avoid ideological and other kinds of extremes. The term "strategy" also requires some qualification. Although the term implies self-consciously chosen and carefully charted paths toward social and personal identity, the motivational reality is more complex. People choose paths, but they also stumble across or drift into them. In the analysis that follows, self-conscious choice and maintenance of a strategy seems more a characteristic of exclusivity and autonomy than of the pragmatic strategy.

2. It should be evident from the discussion of the separation of membership and identification in Chapter IV that not all who are members of a particular religious group are exclusive identifiers. In this and other illustrations in this chapter, I do not assume that the members of any social group or category share uniform levels of identification, or that membership implies any identification whatsoever.

3. There are, to be sure, several varieties of Orthodox Jews, ranging from more

"modern" to more "traditional." For an excellent account of everyday life in a "modern" Orthodox synagogue (and a characterization of the modern-traditional distinction) see Samuel C. Heilman, *Synagogue Life: A Study in Symbolic Interaction* (Chicago: University of Chicago Press, 1976), chap. 1. For an excellent discussion of Jewish identity and of the varieties of Jewish response to modernity, see Steven M. Cohen, *American Modernity and Jewish Identity* (New York: Tavistock, 1983), especially chaps. 1 and 2.

4. There is no effort or intent here to *explain* the theology of Christianity as the result of a quest for identity or for the construction of community. Rather, the theology makes Jesus available as a figure around whom a community and a social identity can be constructed under particular modern conditions.

5. See Robert K. Merton, *Social Theory and Social Structure* (Glencoe, Ill.: Free Press, 1957).

6. See Lawrence Kohlberg, "State and Sequence: The Cognitive-Developmental Approach to Socialization," in David Goslin, ed., *Handbook of Socialization Theory and Research* (Chicago: Rand-McNally, 1969).

7. See George Herbert Mead, *Mind, Self, and Society* (Chicago: University of Chicago Press, 1934).

8. The similarities—but also the differences—between this analysis and that of Christopher Lasch in *The Culture of Narcissism* (New York: Basic Books, 1978) are crucial and demand some comment. The quest for autonomy easily turns into narcissism, for where there is an identity of self with the generalized other, where the person identifies only with self and is differentiated from all others, there is, in fact, *no* self, or at best an attenuated self. But this approach to narcissism is a theoretically more satisfying one than Lasch's for several reasons. First, where Lasch uses narcissism as his sole metaphor for understanding the culture, my analysis shows it to reflect only one extreme of the culture, the other extreme being excess identification with community. Second, Lasch sees narcissism as originating in the decline of authority and in the experiences of childhood; but narcissism, which is a less widespread phenomenon than Lasch imagines, is continuously generated by the circumstances under which some people choose to construct themselves. Third, this approach to narcissism brings it closer to "selfishness"; that is, the social mechanisms that produce selfishness (interest only in individual goals and purposes) are also those that produce narcissism (projection of the self as the generalized other).

9. There is not space here to explore every strategy of self-construction; *migration* and *rejection* are two strategies that provide alternatives to the mainstay strategy for those who abandon exclusivity or autonomy.

10. Seymour Epstein has argued persuasively for the recasting of "self-concept" as "self-theory," an approach that is in some ways close in spirit to my characterization of pragmatic identification. In Epstein's terms, a self-theory is "a theory that the individual has unwittingly constructed about himself as an experiencing,

functioning individual, and it is a part of a broader theory which he holds with respect to his entire range of significant experience." But where his "self-theory" is defined largely in psychological terms—it is the person's theory of *self*—I conceive the pragmatic strategy of identification as a theory of both self and society. The pragmatic strategy, like the exclusive and autonomous strategies, is a theory driven by fundamental ideas about where one fits in society and community as well as basic notions about what one *is* as a human being. See Seymour Epstein, "The Self-Concept Revisited: Or, a Theory of a Theory," *American Psychologist* 28 (May 1973): 404–416; also see his "The Self-Concept: A Review and the Proposal of an Integrated Theory of Personality," pp. 82–132 in Ervin Staub, ed., *Personality: Basic Issues and Current Research* (Englewood Cliffs, N.J.: Prentice-Hall, 1980).

11. See C. Wright Mills, "Situated Actions and Vocabularies of Motive," *American Sociological Review* 5 (October 1940): 904–913; Marvin Scott and Stanford Lyman, "Accounts," *American Sociological Review* 33 (December 1968): 46–62; John P. Hewitt and Randall G. Stokes, "Disclaimers," *American Sociological Review* 40 (February 1975): 1–11.

12. Many symbolic interactionists would find any discussion of motivation, as opposed to motive, objectionable, on the grounds that we can attend only to what is directly observable and must eschew any "motive mongering," that is, any temptation to substitute hypothetical hidden motivations for announced and observable motives. But if we are to take Mead's pragmatism seriously, we must attend to—and by and large this means we must theorize about—the *sensitivities* of human beings and their impulses seeking release. In other words, we must theorize about motivation, and that is what we are doing when we postulate social and personal identity.

13. See Louis A. Zurcher, *The Mutable Self: A Self-Concept for Social Change* (Beverly Hills, Calif.: Sage, 1977). Also see Zurcher, "The Bureaucratizing of Impulse: Self-Conception in the 1980s," *Symbolic Interaction* 9 (Fall 1986): 169–178.

14. Joseph R. Gusfield, *Community* (New York: Harper and Row, 1975).

BIBLIOGRAPHY

Arditi, George. "Role as a Cultural Concept." *Theory and Society* 16 (July 1987): 565–591.

Baumeister, Roy F. *Identity: Cultural Change and the Struggle for Self*. New York: Oxford University Press, 1986.

Bellah, Robert N., Richard Madsen, William M. Sullivan, Ann Swidler, and Steven M. Tipton. *Habits of the Heart: Individualism and Commitment in American Life*. Berkeley: University of California Press, 1985.

Bercovitch, Sacvan. *The American Jeremiad*. Madison: University of Wisconsin Press, 1978.

———. *The Puritan Origins of the American Self*. New Haven, Ct.: Yale University Press, 1975.

Berger, Peter L., and Thomas Luckmann. *The Social Construction of Reality*. New York: Doubleday Anchor, 1967.

Berthoff, Rowland. *An Unsettled People: Social Order and Disorder in American History*. New York: Harper and Row, 1971.

Blau, Peter M., and W. Richard Scott. *Formal Organizations*. San Francisco: Chandler, 1962.

Brown, Richard D. "Modernization and the Modern Personality in Early America, 1600–1865: A Sketch of a Synthesis." *Journal of Interdisciplinary History* 2 (1972): 201–228.

Burke, Peter J. "The Link Between Identity and Role Performance." *Social Psychology Quarterly* 44 (1981): 83–92.

———. "The Self: Measurement Requirements from an Interactionist Perspective." *Social Psychology Quarterly* 43 (1980): 18–29.

Burke, Peter J., and Judy Tully. "The Measurement of Role/Identity." *Social Forces* 55 (1977): 881–897.

Burns, Rex. *Success in America: The Yeoman Dream and the Industrial Revolution*. Amherst: University of Massachusetts Press, 1976.

Carveth, Donald L. "Psychoanalysis and Social Theory: The Hobbesian Problem Revisited." *Psychoanalysis and Contemporary Thought* 7 (1984): 43–98.

Cawelti, John. *Apostles of the Self-Made Man*. Chicago: University of Chicago Press, 1965.

Cohen, Steven M. *American Modernity and Jewish Identity*. New York: Tavistock, 1983.

Cooley, Charles H. *Human Nature and the Social Order*. New York: Scribners, 1902.

Cuba, Lee J. *Identity and Community on the Alaskan Frontier*. Philadelphia: Temple University Press, 1987.

Degler, Carl N. "The Sociologist as Historian: Riesman's *The Lonely Crowd*." *American Quarterly* 15 (Winter 1963): 483–497.

Durkheim, Emile. *The Division of Labor in Society*, trans. George Simpson. Glencoe, Ill.: Free Press, 1964.

Elliot, Gregory C. "Self-Esteem and Self-Consistency: A Theoretical and Empirical Link Between Two Primary Motivations." *Social Psychology Quarterly* 49 (1986): 207–218.

Emerson, Ralph Waldo. *The Collected Works of Ralph Waldo Emerson*, ed. Robert E. Spiller and Alfred R. Ferguson, vol. 1. Cambridge, Mass.: Harvard University Press, 1971.

Epstein, Seymour. "The Self-Concept: A Review and the Proposal of an Integrated Theory of Personality." Pp. 82–132 in Ervin Staub, ed., *Personality: Basic Issues and Current Research* (Englewood Cliffs, N.J.: Prentice-Hall, 1980).

———. "The Self-Concept Revisited: Or, a Theory of a Theory." *American Psychologist* 28 (May 1973): 404–416.

Erikson, Erik H. *Childhood and Society*. 2nd ed. New York: Norton, 1958.

Erikson, Kai T. *Everything in Its Path*. New York: Simon and Schuster, 1976.

Featherstone, Joseph. "John Dewey and David Riesman: From the Lost Individual to the Lonely Crowd." Pp. 3–39 in Herbert Gans, Nathan Glazer, Joseph R. Gusfield, and Christopher Jencks, eds., *On the Making of Americans: Essays in Honor of David Riesman* (Philadelphia: University of Pennsylvania Press, 1979).

Fischer, David H. *Growing Old in America*. New York: Oxford University Press, 1977.

Foote, Nelson. "Identification as the Basis for a Theory of Motivation." *American Sociological Review* 26 (1951): 14–21.

Furay, Conal. *The Grassroots Mind in America: The American Sense of Absolutes*. New York: New Viewpoints, 1977.

Gans, Herbert, Nathan Glazer, Joseph R. Gusfield, and Christopher Jencks, eds. *On the Making of Americans: Essays in Honor of David Riesman*. Philadelphia: University of Pennsylvania Press, 1979.

Geertz, Clifford. *The Interpretation of Cultures*. New York: Basic Books, 1973.

Goffman, Erving. *Encounters*. Indianapolis: Bobbs-Merrill, 1961.

———. *The Presentation of Self in Everyday Life*. New York: Doubleday, 1959.

———. *Stigma: Notes on the Management of Spoiled Identity*. Englewood Cliffs, N.J.: Prentice-Hall, 1963.

Goode, William J. *Explorations in Social Theory*. New York: Oxford University Press, 1973.

———. "A Theory of Role Strain." *American Sociological Review* 25 (1960): 483–496.

Gordon, Steven. "The Sociology of Sentiments and Emotion." Pp. 562–592 in Morris Rosenberg and Ralph H. Turner, eds., *Social Psychology: Sociological Perspectives* (New York: Basic Books, 1982).

Greven, Philip. *The Protestant Temperament: Patterns of Child-Rearing, Religious Experience, and the Self in Early America.* New York: Knopf, 1977.

Gusfield, Joseph R. *Community.* New York: Harper and Row, 1975.

———. "The Sociological Reality of America." Pp. 41–62 in Herbert Gans, Nathan Glazer, Joseph R. Gusfield, and Christopher Jencks, eds., *On the Making of Americans: Essays in Honor of David Riesman* (Philadelphia: University of Pennsylvania Press, 1979).

———. *Symbolic Crusade.* Urbana: University of Illinois Press, 1963.

Hamilton, Richard, and James D. Wright. *The State of the Masses.* New York: Aldine, 1986.

Heilman, Samuel C. *Synagogue Life: A Study in Symbolic Interaction.* Chicago: University of Chicago Press, 1976.

Hewitt, John P. "Review Essay on *Five Bodies: The Human Shape of Modern Society* by John O'Neill." *Symbolic Interaction* 9 (Fall 1986): 276–280.

———. *Self and Society: A Symbolic Interactionist Social Psychology.* 4th ed. Boston: Allyn and Bacon, 1988.

———. "Symbolic Interactionism and the Study of Communication." Pp. 1–37 in Thelma McCormack, ed., *Culture, Code, and Content Analysis: Studies in Communication,* vol. 2 (Greenwich, Ct.: JAI Press, 1982).

Hewitt, John P., and Randall G. Stokes. "Disclaimers." *American Sociological Review* 40 (February 1975): 1–11.

Hochschild, Arlie R. "Emotion Work, Feeling Rules, and Social Structure." *American Journal of Sociology* 85 (November 1979): 551–575.

———. *The Unexpected Community.* Englewood Cliffs, N.J.: Prentice-Hall, 1973.

Howe, Irving. *The American Newness.* Cambridge, Mass.: Harvard University Press, 1986.

James, William. *The Principles of Psychology.* New York: Henry Holt, 1890.

Klapp, Orrin E. *The Collective Search for Identity.* New York: Holt, Rinehart, Winston, 1969.

———. *Heroes, Villains, and Fools: The Changing American Character.* Englewood Cliffs, N.J.: Prentice-Hall, 1962.

Kohlberg, Lawrence. "State and Sequence: The Cognitive-Developmental Approach to Socialization." Pp. 347–480 in David Goslin, ed., *Handbook of Socialization Theory and Research* (Chicago: Rand-McNally, 1969).

Kotarba, Joseph A., and Andrea Fontana, eds. *The Existential Self in Society.* Chicago: University of Chicago Press, 1984.

Kreilkamp, Thomas. *The Corrosion of the Self.* New York: New York University Press, 1976.

Kubler-Ross, Elisabeth. *On Death and Dying*. New York: Macmillan, 1969.

Lasch, Christopher. *The Culture of Narcissism*. New York: Basic Books, 1978.

———. *The Minimal Self: Psychic Survival in Troubled Times*. New York: Norton, 1984.

Levy, Marion J. *The Structure of Society*. Princeton, N.J.: Princeton University Press, 1951.

Lewis, R. W. B. *The American Adam: Innocence, Tragedy, and Tradition in the Nineteenth Century*. Chicago: University of Chicago Press, 1955.

Lipset, Seymour Martin. *The First New Nation*. New York: Basic Books, 1963.

Luker, Kristin. *Abortion and the Politics of Motherhood*. Berkeley: University of California Press, 1984.

Lukes, Steven. *Individualism*. New York: Harper and Row, 1975.

Marin, Peter. "The New Narcissism." *Harper's Magazine*, October 1975, pp. 45–50.

Martineau, Harriet. *Society in America*. New York: Saunders and Otlay, 1837.

McCall, George J., and J. L. Simmons. *Identities and Interactions*. Rev. ed. New York: Free Press, 1978.

McDermott, John J. *Streams of Experience: Reflections on the History and Philosophy of American Culture*. Amherst: University of Massachusetts Press, 1986.

Mead, George Herbert. *Mind, Self, and Society*. Chicago: University of Chicago Press, 1934.

———. *The Philosophy of the Act*. Chicago: University of Chicago Press, 1938.

Merton, Robert K. *Social Theory and Social Structure*. Glencoe, Ill.: Free Press, 1957.

———. *Sociological Ambivalence and Other Essays*. New York: Free Press, 1976.

Meyer, Donald. *The Positive Thinkers: Religion as Pop Psychology from Mary Baker Eddy to Oral Roberts*. New York: Pantheon, 1980.

Mills, C. Wright. "Situated Actions and Vocabularies of Motive." *American Sociological Review* 5 (October 1940): 905–913.

O'Neill, John. *Five Bodies: The Human Shape of Modern Society*. Ithaca, N.Y.: Cornell University Press, 1985.

Page, Charles H. "Bureaucracy's Other Face." *Social Forces* 25 (1946): 88–95.

Podhoretz, Norman. *Making It*. New York: Random House, 1967.

Potter, David M. *People of Plenty: Economic Abundance and the American Character*. Chicago: University of Chicago Press, 1954.

Reich, Charles A. *The Greening of America*. New York: Random House, 1970.

Reynolds, Charles H., and Ralph V. Norman, eds. *Community in America: The Challenge of Habits of the Heart*. Berkeley: University of California Press, 1988.

Rieff, Philip. *The Triumph of the Therapeutic*. New York: Harper and Row, 1966.

Riesman, David. *Individualism Reconsidered*. Repr. New York: Free Press, 1964.

Riesman, David, with Nathan Glazer and Ruel Denney. *The Lonely Crowd: A*

Study of the Changing American Character. New Haven, Ct.: Yale University Press, 1950.

Robertson, Roland, and Burkart Holzner, eds. *Identity and Authority*. London: Basil Blackwell, 1979.

Rochberg-Halton, Eugene. *Meaning and Modernity: Social Theory in the Pragmatic Attitude*. Chicago: University of Chicago Press, 1986.

Rogers, Carl. *Carl Rogers on Personal Power*. New York: Delacorte, 1977.

———. *Client-Centered Therapy*. Boston: Houghton Mifflin, 1951.

———. *A Way of Being*. Boston: Houghton Mifflin, 1980.

Rose, Arnold M., ed. *Human Behavior and Social Process*. Boston: Houghton Mifflin, 1962.

Rosen, R. D. *Psychobabble: Fast Talk and Quick Cure in the Era of Feeling*. New York: Atheneum, 1977.

Rosenberg, Morris. *Conceiving the Self*. New York: Basic Books, 1979.

———. *Society and the Adolescent Self-Image*. Princeton, N.J.: Princeton University Press, 1965.

Rosenberg, Morris, and Ralph H. Turner, eds. *Social Psychology: Sociological Perspectives*. New York: Basic Books, 1982.

Sarbin, Theodore R., and Karl E. Scheibe, eds. *Studies in Social Identity*. New York: Praeger, 1983.

Saum, Lewis O. *The Popular Mood of Pre-Civil War America*. Westport, Ct.: Greenwood, 1980.

Schur, Edwin. *The Awareness Trap: Self-Absorption Instead of Social Change*. New York: Quadrangle-New York Times, 1976.

Scott, Marvin, and Stanford Lyman. "Accounts." *American Sociological Review* 33 (December 1968): 46–62.

Sennett, Richard. *The Fall of Public Man*. New York: Knopf, 1977.

———. *The Uses of Disorder: Personal Identity and City Life*. New York: Knopf, 1970.

Shibutani, Tamotsu. "Reference Groups as Perspectives." *American Journal of Sociology* 60 (1955): 562–569.

———. *Society and Personality*. Englewood Cliffs, N.J.: Prentice-Hall, 1961.

Slater, Philip. *The Pursuit of Loneliness*. Boston: Beacon, 1974.

Snow, David A., and Leon Anderson. "Identity Work Among the Homeless." *American Journal of Sociology* 92 (May 1987): 1336–1371.

Stokes, Randall G., and John P. Hewitt. "Aligning Actions." *American Sociological Review* 41 (October 1976): 838–849.

Stone, Gregory P. "Appearance and the Self: A Slightly Revised Version." Pp. 187–202 in Gregory P. Stone and Harvey A. Farberman, eds., *Social Psychology Through Symbolic Interaction* (2nd ed.; New York: Wiley, 1981).

Stout, Jeffrey. "Liberal Society and the Languages of Morals." Pp. 127–146 in Charles H. Reynolds and Ralph V. Norman, eds., *Community in America:*

The Challenge of Habits of the Heart (Berkeley: University of California Press, 1988).

Strauss, Anselm L. *Mirrors and Masks: The Search for Identity*. Glencoe, Ill.: Free Press, 1959.

Strauss, Anselm L., ed. *George H. Mead: On Social Psychology*. Chicago: University of Chicago Press, 1964.

Stryker, Sheldon. *Symbolic Interactionism: A Social Structural Version*. Menlo Park, Calif.: Benjamin/Cummings, 1980.

Stryker, Sheldon, and Anne Statham. "Symbolic Interactionism and Role Theory." Pp. 311–378 in Gardner Lindzey and Elliot Aronson, eds., *Handbook of Social Psychology* (New York: Random House, 1985).

Susman, Warren I. "Personality and the Making of Twentieth-Century Culture." Pp. 271–290 in his *Culture as History* (New York: Pantheon, 1984).

Tocqueville, Alexis de. *Democracy in America*, ed. Phillips Bradley, vols. 1 and 2. New York: Vintage, 1945.

Trilling, Lionel. *Sincerity and Authenticity*. Cambridge, Mass.: Harvard University Press, 1972.

Turner, Ralph H. "Is There a Quest for Identity?" *Sociological Quarterly* 16 (Spring 1975): 148–161.

————. "The Real Self: From Institution to Impulse." *American Journal of Sociology* 81 (March 1976): 989–1016.

————. "Role-Taking: Process versus Conformity." Pp. 20–40 in Arnold M. Rose, ed., *Human Behavior and Social Process* (Boston: Houghton Mifflin, 1962).

————. "Role-Taking, Role-Standpoint, and Reference Group Behavior." *American Journal of Sociology* 61 (1956): 316–328.

Turner, Ralph H., and Lewis M. Killian. *Collective Behavior*. 3rd ed. Englewood Cliffs, N.J.: Prentice-Hall, 1987.

Varenne, Herve. *Americans Together: Structured Diversity in a Midwestern Town*. New York: Teachers College Press, 1977.

Veroff, Joseph, Elizabeth Douvan, and Richard Kulka. *The Inner American: A Self-Portrait from 1957 to 1976*. New York: Basic Books, 1981.

Wagner, Helmut R., ed. *Alfred Schutz: On Phenomenology and Social Relations*. Chicago: University of Chicago Press, 1970.

Weigert, Andrew J. "Identity: Its Emergence Within Sociological Psychology." *Symbolic Interaction* 6 (Fall 1983): 183–206.

Weigert, Andrew J., J. Smith Teitge, and Dennis W. Teitge. *Society and Identity: Toward a Sociological Psychology*. Cambridge, Eng.: Cambridge University Press, 1986.

Wheelis, Allen. *The Quest for Identity*. New York: Norton, 1958.

Whyte, William H. *The Organization Man*. New York: Simon and Schuster, 1956.

Williams, Raymond. *Culture and Society, 1780–1950*. Garden City, N.Y.: Doubleday Anchor, 1960.

———. *Keywords: A Vocabulary of Culture and Society*. New York: Oxford University Press, 1976.

Wood, Michael R., and Louis A. Zurcher. *The Development of a Postmodern Self: A Computer-Assisted Analysis of Personal Documents*. Westport, Ct.: Greenwood, 1988.

Wrong, Dennis. "The Idea of 'Community': A Critique." Pp. 254–263 in Irving Howe, ed., *Twenty-Five Years of Dissent: An American Tradition* (New York: Methuen, 1979).

Zurcher, Louis A. "The Bureaucratizing of Impulse: Self-Conception in the 1980s." *Symbolic Interaction* 9 (Fall 1986): 169–178.

———. *The Mutable Self: A Self-Concept for Social Change*. Beverly Hills, Calif.: Sage, 1977.

INDEX